You're Invited

D1397392

Please join the Junior League of Raleigh, Inc.
for a celebration of
North Carolina's finest recipes.

The Junior League of Raleigh is an organization of women committed to promoting voluntarism, developing the potential of women, and improving communities through the effective action and leadership of trained volunteers. Its purpose is exclusively educational and charitable. All proceeds from the sale of *You're Invited* will benefit the community and charitable activities of the Junior League of Raleigh, Inc.

Copies of *You're Invited* may be obtained by sending $21.95 plus $4.00 shipping and handling to the following address. North Carolina residents should add $1.32 sales tax. For your convenience, order forms are located in the back of the cookbook.

Junior League of Raleigh, Inc.
4020 Barrett Drive, Suite 104
Raleigh, North Carolina 27609
(919) 785-0530 Cookbook fax
(919) 787-1103, pound (#) 120 Cookbook voice mail

The Junior League of Raleigh commissioned artist Marriott Little to convey the spirit of *You're Invited* for our cover artwork. We thank her for so graciously illustrating our theme.

Printed in the USA by
WIMMER
The Wimmer Companies
Memphis
1-800-548-2537

Table of Contents

Breakfast—Dappled Shade

Fleur-de-lis

Megg's Cups

Still Life With Peaches And Melons

Summer Spread

Places I Have Been

Provence Luncheon

The Dining Room

denotes recipes that can be prepared
and served in 45 minutes or less.

You're Invited 3

You're Invited

An engagement awaits you: blue jean or white tie, simple or elaborate, an event to salute tradition though enhanced with contemporary flair.

The Junior League of Raleigh requests the honor of your presence as we celebrate the many flavors of our community. Both chic sophistication and down-home style portray North Carolina's capital city, as graciousness is equally proffered in either case.

In Raleigh, as throughout the south, hospitality is preeminent. It is a custom that embraces all: friends, friends of friends, relatives, neighbors, strangers. Initiated when the first passing traveler was offered the very best as he crossed an early Raleigh threshold, the rite of hospitality thrives.

In fact, so many travelers are captivated by our southern hospitality that they, too, have become settlers. Raleigh's population has more than doubled in the last 25 years, enriching our lives even as the skyline rises.

Of course, it's more than sumptuous food and the convivial atmosphere that charms some folks. They are further enticed by the beauty of our four distinct seasons and the celebrations that each one affords.

In March and April we see the rebirth of spring. Raleigh streets become canopied with dogwood blossoms and lined with thousands of azaleas that burst into every shade of pink and white and red. It is no accident that corporate employee candidates are invited to visit us then, when the deepest south seems to have jumped directly from winter into summer and much of the country is blanketed still with reminders of what now is tiresome snow.

Summer? Well, yes, it's hot, but not so hot as to dampen our zest for barbecues, baseball, and concerts outdoors. And since the drive is equally short to Atlantic beaches or the Smoky mountains, the catch of the day could as easily be mountain trout as grilled yellowfin tuna.

In fall the City of Oaks turns to deepest hues of purple, red and gold. Team flags fly and autos bear the burgeoning weight of delectable foods destined for tailgating fun. Markets abound with colorful produce – the last of the okra and Silver Queen corn, the first sweet potatoes and bright orange pumpkins, red Stayman apples, the green of beans and down-home greens.

Winter may offer a snow or two, but rarely turns bitter. As snow appears, so do road blocks for the steepest streets, followed by sleds from every corner. Four-wheel-drive owners attend to stranded motorists, and children celebrate their freedom from school. Neighborhood parties feature freshly baked bread and four kinds of soup on the stove, planting warm memories even as the snow melts into rain.

To choose, prepare and serve the best from each season has ever been the Raleigh way. Honoring this tradition, our League presents the following recipes and entertaining ideas. An invitation is implicit in each: to celebrate time-tested, oft-requested dishes prepared with contemporary techniques; to celebrate both local bounty and harvests from far away; to celebrate both preservation and progress; to celebrate the spirit of hospitality.

We are pleased to send you this invitation to sample the best of our community. The door is open, and You're Invited.

Linda Turner

Breakfast—Dappled Shade
oil on canvas, 1997

From the private collection of
Dr. and Mrs. E. Ruffin Franklin, Raleigh, NC.

Menus

New Year's Day Brunch

Bloody Marys or Hot Buttered Rum, page 55

Country Ham with Red-Eye Gravy, page 85
Gruyère Cheese Grits, page 85
Good Luck Black-Eyed Peas, page 211
Fresh Collard Greens, page 211

Smithfield Biscuits, page 61

Bread Pudding with Blueberries and Warm Whiskey Sauce, page 247

If you are a true southerner, then you are familiar with the New Year's Day menu. It is not one to be altered. Black-eyed peas bring good luck for the year ahead, and collards bring money. Grits are served because we are, after all, southern. Country ham with gravy and biscuits is simply the best. Finally, bread pudding is the resourceful and most delicious way to finish leftover bread from last year!

You're Invited
Junior League of Raleigh, NC

Romantic Valentine's Dinner for Two

Madeira Mushroom Soup, page 102

Fresh Romaine with Caesar Salad Dressing, page 126

Champagne Steak, page 177
Garlic Broccoli, page 217
Roasted Roquefort Potatoes, page 224

Coffee Crème Brûlée , page 251
Heart-shaped Chocolate Peanut Butter Bark, page 276

Do not fall in with the Valentine's Day skeptics. It is not just for greeting card companies and florists. Why not take advantage of every excuse possible to share a cozy evening with the one you love? This intimate menu is the right blend of sumptuous, quick and make-ahead, allowing you to focus on the romance.

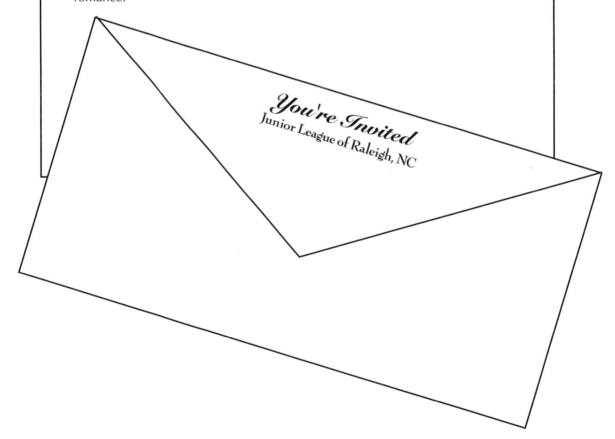

You're Invited
Junior League of Raleigh, NC

ACC Tournament Party

Spicy Corn Dip, page 38
and
Sassy Salsa, page 36
with Blue (Devil) Corn Chips

Red & White Chicken Chili, page 93

Carolina Cornbread, page 63

Frosted Chocolate Kahlúa Bars, page 271

March Madness is an apt description for the mayhem that ensues around Atlantic Coast Conference tournament time. Loyalties are fierce in the Triangle, as three of the country's legendary basketball programs are a stone's throw from one another. Because the fans can be testy, we suggest a menu with dishes to placate fans of Duke University, North Carolina State University and the University of North Carolina at Chapel Hill. The key to a successful tournament party is to prepare food that is easy to make ahead and easy to serve, so that no one misses a minute of the action. Time-outs should be reserved for breaks to the cooler — not cooking or cleaning up!

You're Invited
Junior League of Raleigh, NC

Family Sunday Supper

Honey Bear Chicken, page 162
Apple Slices with Creamy Caramel Dip, page 37
Tossed Green Salad with Poppy Seed Dressing, page 128
Grilled Corn on the Cob

Parmesan Twists, page 67

Painted Sugar Cookies, page 275

Devote the entire day to your family by enlisting their help in every aspect of creating the evening meal, preparation to cleanup. The menu items suggested here are guaranteed child-pleasers, if not the month's recommendation from *Gourmet* magazine.

To grill corn on the cob, remove only the outer husks and tear into thin strips. Peel back the remaining husks, remove silks and rewrap husks. Tie with reserved corn husk strips. Soak corn in a clean bucket of cold water for an hour. Place directly on grill over medium-hot coals for 15 to 20 minutes, turning frequently. As the corn steams in its husks, your children may be having too much fun to realize this is quality time!

You're Invited
Junior League of Raleigh, NC

The Junior League of Raleigh also recommends the following recipe from its signature project, SAFE*child*, an agency dedicated to supporting and strengthening families in Wake County.

SAFE*child's* Recipe
for Positive Parenting

2	cups	**Unconditional Love**
1	cup	**Reasonable Expectations**
½	cup	**Careful Listening**
½	cup	**Time Together**
2	tablespoons	**Encouragement**
1	teaspoon	**Limit-Setting**
		Dash of Humor

• Gather your children together. Sprinkle liberally with unconditional love. In a bowl sift together reasonable expectations and careful listening. Add time together. Alternately add encouragement and limit-setting, ending with a dash of humor. Surround children with this mixture daily, appreciating the uniqueness of each child.

Remember: No one is born knowing how to be an effective parent. Seek support, information and community resources, and learn to be the best parent you can be!

SAFE*child*

SAFEchild is committed to eliminating child abuse in Wake County by helping adults and children create nurturing environments free from abuse and neglect. Established in 1992 by the Junior League of Raleigh Inc.

Easter Lunch

Grilled Lamb with Rosemary & Red Wine, page 202
Served with Assorted Chutneys

Front Porch Frittata, page 83
Patchwork Quilt Rice, page 231
Marinated Asparagus, page 214

Herbed Carrot Biscuits, page 62

Fresh Lemon Pie, page 258

By Easter, spring fever is an epidemic. The sheer force of color in Raleigh in the springtime—dogwoods, azaleas, pansies, forsythia, hyacinths, tulips and Lenten roses — draws everyone out of doors. The air is fragrant; the breezes cool, stirring frequent play with the musical wind chimes. Tranquility reigns as even the grumpiest of souls is lulled into cordiality.

Take advantage of the contagion and invite any elder or younger neighbors with distant families to share in your celebration. Serve this elegant luncheon at your most spectacular outdoor spot. Delight the children by adding bunny-shaped peanut butter and jelly sandwiches to the menu.

Following lunch, encourage unanimous participation in games of croquet or badminton, or an old-fashioned Easter egg hunt.

You're Invited
Junior League of Raleigh, NC

Bridal Tea

Fine Quality Loose Teas
such as Earl Grey, English Breakfast or Darjeeling

Champagne Brunch Punch, page 56

Variety of Canapés, page 50
Provençal Palmiers, page 31

Currant Scones (page 77) with Whipped Butter and Strawberry Preserves

Raspberry Trifle with Custard Sauce, page 245
Chocolate Seduction Tarts, page 256

Every aspect of the southern bridal tea is steeped in tradition. Honor your own traditions by pulling out all the stops and all the family heirlooms. Tradition dictates the use of fine, loose teas, a sterling tea ball and the dainty, antique teapot or the sterling service. Canapés, scones and sweets are necessary; palmiers and champagne punch lend an elegant touch.

Consider showering the bride at tea. It is likely that guests span three generations and may have never met. The gifts will serve as a focal point and shared conversation topic.

You're Invited
Junior League of Raleigh, NC

Elegant Dinner Party

Cream of Six Onion Soup, page 89

Salad of Lettuce and Braised Quail, page 121

Refreshing Berry Sorbet, page 269

Salmon with Herb Sauce, page 151
Julienne of Carrots and Zucchini, page 219
Roasted Rosemary Potatoes, page 221

Chocolate Cloaked Pears, page 263

The desire to be among friends is the only excuse needed to have an elegant dinner party. Rather than being daunted by the affair, take enough time to delight in the process. During the week prior, wash and iron your favorite table linens and polish your silver. Once the table is set, so is your anticipatory mood. Spend a day at the flea market or antique warehouse to find unusual items to use for food service or decoration. Purchase all nonperishable food items and order the quail and salmon. Finally, hire a local student to help you clean and serve so that you can devote the day of the party to the joy of cooking, and the evening to your guests.

You're Invited
Junior League of Raleigh, NC

Luncheon with the Ladies

Lemon Tea Refresher, page 57

Elegant Stuffed Pea Pods, page 32

Tropical Fruit Gazpacho, page 104

Carolina Deviled Crab, page 137
Asparagus and Prosciutto Bundles, page 213

Quick & Incredible Cheese Biscuits, page 62

Strawberry Soufflé, page 252

Numerous opportunities exist to entertain the ladies at luncheon. Perhaps it is your turn to entertain your investment, book or garden club. Likewise, you may wish to host your bridge, golf or tennis club, or fellow board members. Your hospitality is demonstrated here by offering a menu replete with colorful fare, both light and sinful. Guests feel good, but not too guilty.

You're Invited
Junior League of Raleigh, NC

Come-on-Over Cookout

Watermelon Granita, page 58

Shrimp & Lime Tostadas, page 41

Grilled Rib-eyes with Mango Salsa, page 180
Tiger-Stripe Potato Kebabs, page 226
Honey-Ginger Green Beans, page 214

Quick Herbed Focaccia, page 67

Summer Fruit Ice Cream, page 268

Grilling is perhaps the easiest way to entertain. The grill is a good gathering place, and cooking is part of the event rather than a task that must be completed in advance. The casual atmosphere obliges both hosts and guests to unwind and enjoy. No one seems to notice what time the meal begins or ends, and, what's more, no one seems to care.

Fortunately, Raleigh's climate does not restrict grilling to a summer activity. Grills are in use from March to October, or all year for those more hardy. From across the hedge or over the phone, the "Come on over" call is frequently heard and most often answered with a quick and resounding, "Be right there."

You're Invited
Junior League of Raleigh, NC

Fourth of July Picnic

Carolina Country Ham Crostini, page 32

Southern Fried Chicken, page 159
Parslied Potato Salad, page 115
Black Bean and Corn Salad, page 111
Tomato Basil Tart, page 227

Traditional Southern Cornbread, page 64

1 Ripe Watermelon

Raleigh's Best Ever Cookies, page 273

No summer picnic is complete without an ice-cold, ripe watermelon and an old-fashioned seed-spitting contest. It is just as simple as it sounds: first, select a judge, then line up the contestants and see which one spits his or her watermelon seeds the farthest.

Likewise, no Fourth of July picnic is complete without a blazing fireworks display. Residents and visitors to Wake County have two sensational events from which to choose: a relaxed evening at the Pops with the North Carolina Symphony in Cary's Regency Park or a more action-packed affair at the State Fairgrounds. Both events incorporate a grand finale of rousing fireworks.

You're Invited
Junior League of Raleigh, NC

Beach Weekend Supper

Gambler's Slush, page 59

Bacon and Cheddar Triangles, page 30
Classic Guacamole (page 38) with Tortilla Chips

Shrimp with Tabasco Butter, page 130
and/or
Citrus Baked Mahi Mahi, page 148
Margarita Berry Slaw, page 114
Fresh Corn Fritters, page 221

Key Lime Cheesecake, page 250

Raleigh's proximity to Atlantic beaches provides the population with an escape for much needed getaway weekends. In a couple of hours, you will have fewer worries and scenic views. Our featured menu is sure to satisfy your weekend crowd after a day of surf and sun. Serve it at home to attain that getaway feeling, minus the salt and sand.

You're Invited
Junior League of Raleigh, NC

Fall Football Tailgate

Tomato Bisque, page 103

Curried Chicken Salad (page 117) in Croissants
Sweet Potato Biscuits (page 61) with Country Ham
Tailgate Tortillas, page 36
Savory Rice Salad, page 118

Sinful Caramel Squares, page 270
Glazed Apple Cookies, page 274

Come September, thoughts turn to friendly rivalries, cooler weather, college days, college friends and movable feasts. The first brisk game day is heaven, and that thermos of tomato bisque is your ticket. Curried chicken salad, sweet potato biscuits and glazed apple cookies are the essence of fall, while the tortillas, rice salad and caramel squares must have been created with tailgate parties in mind. In fact, this mix of palatable and portable fare might incline you to feel so generous that you offer to share with fans of the opposing team.

You're Invited
Junior League of Raleigh, NC

Supper Club Spread

Green Chile Wonton Cups, page 49

Veal Chops with Wild Mushrooms, page 190
Risotto with Grilled Vegetables, page 230

Savory Onion Scones, page 63

Frozen Mocha Torte with Amaretto Cinnamon Sauce, page 267

Life seems so hectic at times that months go by before you realize that you have new neighbors and that you don't know what your friends are up to. A popular way to stay connected with old friends and to make new ones is to form a supper, gourmet or wine tasting club. Here are several suggestions for starting a supper club:

- Invite a number of folks to your home, close friends and casual acquaintances. Divide into teams of two, the pairs taking turns throughout the year preparing and serving the other members. If you are shy of twelve pairs, choose some months to meet at restaurants.

–or–

- Select your group and your schedule for hosts. Each month the host prepares the entrée while the others bring the remaining courses for the meal and the drinks.

–or–

- Begin by inviting one person or couple you know and asking them to invite one unknown to you. For the second gathering, you bring guests unknown to the others. Carry on until you have a large group of new friends.

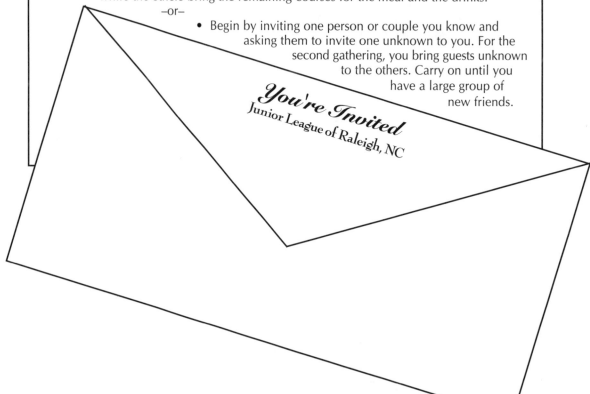

You're Invited
Junior League of Raleigh, NC

Good Neighbor Provisions

Clove Studded Ham with Orange-Rum Glaze, page 195
Creamy Scalloped Potatoes, page 224
Baked Butter Beans, page 216
Cranapple Bake, page 88

Rustic Honey Wheat Bread, page 70

Coconut Chess Pie, page 257

Words are not equal to many of life's events. Since southerners hate to be without adequate words, we arrive at such times laden with food. Whether celebrating the arrival of a child or offering condolences, the generous gift of refreshment goes far in relaying the message that you care.

An essential component of comfort fare is that it be simple to prepare and serve. Later, when the family has time to think, they will recall your kind gesture with gratitude.

You're Invited
Junior League of Raleigh, NC

Traditional Holiday Dinner

Old-fashioned Roasted Turkey, page 170
Stuffing with Swiss Chard & Sausage, page 170

Scalloped Oysters, page 135
Grated Sweet Potato Custard, page 209
Broccoli with Balsamic Butter, page 216
Nutted Mushroom Rice, page 226
Fresh Fruit Salad, page 112

Old-fashioned Dinner Rolls, page 65

Peppermint Ice Cream in Meringue Cups, page 266
Pumpkin Pecan Cake, page 237
Cranberry Pie, page 259

Time-honored traditions become such for a reason: they work. In the instance of food traditions, some dishes are honored because they are the favorites, no matter how difficult and time-consuming they are to prepare. Others make the short list strictly for simplicity's sake.

When planning your holiday feast, balance is the key. Keep the sentimental favorites; use the freshest seasonal fare; and finally, add at least one new element, for the surprise you serve this year may become the time-honored staple for generations to come.

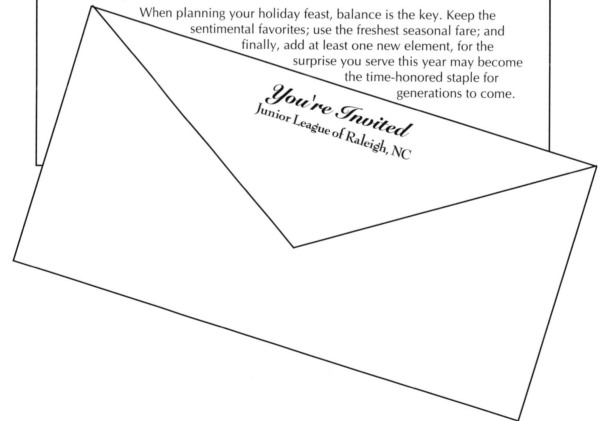

You're Invited
Junior League of Raleigh, NC

Christmas Cocktails

Eggceptional Eggnog, page 54

Elegant Beef Tenderloin (page 178) with assorted rolls

Chile-Lime Shrimp Kebabs, page 33
Mushroom and Gruyère Puffs, page 29
Salmon and Caper Canapés, page 50
Crudité Basket with Roasted Red Pepper Dip, page 35

Chocolate Hazelnut Truffles, page 277
Angel Kisses, page 273

Amid all the holiday revelry, three productions from local Thespians are events to add to the calendar. Build a spectacular evening around the annual re-creation of "A Christmas Carol," "The Nutcracker " or "Cinderella." Before the theatre, gather your group to enjoy drinks and light fare at any of the area's restaurants, pubs or bistros. Notice the City of Oaks' distinctive acorn lights and other festive decorations as you make your way to the play. Your post-theatre cocktail party will be the final in a series of hits.

You're Invited
Junior League of Raleigh, NC

There are as many ways to cook a North Carolina pig as there are ways to make biscuits, or ways to catch a speckled trout, or ways to spot a Wompus Cat. (Ask me about that later, that's another story!) But let me tell you one of those ways that has worked pretty well for me over the years.

First of all, you must order a freshly slaughtered pig from your butcher. In order to know what size to choose, you must know how many guests will be salivating over this succulent dish. Most expert pig cookers agree that a ninety-pound pig that has been "dressed out" (cleaned) for cooking will feed about fifty normally hungry people, if they "pick" it from the grill. (Picking means pulling the meat off the bones and eating it with your fingers, not caring if the grease drizzles down your chin.) It will feed seventy-five or eighty when chopped and served. Furthermore, these same experts agree that this ninety-pound pig will produce a more tender and tasty meat than any other size. While you can cook a larger pig and have a bigger crowd, I must warn you that a one hundred twenty-pound or more pig can be mighty fatty. So remember, never invite more than eighty people to your party. Now, let's get to the cooking equipment...

First you get a 250-gallon oil drum. For many years North Carolina farmers have converted a 250-gallon oil drum, a set of axles and wheels from an old Volkswagen or such, and some pretty solid welding skills, into a pig cooker. (Note that the cooking apparatus and the chef are known by the same name.) Pig cookers are shared among friends, relatives, churches and volunteer fire departments and are easily found in eastern North Carolina, but might be scarce in other locales. I even heard a story about a couple of N.C. guys pulling a red pig cooker all the way to Washington, D.C. to cook pigs for senators. Washington's popular catering company, "Entertaining with Elegance," paid those fellas $1000 to cook just one pig! Now, let's examine the cooking method...

Local experts have found the pigs that consistently win tasting contests are cooked "right at" nine hours, over medium-hot coals, using any combination of the following: oak wood, hickory wood, and/or fine quality charcoal briquettes. To start, rise before the sun and go get the pig. Place the pig face down, skin side up on the cooker. Next, you should line the bottom of your grill with the coals, forming a circle around the outer edges of the pig. To get an idea of how many coals to use, start with 10 pounds of charcoal briquettes and wait until they are 100% white ash. The amount of heat that the charcoal generates would be your

guideline for using alternative coals from oak or hickory wood. (Keep the heat about the same no matter what your heat source.) In about forty-five minutes it will be time to add some more coals, but don't add as many as you started with. The trick is to keep a good medium-hot temperature for nine hours without letting the pig flame or burn.

After about seven hours, two men (one at each end of the pig) take hold of the legs of the pig with their arms in a criss-crossed position and, on the count of three, flip the pig over onto its skin side (stomach up), revealing beautiful, golden, oak-colored ribs, hams, shoulders and tenderloin. At this time the pig cooker and his helpers test the tenderness and succulence of those mouth-watering ribs. Then you "sauce down" the pig with your award-winning barbecue sauce. Let the skin get nice and crisp and the pig simmer in all its juices. After about two more hours, the pig should be good and done. All that is left to do is "pick" it.

Note: I recommend "pickin" half of the pig and chopping the other half along with the skin — the best of both worlds.

THE COOKER

Jerry Oates

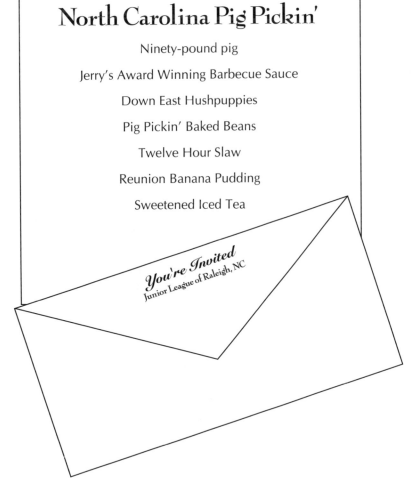

North Carolina Pig Pickin'

Ninety-pound pig

Jerry's Award Winning Barbecue Sauce

Down East Hushpuppies

Pig Pickin' Baked Beans

Twelve Hour Slaw

Reunion Banana Pudding

Sweetened Iced Tea

You're Invited
Junior League of Raleigh, NC

Not only a popular *The News & Observer* columnist, Dennis Rogers is also North Carolina's self-proclaimed barbecue aficionado. He is adamant about one aspect of the cuisine, "Y'all is plural, there is no such thing as one grit and barbecue—for the thousandth time—is a noun. It is not a verb or an adjective. You cook a pig and you get barbecue. You grill steaks and burgers. You do not 'barbecue' anything." *(The News & Observer,* April 1977)

Jerry's Award-Winning Barbecue Sauce

For smaller crowds or inclement weather, we offer a Slow Cooker Barbecue recipe (p. 201)

64	ounces apple cider vinegar
32	ounces ketchup
1	tablespoon Worcestershire sauce
1	tablespoon cayenne pepper (more to taste)
3	ounces crushed red pepper flakes
6	ounces honey
2	teaspoons salt
2	teaspoons black pepper
	juice from ½ lemon
½	teaspoon coriander

- Place all ingredients in a large stockpot and heat until well combined.
- Remove from heat and let stand 2 to 3 hours at room temperature before using to let flavors mix.

Yield: dresses 1 pig

Down East Hushpuppies

If you are unfamiliar with the story, those deep-fried morsels were invented to keep the plantation dogs quiet, "Hush puppies." They have kept quite a few people quiet, too.

2	cups white cornmeal
1	teaspoon salt
2	tablespoons chopped green onions
1	cup buttermilk or more as needed
2	eggs
¼	cup lard, bacon drippings or shortening, melted
4	cups vegetable oil

- In a medium bowl, combine cornmeal, salt and green onions. Mix well. Add buttermilk, eggs and shortening. Mix again. If the mixture is crumbly, add buttermilk, one tablespoon at a time, until batter holds together.
- Heat oil in a large pot or deep-fat fryer to 375°F.
- Form batter into 1½-inch pieces and fry, a few at a time, until they are golden brown, 2 to 3 minutes.
- Drain on paper towels and serve at once.

Note: Lard or bacon drippings make a crisper hushpuppy than vegetable oil.

Yield: 48 hushpuppies

Pig Pickin' Baked Beans

4   slices bacon
½   cup chopped onion
2   (16-ounce) cans pork and beans
2   tablespoons brown sugar
2   tablespoons ketchup
2   tablespoons Worcestershire sauce
1   tablespoon prepared mustard

- Preheat oven to 350°F.
- Cook bacon in skillet until crisp. Remove, cool and crumble.
- Add onion to 2 tablespoons reserved drippings and sauté 5 minutes. Combine sugar, ketchup, Worcestershire sauce and mustard in large bowl. Add beans and onion with drippings. Mix in bacon.
- Pour into 1½-quart casserole.
- Bake for 1½ hours.

Yield: 6 servings

Twelve Hour Slaw

1   large cabbage, shredded
1   onion, thinly sliced (Vidalia or Spanish)
1   cup chopped green bell pepper
1   cup plus 1 tablespoon sugar, divided
1   cup vinegar
1   tablespoon salt
1   tablespoon celery seed
¾   cup salad oil
1   teaspoon dried mustard.

- Arrange cabbage, onion and green pepper in a bowl in layers until bowl is full. Top with 1 cup of sugar. (Do not stir.)
- Mix vinegar, salt, celery seed, salad oil, dried mustard and 1 tablespoon sugar in a medium saucepan.
- Let ingredients come to a boil.
- Pour over cabbage and seal tight with lid. Let stand overnight in refrigerator. Toss next day.

Yield: 10 servings

Debate, after the preferred type of barbecue and the best sauce, turns to slaw. There are two types for consideration, mayonnaise- or vinegar-based. Vinegar wins our debate for unbeatable flavor and for the make-ahead factor.

Reunion Banana Pudding

A creamy comfort food with an old-fashioned taste that has made it a Carolina favorite for generations.

⅓ **cup all-purpose flour**
   dash of salt
¾ **cup sugar, divided**
4 **eggs, separated**
3 **cups milk**
½ **teaspoon vanilla extract**
40 **vanilla wafers**
6 **ripe bananas, sliced**

- Combine flour, salt and ½ cup sugar in top of double boiler. Stir in egg yolks and milk. Blend well. Stirring constantly, cook uncovered until thickened. Reduce heat to low and cook 5 minutes.
- Remove from heat and add vanilla.
- Alternate layers of vanilla wafers, bananas and pudding in a 1½-quart casserole, ending with pudding.
- Preheat oven to 425°F.
- Beat egg whites until foamy. Gradually add ¼ cup sugar and beat until stiff peaks form. Spread on pudding.
- Bake for 5 minutes.
- Let cool and chill before serving.

Yield: 6 servings

Tracey Parker
Fleur-de-lis
oil on canvas, 1998

Appetizers and Beverages

Hors d'oeuvres

Appetizers

Dips

Crostini

Wonton Wraps

Beverages

Mushroom and Gruyère Puffs

A buttery puff pastry filled with mushrooms, walnuts and sweet Gruyère cheese

3	tablespoons butter
2	tablespoons finely chopped shallots
1	pound mushrooms, chopped
1	teaspoon salt
1	teaspoon pepper
2	teaspoons minced fresh tarragon or oregano
½	cup dry white wine
½	cup finely chopped scallions
⅓	cup minced fresh parsley
1	tablespoon freshly squeezed lemon juice
1⅓	cups walnuts or pecans, lightly toasted and finely chopped
½	pound Gruyère cheese, grated (about 2 cups)
1	(17½-ounce) box frozen puff pastry dough, thawed

- Melt butter in sauté pan. Add shallots, mushrooms, salt, pepper and fresh herbs. Cook over medium heat until most of the liquid has evaporated.
- Add wine and cook until evaporated, stirring occasionally.
- Remove from heat and put into a bowl. Stir in scallions, parsley and lemon juice.
- Let cool, then add walnuts and cheese. Blend thoroughly.
- To make the puffs, lay the pastry sheet flat and use a pizza cutter to cut into small squares.
- Press into mini muffin tins and fill with the mushroom filling.
- Bake at 350°F for 10 minutes.

Yield: 30 puffs

Wine Recommendations: Unoaked Macon, Red Côtes du Rhone or Beaujolais

Appetizers

Appeteasers

Enticing tidbits

Premier crowd pleasers

Puréed, diced, quartered, whole

Dipped or skewered, in wrappers or rolls

Chewy, crunchy, salty, sweet

Grilled, smoked, baked, broiled, frozen treats

Cutout circles, hearts or stars

On buffet tables, along raw bars

Tempting morsels, savory bites

Whatever whets your appetite

Raleigh, Durham and Chapel Hill form North Carolina's Triangle area. Each city is home to an esteemed university and each has a distinct personality. The cities lie in three separate counties; yet they share much in common, namely, the cutting edge technology that streams from the midst of all three — the Research Triangle Park.

Bacon and Cheddar Triangles
Happily served in the Triangle and beyond

1	loaf very thin white bread (Remove crusts if desired.)
½	pound extra sharp cheddar cheese, grated
8	slices bacon, cooked and crumbled
1	(2-ounce) package slivered almonds sautéed in 1 tablespoon butter
1	cup mayonnaise
2	tablespoons Worcestershire sauce
1	small onion, grated
	orange marmalade, peach preserves or fresh strawberries to garnish

- Combine cheese, bacon, almonds, mayonnaise, Worcestershire sauce and onion. Spoon onto bread slices. Cut bread into quarters. (May be frozen at this stage.)
- Bake at 400°F for 5 minutes (or longer if frozen). Serve hot.
- Garnish with a dollop of orange marmalade, peach preserves or a fresh strawberry.

Yield: 30 pieces

Crab tartlets are the crowning touch of your appetizer menu. They are both elegant and easy to pass around.

Carolina Crab Tartlets
Sophisticated east coast cuisine

½	cup butter, softened (not margarine)
1	(3-ounce) package cream cheese, softened (not lowfat)
1	cup all-purpose flour
½	teaspoon salt
1	pound fresh backfin crabmeat
½	cup mayonnaise
1	tablespoon freshly squeezed lemon juice
¼	cup finely chopped celery
4	green onions, finely chopped
½	cup grated Swiss cheese
½	teaspoon Worcestershire sauce
¼	teaspoon garlic salt
¼	teaspoon cayenne pepper (optional)

- Cream butter and cream cheese. Stir in flour and salt.
- Roll into 24 small balls and chill 1 hour.
- Press into tiny muffin tins, about 1¾-inch diameter.
- Mix crab with remaining ingredients.
- Spoon into unbaked shells and bake at 350°F until golden, approximately 30 minutes.

Yield: 24 pieces

Provençal Palmiers

For a taste à la Provençal

1   **cup black olives, chopped**
¼   **cup sun-dried tomatoes in oil, drained and chopped**
2   **teaspoons finely chopped garlic**
2   **teaspoons dried basil**
1½ **teaspoons dried thyme**
1   **teaspoon fennel seeds, lightly crushed**
1¼ **cups fresh Parmesan cheese, divided**
1   **(17¼-ounce) package frozen puff pastry, thawed**
    Fresh basil and thyme to garnish

- Combine olives, tomatoes, garlic, basil, thyme, fennel and ½ cup Parmesan cheese. Stir well.
- Flour the work surface. Place one puff pastry sheet on it. Sprinkle with 1 tablespoon cheese. Press cheese into pastry with a rolling pin. Turn pastry over and repeat.
- Spread ½ of the olive and tomato mixture over the pastry. Cover with waxed paper and roll evenly with rolling pin.
- Starting with the longer sides, roll tightly like a jelly-roll, stopping at the center. Repeat with the other side so the 2 rolls meet in the center.
- Repeat using the remaining half of the olive and tomato mixture with the other pastry sheet.
- Cut rolls into ⅜-inch slices (26 to 28 per roll).
- Place on cookie sheet coated with cooking spray, cover with plastic, and refrigerate for 30 minutes.
- Preheat oven to 450°F.
- Sprinkle each slice with ¼ teaspoon Parmesan cheese. Bake 6 to 8 minutes.
- Turn slices over, sprinkle with ¼ teaspoon Parmesan cheese, and bake 4 to 6 minutes longer.
- Serve warm or at room temperature.
- Garnish with fresh basil and thyme.

Yield: 10 to 12 servings

Wine Recommendations: Dolcetto d'Alva, Pinot Grigio or Unoaked Sauvignon Blanc

Provence is that southern region of France synonymous with food and beauty. As in Italian cooking, garlic, tomatoes and olive oil comprise the staple ingredients. Additionally, onions, olives, mushrooms, anchovies and eggplant are typical in Provençal dishes.

Translated, crostini are "little toasts," typically brushed with olive oil. A couple of steps distinguish crostini from bruschetta, a garlic bread appetizer also of Italian origin. Bruschetta begins with toasted bread which is then rubbed with halved garlic cloves and drizzled with olive oil. The toasts are seasoned with salt and pepper, heated and served warm.

Carolina Country Ham Crostini
Little toasts with big taste

1   large ripe tomato
1   medium green bell pepper
3   cloves garlic, pressed
3   tablespoons olive oil
2   tablespoons minced fresh parsley
    salt and pepper to taste
1   baguette, sliced ¼-inch thick on a sharp bias
    unsalted butter as needed
    thinly sliced Virginia ham
    kalamata olives

- Peel and dice the tomato, discarding seeds. Remove seeds and ribs from green pepper and dice. Combine the tomato, pepper, garlic, oil, parsley, salt and pepper. Toss thoroughly and marinate several hours.
- Brush the baguette slices with olive oil. Toast on both sides and allow to cool. Spread each crouton lightly with butter. Top each with a slice of ham trimmed to fit the crouton.
- Drain the tomato/pepper mixture of excess moisture, and place a half teaspoonful on top of each slice of the ham. Garnish with a slice of black olive.

Yield: approximately 10 servings

Blanching vegetables and fruits sets peak color and flavor. It will also firm the flesh and loosen the skins for easy peeling, as with tomatoes or peaches. Begin timing as soon as vegetables or fruits are placed in boiling water; do not wait for the water to return to boiling, or food may overcook. Quickly refresh under cold water or in an ice water bath.

Elegant Stuffed Pea Pods
Vibrant and light with luncheons or cocktails

½   pound snow pea pods
1   cup unsalted butter
1   (8-ounce) package cream cheese, softened
16 ounces sharp cheddar cheese, grated
2   tablespoons prepared horseradish, squeezed dry
1   teaspoon dry mustard, dissolved in 2 tablespoons Worcestershire sauce
2   tablespoons beer
½   cup unsalted cashews or toasted walnuts, chopped

- Blanch pea pods for 1 minute in boiling water. Refresh in ice water.
- With a sharp knife, trim ends and split open along one side.
- Mix together cream cheese and cheddar cheese and then other ingredients except pea pods.
- Pipe cheese mixture into pea pods until full, using a pastry bag.
- Chill and serve.

Yield: approximately 50 pieces

Wine Recommendations: Alsace Pinot Blanc, Loire Sauvignon Blanc or Brut Champagne

Chile Lime Shrimp Kebabs

Piquant sparks from the grill fire

10	**large shrimp (about 12 ounces)**
2	**tablespoons minced fresh cilantro**
1	**tablespoon minced seeded jalapeño pepper**
2	**tablespoons freshly squeezed lime juice**
1	**teaspoon dried oregano**
1	**teaspoon chili powder**
1	**teaspoon olive oil**
½	**teaspoon salt**
½	**teaspoon pepper**
1	**clove garlic, minced**

- Peel shrimp, leaving tails intact.
- Combine cilantro and next 8 ingredients (cilantro through garlic) in a bowl; stir well. Add shrimp and toss to coat. Cover and marinate in refrigerator 1 hour, stirring occasionally. Remove shrimp from bowl; reserve marinade.
- Thread 3 shrimp onto each skewer. Prepare grill or broiler. Place kebabs on grill rack or broiler pan coated with cooking spray. Cook 3 minutes on each side or until done, basting occasionally with reserved marinade.

Variation: To serve as an entrée, add 8 cherry tomatoes, threading them alternately with shrimp on the skewers. Serve over rice for a light yet satisfying meal.

Note: If using wooden skewers, soak them first for 30 minutes to prevent food from sticking to the skewer.

Yield: 4 servings

Wine Recommendations: Demi-sec Loire Chenin Blanc, Alsace Pinot Blanc or Moscato d'Asti

Bedecking the outdoors need not be elaborate or expensive. Fill your wheelbarrow with ice to chill drinks. Create bouquets using skewered whole vegetables in terra cotta planters instead of the usual flower arrangements. Run your watering can through the dishwasher and use it to pour drinks. With imagination, ordinary household objects become memorable decorations.

Portobello Mushrooms with Hummus and Roasted Garlic Aïoli

A signature appetizer at Portobello's, a north Raleigh restaurant of eclectic Italian cuisine

1	**cup plus 2 tablespoons olive oil**
½	**cup balsamic vinegar**
	salt and pepper to taste
16	**ounces portobello mushrooms, sliced ½-inch thick**
¼	**cup all-purpose flour**
	Hummus (recipe follows)
	Roasted Garlic Aïoli (recipe follows)

- Whisk together 1 cup olive oil, balsamic vinegar, salt and pepper to form vinaigrette. Marinate mushrooms in vinaigrette, and refrigerate for at least 24 hours.
- Coat mushrooms with flour, shaking off excess.
- Sauté mushrooms in 2 tablespoons olive oil until tender and browned.
- Serve with a dollop of Hummus and Roasted Garlic Aïoli on each side.

Hummus

1	**(10-ounce) can chickpeas, drained, liquid reserved**
2	**tablespoons vinaigrette dressing**
	juice of ½ lemon
½	**teaspoon chopped garlic**
½	**teaspoon tahini paste**
	salt and pepper to taste

- Combine chickpeas, vinaigrette, lemon juice, garlic and tahini in the bowl of a food processor with half of the reserved chickpea liquid. Process until smooth. Season with salt and pepper.

Roasted Garlic Aïoli

1	**large or 2 small heads garlic**
¾	**cup mayonnaise**
	juice of ¼ lemon
	salt and pepper to taste

- Preheat oven to 325°F.
- Roast garlic head in a small dish until golden brown, about 20 minutes.
- Remove garlic cloves and place in a food processor fitted with a steel blade. Add mayonnaise and lemon juice and process until smooth.
- Season with salt and pepper.

Yield: 4 servings

White Pizza

It's in the cheese.

4 to 5	cloves garlic, minced
1	tablespoon dry oregano
1/3	cup olive oil
1	pound fontina cheese, freshly shredded
	Biscuit Pizza Crust (see below)

- Sauté the garlic and oregano in the olive oil until garlic is pale yellow but not brown.
- Brush this mixture onto prepared crusts, dividing equally.
- Top with equal portions of shredded fontina cheese.
- Bake in preheated 425°F oven for 8 to 10 minutes.
- Cut into squares and serve in a basket lined with a red bandana.

Biscuit Pizza Crust

1	(1/4-ounce) package active dry yeast
3/4	cup warm water, 110° to 115°F
2 1/2	cups packaged biscuit mix
	olive oil, salad dressing or cooking spray

- Soften yeast in warm water. Add biscuit mix and beat vigorously for 2 minutes.
- Dust counter surface with extra biscuit mix. Knead dough until smooth (25 strokes).
- Divide dough in half and roll each piece of dough into a 12-inch circle. Place dough circles onto baking sheets oiled with cooking spray. Crimp edges.

Yield: approximately 32 pieces

> "When my husband and I were courting, back in the Dark Ages, we loved to dine at an authentic Italian restaurant where rude waiters served exceptional food. White pizza became our standard appetizer. We ordered it again and again before discovering that fontina cheese is the secret to its sharp, rich taste."

Roasted Red Pepper Dip

Serve with raw, peeled jicama sticks or blanched green beans instead of the usual crudités.

1	(7 1/2-ounce) jar roasted red peppers, including juice
1	cup nonfat mayonnaise
1/3	cup Parmesan cheese
1	clove garlic, minced
3	tablespoons chopped fresh basil
	freshly ground pepper to taste

- Purée all ingredients in a blender or food processor.
- Serve chilled.

Yield: 1 1/2 cups

Roast red peppers over the open flame of your gas stove or grill, or char under the broiler, turning to blacken every side. When the skins are charred, remove peppers from heat and place in a paper bag for about 20 minutes. Remove peppers and peel the blackened skins. Two peppers is roughly equivalent to a 7 1/2 ounce jar.

Tailgate Tortillas

Take plenty along since tortilla roll-ups are awfully easy to eat.

Give your tailgate party a lift by using roasted red pepper or vegetable tortillas. These more colorful varieties are usually sold in the grocer's dairy case.

2   (8-ounce) packages Neufchâtel cheese, softened
1   cup chopped almonds, toasted
½   cup sliced green onions
2   tablespoons Dijon mustard
2   cloves garlic, minced
1   teaspoon dill weed
1   teaspoon dried, sweet basil
2   large cracker bread rounds or 6 large flour tortillas
1   pound thinly sliced ham
8   leaves red leaf lettuce

- Blend cheese with almonds, green onions, mustard, garlic, dill weed and basil.
- Soften cracker bread according to package directions or lightly steam tortillas.
- Spread cheese mixture on one side of each cracker bread or flour tortilla. Top with ham slices and lettuce, dividing equally.
- Roll tightly, sealing edges. Roll in aluminum foil and chill until ready to serve.
- To serve, cut in long diagonal slices placing cut-side down on serving plate.

Yield: 6 to 8 servings

Sassy Salsa

Good for more than chips and talking back

Salsas are spicy and low- or nonfat, so add them freely to a variety of dishes. Use as a topping for baked potatoes or black bean soup. Add to omelets and egg casseroles. Mix into a paste with goat cheese to top toasted pita bread. First brush pita with olive oil and lemon juice, then cut into wedges. Add salsa and goat cheese paste then sprinkle with cooked, crumbled bacon and a sliver of avocado.

2   large, ripe tomatoes cut into large wedges
1   small Vidalia onion
½   medium green bell pepper, cut into large slices
3   cloves garlic
4   pickled jalapeño peppers, seeded, and 2 teaspoons of the juice from the jar
½   cup chopped fresh cilantro
½   cup vegetable juice
½   teaspoon salt

- In a food processor, chop the tomatoes, onion, green pepper, garlic, jalapeño pepper and pepper juice. Do not purée.
- Add cilantro, vegetable juice and salt and pulse the processor until mixture is well blended and chunky.
- Serve with chips.

Yield: 3 cups

Grand Marnier Dip

Exquisite dip to serve with chocolate wafers or crackers, graham crackers, chocolate chunks, ladyfingers or bananas

- ½   **cup crushed strawberries**
- ¼   **cup finely chopped walnuts**
- ¼   **cup dark brown sugar**
- ⅓   **cup Grand Marnier liqueur**
- 1   **(8-ounce) package cream cheese, softened**
- 1   **cup sour cream**

- Reserve 1 tablespoon each of the strawberries and walnuts for garnish.
- In a small bowl, mix remaining strawberries, brown sugar and liqueur. Set aside.
- Blend cream cheese and sour cream until smooth. Add the strawberry mixture, blending well.
- Fold in remaining walnuts.
- Mound reserved strawberries in the center, and ring with reserved walnuts.
- Cover and chill.

Yield: 3½ cups

Wine Recommendations: Moscato d'Asti or Demi-Sec Champagne

Creamy Caramel Dip

Sweet, creamy dip and edible PlayDough

- 1   **(8-ounce) package cream cheese, softened**
- ¾   **cup packed brown sugar**
- 1   **cup sour cream**
- 2   **teaspoons vanilla extract**
- 2   **teaspoons freshly squeezed lemon juice**
- 1   **cup cold milk**
- 1   **(3.4-ounce) package instant vanilla pudding mix**
  assorted fresh fruit for dipping

- In a mixing bowl, beat cream cheese and brown sugar until smooth.
- Add the sour cream, vanilla, lemon juice, milk and pudding mix, beating well after each addition.
- Cover and chill for at least 1 hour.
- Serve as a dip for assorted fruit.

Yield: 3½ cups

Sponge Fingers

3 eggs, separated

½ cup sugar, divided

½ cup flour, sifted confectioner's sugar for dusting

- **Grease a baking sheet and line with parchment paper. Beat egg whites to soft peak stage, then gradually whisk in half the sugar until stiff and glossy. Lightly beat egg yolks with remaining sugar. Fold into meringue followed by flour. Pipe onto prepared baking sheet and dust with confectioner's sugar in two additions. Bake in a 350° oven until golden brown, about 10 minutes. Cool on wire rack. Makes 10-12.**

Marzipan Pine Cones

Spoon marzipan, about the size of a quarter, into the hands of your child. Let her form into a cone shape and then stick almonds in at an angle. Dip the cones in Creamy Caramel Dip, and you have marzipan pine cones.

Complete your Mexican theme dinner by using hollowed out pattypan squashes as serving dishes for guacamole, sour cream, salsa, or chopped onion and peppers. The round, curvy shape and greenish hues team well with Mexican pottery and fabrics.

Classic Guacamole

6 to 8	ripe avocados
2	medium tomatoes, chopped
3	serrano or jalapeño chiles, ribbed, seeded and minced
	garlic salt
	salt and pepper to taste
1	lime

- Peel and seed avocados. Mash roughly with a fork, just enough to break up the meat.
- Add tomatoes and chiles, and season with garlic salt, salt and pepper.
- Squeeze the juice of the lime over the mixture and mix well.
- Can be made ahead 2 hours and refrigerated.

Yield: 8 servings

Some like it hot, and some like it hotter. The Scoville scale, devised in 1919, assigns numbers to various chiles based on the degree of heat, 1 (mildest) to 10 (hottest).

Fresh Chiles:
Anaheim, 2
Habanero, 10
Jalapeño, 7
Poblano, 3
Serrano, 7
Thai, 8
Teppin, 8

Dried Chiles:
Ancho, 4
Chipotle, 6
Chile De Arbol, 8
New Mexico, 3
Pasilla, 4
Pequin, 8

Spicy Corn Dip

Make it hotter by using pickled habaneros instead of jalapeños and by adding juice from the jar.

1	(16-ounce) bag frozen white corn
1	(8-ounce) package cream cheese, softened
¼	cup butter or margarine, softened
2	tablespoons cumin
2	tablespoons chopped pickled jalapeño pepper
	salt and pepper to taste
	tortilla chips

- Cook corn approximately 5 minutes. Drain.
- Combine corn with softened butter and cream cheese, stirring until blended.
- Add cumin and jalapeño pepper to taste. Season with salt and pepper.
- Serve warm or at room temperature with tortilla chips.

Yield: 10 to 15 servings

Fireside Fondue

4   slices bacon
2   tablespoons minced onion
1   teaspoon all-purpose flour
8   ounces sharp cheese, shredded (2 cups)
1   cup sour cream
½   teaspoon Worcestershire sauce
    dash of hot sauce

- In saucepan, fry bacon until crisp; drain, reserving 1 tablespoon drippings. Crumble bacon and set aside.
- Cook onions in reserved drippings until tender and translucent. Stir in flour.
- Stir in remaining ingredients.
- Cook over low heat, stirring constantly, until cheese is melted.
- Pour into fondue pot, and top with bacon. Place over fondue burner.
- Suggested dippers include celery sticks, red bell pepper strips, jicama sticks and toasted bread triangles.

Yield: 8 to 10 servings

Wine Recommendations: Cru Beaujolais or Lightly Oaked Australian Chardonnay

Fold leftover fireside fondue into scrambled eggs for a creamy, fluffy change of pace. Top with fresh chives.

Layered Italian Pepperoni Dip

Serve with homemade melba toast.

1   (8-ounce) package cream cheese, thinly sliced
¾   (26-ounce) jar purchased spaghetti sauce
1   bunch green onions, chopped
8   ounces mozzarella cheese, shredded
1   (4-ounce) jar black olives, drained and chopped
1   (14-ounce) can artichoke hearts, drained and chopped
    garlic salt to taste
1   (3-ounce) package pepperoni slices
4   ounces Parmesan cheese, grated

- Layer all ingredients, beginning with the cream cheese, in an 11x7x1½-inch baking dish.
- Bake at 350°F until hot and bubbly, about 20 minutes.
- Serve with toasted bread or crackers.

Yield: 10 to 12 servings

Small gestures, like making homemade melba toast, are memorable ones for guests. To make, remove crusts from thin slices of white or brown bread and cut into serving sized pieces. Place on baking sheet and bake at 275° for about 20 minutes, turning once. Remove when brown and crisp.

Simple Salmon Dip

Necessarily do-ahead

Bring Simple Salmon Dip and a bottle of wine to express thanks to your weekend hosts. A Loire Sauvignon Blanc, an Alsace Auxerrois or a Chablis will complement the dip, and your hosts will compliment you.

³/₄ teaspoon dill
³/₄ cup sour cream
1 tablespoon prepared horseradish
1 tablespoon mayonnaise
¹/₄ cup chopped green onions
6 ounces smoked salmon, chopped

- Mix together first 4 ingredients.
- Fold in salmon and green onions.
- Refrigerate 1 to 2 days before serving.
- Serve with crackers.

Yield: approximately 1 cup

Marinated Seafood Antipasto

Meets minimum effort and maximum taste requirement.

Antipasto baskets provide a mouth-watering array of foods from which to select. Line a long, shallow basket or platter with lettuce leaves and arrange cheeses, olives, cured meats, roasted peppers and cooked shrimp in rows. Drizzle with balsamic vinegar if desired, and garnish with fresh herb sprigs. Serve an assortment of bread sticks and focaccia as well.

1¹/₂ pounds shrimp, peeled, deveined and cooked
6 ounces provolone cheese, cubed
1 (6-ounce) can pitted black olives, drained
¹/₂ cup sliced scallions
²/₃ cup lemon juice
2 tablespoons Dijon mustard
2 teaspoons sugar
1¹/₂ teaspoon dried thyme (or 2¹/₂ tablespoons fresh)
1 teaspoon salt
4 ounces Genoa salami, cubed
1 red bell pepper, seeded and diced
1 yellow bell pepper, seeded and diced

- Place shrimp, cheese, olives and onions in a shallow dish.
- Combine remaining ingredients except salami and peppers. Pour over shrimp mixture.
- Cover and refrigerate 6 hours or overnight, stirring occasionally.
- Add salami and peppers. Toss well. Drain.

Yield: 8 to 10 servings

Wine Recommendations: Prosecco, Pinot Grigio or Alsace Pinot Blanc

Shrimp and Lime Tostadas

Three of the four steps here can be completed the day before.

9   **(5 to 6-inch) corn tortillas, each cut into 6 wedges**
    no stick vegetable cooking spray
3   **cloves garlic, unpeeled**
1   **tablespoon cumin seeds**
1½ **pounds uncooked medium shrimp, peeled and deveined**
3½ **teaspoons finely grated lime peel**
6   **tablespoons freshly squeezed lime juice**
6   **tablespoons plain yogurt**
6   **tablespoons chopped fresh cilantro**
2½ **teaspoons minced, seeded serrano or jalapeño chiles**
    salt and pepper to taste

- Preheat oven to 325°F. Place tortilla wedges in single layer on 2 large baking sheets. Bake until crisp, turning once, about 30 minutes. Cool on baking sheet.
- Spray small baking dish with vegetable spray. Add garlic; cover with foil. Bake until tender, about 30 minutes. Cool slightly. Peel garlic and mash in small bowl.
- Heat small skillet over medium heat. Add cumin seeds; stir until fragrant, about 1 minute. Grind in spice grinder or in mortar with pestle. Add to garlic.
- Bring large pot of water to boil. Add shrimp and lime peel and cook until shrimp are opaque, about 3 minutes. Drain shrimp and lime peel in fine strainer. Cool. Coarsely chop shrimp. Transfer shrimp and lime peel to bowl.
- Tortillas, garlic mixture and shrimp can be made 1 day ahead. Store tortillas in airtight containers at room temperature. Chill garlic mixture and shrimp separately.
- Add lime juice, yogurt, chopped cilantro, chiles and garlic mixture to shrimp. Season with salt and pepper. Spoon atop tortilla chips and serve.

Yield: 6 to 8 servings

Scallops with Jamaican Tartar Sauce

Jamaican Tartar Sauce

½ cup light mayonnaise

½ teaspoon hot pepper sauce

2 tablespoons peeled and finely chopped lime sections

2 tablespoons finely chopped green onions

1 tablespoon finely minced cilantro

1 stalk celery, finely minced

- **Combine all ingredients and refrigerate 1 hour to blend flavors.**

1 egg
2 tablespoons nonfat yogurt
½ teaspoon hot pepper sauce
¼ teaspoon salt
1 cup fine dry bread crumbs
⅓ cup white cornmeal or fine yellow cornmeal
no stick vegetable cooking spray
1⅓ pounds large scallops, patted dry with paper towels
2 teaspoons margarine, melted
Jamaican Tartar Sauce (see sidebar)

- Preheat oven to 475°F.
- Whisk together egg, yogurt, pepper sauce and salt. Pour on a plate.
- Combine bread crumbs and cornmeal and spread on a second plate.
- Spray a large, shallow baking pan with cooking spray.
- Dip scallops in egg mixture, then in bread crumb mixture.
- Arrange in the baking pan and drizzle with melted margarine.
- Bake for 8 minutes.
- Remove scallops from the oven; turn the oven to broil. When hot, put scallops on the top rack and broil until golden and cooked through.
- Serve with Jamaican Tartar Sauce.

Yield: 8 to 10 servings

Wine Recommendations: Moscato d'Asti or German Riesling Spatlese

Southern Scallops with Lime Horseradish Sauce

An excellent main dish when paired with Herbed Couscous and Vegetables (page 227)

Lime Horseradish Sauce

½ cup mayonnaise
2 tablespoons drained, bottled horseradish
1½ teaspoons fresh lime juice
½ teaspoon freshly grated lime zest
⅛ teaspoon freshly ground black pepper, or to taste

- **Whisk together sauce ingredients and chill, covered.**

6 5-by 2½-inch graham crackers
1 teaspoon coarse salt
1 pound sea scallops (about 24)
vegetable oil
1 large egg, lightly beaten
Lime Horseradish Sauce (see sidebar)

- Place graham crackers in a resealable plastic bag and lightly crush with a rolling pin until crumbs are coarse.
- In a bowl stir together crumbs and salt.
- Discard small, tough muscle from the side of each scallop and halve any large scallops. Pat scallops dry.

(continued on next page)

Southern Scallops with Lime Horseradish Sauce *(continued)*

- In a 4-quart heavy saucepan or heavy kettle, heat 1½ inches oil until it reaches 365°F on a deep-fat thermometer.
- Working in batches of 6, dip scallops in egg to coat, letting excess drip off, and roll in crumb mixture.
- Fry scallops, stirring gently, 2 minutes, or until browned and cooked through.
- Transfer scallops as cooked with a slotted spoon to paper towels to drain and season with salt and pepper.
- Serve with Lime Horseradish Sauce.

Yield: 6 to 8 servings

Wine Recommendations: Demi-Sec Loire Chenin Blanc or California Off-Dry Riesling

Chicken Saté with Thai Dipping Sauce

2   **boneless, skinless chicken breasts**
½   **(6-ounce) jar dry tandoori spice**
6   **tablespoons olive oil**
1   **teaspoon salt**
1   **teaspoon pepper**
½   **teaspoon ground coriander**
    Thai Dipping Sauce (see sidebar)

- Slice chicken into ¼-inch thick strips.
- In a small bowl, combine tandoori spice, olive oil, salt, pepper and coriander.
- Pour over chicken and toss well. Marinate for 6 hours.
- Thread chicken on skewers.
- Grill over medium coals until done, about 8 minutes.
- Serve with Thai Dipping Sauce.

Yield: 6 servings

Thai Dipping Sauce

6 **tablespoons peanut butter**
1 **cup hot chicken stock**
  Thai pepper paste to taste

- In a small bowl, combine peanut butter, chicken stock and Thai pepper paste. Whisk until smooth.

Sweet and Sour Chicken Lollipops

24 **chicken drumettes**
  salt and pepper to taste
1½ **cups duck or plum sauce, about 2 (10-ounce) jars**
¼ **cup soy sauce**
¼ **cup dry white wine**
  orange slices to garnish

- Preheat oven to 350°F.
- Holding drumette at base and using small sharp knife, push all meat toward top, forming lollipop shape. Repeat with remaining drumettes.
- Space drumettes evenly on baking sheet. Season with salt and pepper. Bake 30 minutes, basting drumettes with pan juices.
- Combine duck or plum sauce, soy sauce and white wine in medium bowl. Remove chicken from oven. Spoon half of sauce over drumettes. Return to oven and bake until chicken is golden and crisp, about 15 minutes. Using tongs, transfer chicken to serving platter.
- Garnish with orange slices and serve remaining sauce separately.

Yield: 24 pieces

Wine Recommendations: Vouvray, Alsace Gewurztraminer or California Viognier

Shrimp and Andouille Sausage Crostini

Flavors from the bayou travel north.

Andouille is the highly seasoned and heavily smoked sausage found in a variety of Cajun dishes. Use it to create a spicier rendition of any dish that calls for smoked sausage, or serve it straight up and cold.

2 **tablespoons olive oil**
½ **cup chopped andouille sausage**
¼ **cup diced shallots or red onion**
6 **ounces uncooked shrimp, peeled, deveined and coarsely chopped**
¼ **cup diced, roasted red peppers (purchased are suitable)**
2 **tablespoons chopped fresh parsley**
1 **tablespoon chopped fresh thyme**
1 **tablespoon Dijon mustard**
  salt and pepper to taste
1 **baguette, cut into 24 slices, each ½-inch thick, toasted**

- Heat oil in heavy skillet over medium-high heat. Add sausage and sauté until golden, about 2 minutes. Transfer sausage to a bowl using a slotted spoon.
- Add shallots or red onion to same skillet and sauté 3 minutes.
- Add shrimp and sauté until cooked through, about 3 minutes.
- Mix in peppers, parsley, fresh thyme, mustard and sausage. Season with salt and pepper.
- Spoon mixture onto bread slices. Arrange on platter and serve.

Yield: 24 pieces

Chèvre Crostini with Fresh Seasonal Herbs

1   baguette, cut into ¼-inch thick slices
8   ounces chèvre, crumbled
¼   cup chopped fresh rosemary, parsley, basil and dill
¼   cup minced sun-dried tomatoes in oil, drained
1   cup extra virgin olive oil

- Place the baguette slices on a baking sheet and toast in a preheated 350°F oven until crisp, about 15 minutes.
- Spread or sprinkle the cheese on the baguette slices and top with your choice of herbs and sun-dried tomatoes.
- Drizzle the olive oil very generously over the top.
- Bake until hot, about 5 minutes.

Yield: approximately 10 servings

Wine Recommendations: Unoaked Sauvignon Blanc, Pinot Grigio or Côtes du Rhone Blanc

Smoked Salmon and Caper Crostini

Capers add the crowning touch to these distinctive crostini.

1   (8-ounce) package cream cheese, softened
¾   cup grated Parmesan cheese
1   teaspoon freshly squeezed lemon juice
    dash of Tabasco sauce
8   slices finely textured white bread, trimmed of crusts
⅓   cup butter, softened
3   ounces thinly sliced smoked salmon
    fresh dill sprigs
    capers

- Combine the cream cheese, Parmesan cheese, lemon juice and Tabasco in the bowl of a food processor and process 30 seconds.
- Preheat the oven to 350°F.
  Spread bread on both sides with 1 teaspoon of butter. Cut each slice into 4 triangles and arrange in a single layer on a baking sheet.
- Bake for 3 to 5 minutes until lightly browned. Remove from the oven, turn over all the pieces and bake 1 to 2 minutes more.
- Top each piece of toast with a small piece of smoked salmon.
- Put the cream cheese mixture in a pastry bag fitted with a number 5 open star tip and pipe rosettes of the cream cheese over the smoked salmon.
- Bake for 5 minutes.
- Garnish each with 3 capers and a sprig of fresh dill.

Yield: 32 large pieces

Wine Recommendations: Brut Champagne, Loire Valley Sauvignon Blanc or Dry Riesling

Chèvre is a distinctively tart and light cheese made from goat's milk. Popular varieties include Banon, Bucheron and Montrachet. Look for the words "pur chèvre" on the label to ensure a cheese that is 100 percent goat's milk. Shapes and textures vary among the chèvre cheeses, and they often come packed in spices and oils. Store tightly wrapped and refrigerated for 2 weeks. When cooking with chèvre, bring to room temperature first for best results.

Kalamatas are intensely
rich and fruity olives from
Greece. They are a deep
purplish color and are
almond-like in shape and
size. These olives are
soaked in a wine vinegar
marinade, and likely
scored to better absorb the
marinade's flavors.

Mediterranean Crostini

Augment the Mediterranean theme with a garnish of kalamata olives.

1	baguette, thinly sliced on the diagonal
1	pound eggplant, peeled and cut into ½-inch cubes
1	large onion, chopped
2	tablespoons red wine vinegar
	salt and freshly ground black pepper to taste
1	(7½-ounce) jar roasted red peppers, drained
¼	cup minced fresh parsley
¼ to ½	pound Monterey Jack cheese, grated
¼	cup grated Romano cheese

- Place the baguette slices on a baking sheet and toast in a preheated 350°F oven until crisp, about 15 minutes. Remove from the oven.
- Raise the oven temperature to 425°F. In a large roasting or baking pan, toss together the eggplant, onion, olive oil, vinegar, salt and pepper. Bake until tender, about 15 minutes.
- Lower the oven temperature to 350°F. Transfer the roasted eggplant mixture to a mixing bowl. Add the remaining ingredients and toss well. Taste and adjust the seasonings.
- Spread each Crostini (the crisped baguette slices) with the eggplant and cheese mixture and return to the baking sheet. Bake until hot, about 7 to 10 minutes.

Yield: approximately 10 servings

Delectable wontons fill the
bill as appetizers, snacks
and even side dishes. The
thin dough wrappers are
prepackaged and available
in the produce section of
most supermarkets and
Chinese markets. The dough
comes in both circles and
squares and a variety of
thicknesses. Once filled
with any of our suggestions
or a creation of your own,
wontons may be steamed,
boiled or deep-fried.

Crispy Wontons with Pork

One among many inventive "wrappetizers"

60	wonton wrappers
½	pound ground pork, cooked and drained
1	(5-ounce) can water chestnuts, drained and chopped
¼	cup finely chopped green onions
1	teaspoon fresh ginger juice
1	teaspoon salt
2	teaspoons soy sauce
	dash of pepper
	vegetable oil for frying

- Combine meat with water chestnuts, green onions and ginger juice. Mix well.
- Add remaining ingredients except wonton wrappers.
- Spread wrappers and place a small portion of filling in the center. Fold and seal.
- Deep-fry in preheated vegetable oil until crisp and golden. Drain on paper towels; serve immediately.

Yield: 60 pieces

Swedish Sirloin Filling

Voted most likely to succeed; superb after work.

1	**pound ground sirloin**
4	**tablespoons minced onions**
2	**cloves fresh garlic, minced**
2	**cups shredded Napa cabbage (Chinese cabbage)**
1	**cup grated fresh carrots**
4	**tablespoons sour cream**
2	**teaspoons caraway seeds**
2	**teaspoons dill weed**
½	**teaspoon salt**
1	**teaspoon freshly cracked black pepper**

- Sauté sirloin, onion and garlic until meat is thoroughly cooked. Add cabbage and sauté for about 10 minutes. Remove from heat and drain well.
- Place meat mixture in a large bowl and add remaining ingredients. Mix well and stuff into wrappers of your choice. Cook according to wrapper instructions.

Yield: Varies depending on wrappers

Tuscan Sausage Filling

Voted most athletic; perfect snack for armchair quarterbacks.

1	**pound Italian sausage, sweet or hot**
1	**medium onion**
1	**pound white mushrooms**
¼	**cup medium-dry sherry**
½	**cup chopped fresh parsley**
½	**cup minced, sun-dried tomatoes**
½	**cup ricotta cheese**
½	**cup freshly grated Parmesan cheese**
½	**cup shredded mozzarella cheese**

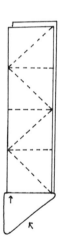

- Preheat oven to 375°F.
- Cook sausage in skillet until no longer pink. Remove from heat and drain, reserving 2 tablespoons of the drippings.
- Add onion and mushrooms to the hot skillet and cook over medium heat until onions are soft and mushrooms' liquid has evaporated.
- Coarsely chop all ingredients and mix well.
- Stuff into wrappers of your choice, such as pizza crust dough or pie crust and bake according to wrapper instructions.

Yield: Varies depending on wrappers

FINISHED
TRIANGLE

Oriental Citrus-Beef Filling

East meets West summit

½ **pound ground beef**
1 **tablespoon frozen orange juice concentrate**
1 **tablespoon soy sauce**
1 **teaspoon sesame oil**
1 **teaspoon rice vinegar**
1 **teaspoon brown sugar**
2 **cloves garlic**
1 **teaspoon grated ginger**
1 **teaspoon grated orange peel**
¼ **teaspoon salt**
¼ **teaspoon cayenne pepper**

- Mix all ingredients in a skillet and cook over medium heat until meat is cooked. Remove from heat and drain.
- Place mixture in ready-made wrappers such as sui mai wrappers or egg roll wrappers. Bake according to wrapper instructions.

Yield: Varies depending on wrappers

Asian Shrimp and Coconut Filling

Sensational served with duck, plum or hoisin sauce and prepared in potsticker wrappers.

1 **pound fresh cooked shrimp, peeled**
2 **cloves garlic**
2 **tablespoons grated ginger**
2 **green onions**
1 **teaspoon crushed red pepper flakes or curry powder**
2 **teaspoons grated orange, lemon, or lime peel**
½ **cup sweetened, flaked coconut**
   fresh cilantro to taste

- Chop all ingredients coarsely.
- Mix well and stuff into ready-made wrappers and bake according to wrapper instructions.

Yield: Varies depending on wrappers

A variety of Asian inspired dipping sauces, such as duck, plum and hoisin, are typically found on the international isle of your supermarket or in oriental markets. Be adventuresome. Experiment with these sauces and others, too.

Fried Wontons with Bacon and Brie

Voted most likely to disappear.

12 **wonton wrappers**
4½ **ounces Brie cheese**
4 **slices bacon, cooked and crumbled**
1 **egg, beaten**
    vegetable oil for frying
    mango chutney

- Remove crust from Brie and discard. Divide Brie into 12 equal parts.
- Place a piece of Brie on top of each wonton wrapper. Top each with about 1 teaspoon of crumbled bacon. Brush 2 adjacent sides of each wrapper with beaten egg, and fold wrapper over to seal into a triangular shape.
- Deep-fry wontons in preheated vegetable oil until golden. Drain on paper towels, then serve hot with mango chutney.

Yield: 12 pieces

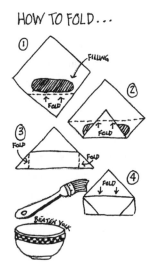

HOW TO FOLD . . .

Green Chile Wonton Cups

Voted most popular — a big winner among testers.

60 **wonton wrappers**
1   **pound Monterey Jack cheese with green chiles, grated**
1   **cup sour cream**
½   **cup pitted black olives, chopped**
⅔   **cup green chiles, seeded, ribbed, and chopped (4-ounce can)**
½   **cup minced green onions**
1   **teaspoon cumin, or more to taste**
1   **teaspoon dried oregano, or more to taste**
    vegetable oil

- Preheat oven to 350°F.
- Combine all ingredients except wonton wrappers and oil. Taste and adjust seasonings.
- To prepare the wontons, oil a mini muffin tin and place 1 wrapper in each cup. Brush each with oil.
- Bake empty wonton wrappers at 350°F until crisp, about 10 to 15 minutes. Remove cups from the muffin tin and place them on a baking sheet.
- Fill the cups with filling and bake at 375°F for about 10 minutes, or until filling is hot and bubbly.

Yield: 60 pieces

Wine Recommendations: New Zealand or Australian Sauvignon Blanc, Alsace Pinot Blanc or Dry Riesling

Canapés are the quintessential hors d'oeuvre, both elegant and simple. Canapés are simple for two reasons. First, canapés consist of only four components; a base, an adhesive, a body and a garnish. The components are a constant, even if the possible combinations for each are many. Second, making canapés requires little measurement; hence they are foolproof. Tip: a classic canapé is ALWAYS crunchy when bitten into, never soft. The following four pages offer various suggestions for making these basic yet impressive appetizers.

Canapés

Canapés consist of four parts: Base, Adhesive, Body and Garnish.

Canapé bases may include:

Thin bread, toasted and cut into shapes
Gladiola blossoms, stamens removed, washed, and shaken dry
Jicama sliced about ¼-inch thick and cut into a star shape
Water crackers
Wonton skins brushed lightly with water, folded diagonally twice into a triangle, then deep-fried and drained
Mushroom caps
Red bell pepper slices cut into heart shapes
Tortilla chips
Toasted pita triangles
Endive leaves
Grilled flour tortillas (brushed with oil first)
Cherry tomato halves, scooped clean
Hard-boiled egg halves, scooped clean
Bliss potatoes
Snow peas
Polenta cakes
English cucumber discs (because they are seedless)
Daikon sliced about ¼-inch thick and cut into ovals or squares

Adhesives may include:

(Note: Adhesives act as a barrier, separating the base and body to keep the base from becoming soggy.)

Mayonnaise or cream cheese flavored with chopped fresh herbs.
Flavored butters (see Side Bars, page 70, 216, 219, 220, 225, 228)
Purchased or homemade pâté

Following are six adhesives that contain five ingredients or fewer:

Lemon Butter

    zest and juice of 1 lemon
1   cup unsalted butter, softened
    salt and white pepper to taste

- Blanch the lemon zest in lightly salted boiling water for 5 minutes. Drain and dry.
- Whip all ingredients together thoroughly.

(continued on next page)

(Canapés continued)

Mustard-Thyme Butter

1   **cup unsalted butter, softened**
2   **tablespoons fresh thyme leaves, minced**
3   **tablespoons Dijon mustard**
    salt and white pepper to taste

• Whip all ingredients together until thoroughly blended.

Tomato-Cilantro Butter

½   **cup unsalted butter, softened**
½   **cup tomato, peeled, seeded, and diced small**
2   **tablespoons fresh cilantro, stems removed, minced**
1   **tablespoon dry white wine**
    salt and white pepper to taste

• Whip all ingredients together until thoroughly blended.

Asian-Style Paste

1   **(8-ounce) package cream cheese, softened**
1   **tablespoon Wasabi (or horseradish)**
1   **tablespoon grated ginger**
1   **tablespoon oyster sauce**
2   **tablespoon soy sauce**

• Purée all ingredients in a food processor until smooth.

Olive Paste

1   **cup kalamata olives, pitted**
2   **cloves garlic**
½   **teaspoon grated lemon zest**
1   **tablespoon lemon juice**
¼   **cup olive oil**
    black pepper to taste

• Purée all ingredients in a food processor or mince very finely and press through a sieve.

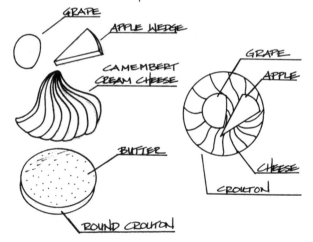

(continued on next page)

Roasted Garlic Paste

1   **garlic bulb (not a clove)**
2   **tablespoons olive oil**
½   **cup unsalted butter, softened**
½   **cup cream cheese, softened**
     salt and white pepper to taste

- Preheat oven to 375°F.
- Break the garlic bulb into cloves, discarding excess skin. Toss the cloves in the olive oil.
- Place in a roasting pan and roast for about 35 minutes. Remove; set aside to cool.
- Squeeze out the soft garlic from the cloves and mash thoroughly with a fork.
- Add the cream cheese and butter. Blend thoroughly and season to taste with salt and white pepper.

The body may include almost anything:

Slices of hard-boiled egg
Strips of rare beef
Grilled lamb
Scallops
Shrimp
Pan-seared tuna
Slices of smoked salmon
Slices of chorizo or andouille sausage
Seasonal vegetables, raw or roasted, such as squashes, zucchini, cucumber or onions
Cooked, mashed sweet potatoes
Slices of cherry tomatoes or larger tomato wedges
Slices of fruit
Cubes of cheese
Slices of ham

Garnish suggestions include:

Radish slice
Slice of kiwi
Slice of pickled gingerroot
Cilantro leaf
Sprig of dill
Carrots cut into matchsticks
Pecan halves
Pistachios
Basil leaf
Olive slice or half
Half a seedless grape

(continued on next page)

(Canapés continued)

Wedge of green apple
Small wedge of pineapple
Red bell pepper strip
Capers
Dollop of caviar
Mint leaf
Spoonful of chutney
Sliver of almond
Melon cube
Snipped chives
Bacon pieces
Chopped egg
Curly lettuce

Sample canapés include:

Gorgonzola Bites
- Water cracker topped with a mixture of equal parts Gorgonzola cheese, cream cheese and butter blended into a smooth paste. Garnish with a half slice of seedless grape and a toasted walnut.

Grecian Morsels
- Diamond-shaped crouton spread with a thin layer of Olive Paste, garnished with a half cherry tomato that is scooped out and filled with feta cheese blended into a paste with garlic, oregano and black pepper.

Greek Tomato Canapés
- Oval crouton spread with goat cheese, topped with a slice of Roma tomato, then a mixture of crumbled feta cheese, goat cheese, basil, olive oil and garlic. Garnish with a small wedge of kalamata olive.

Ham Cornets
- Cut thin-sliced ham into 1½-inch circles, and make an incision from the center to the edge. Roll into a cone shape and fill with cream cheese flavored with Dijon-style mustard and tarragon. Spread a square crouton with a thin layer of the same spread and place the cornet on top. Garnish with a small wedge of pineapple.

Jicama and Chorizo Canapés
- Spread a ¼-inch thick slice of Jicama, cut into a star, with a paste made from goat cheese and salsa verde. Top with a slice of chorizo. Garnish with a red bell pepper spear.

"*I remember striking out on my own. My two best buddies loading my possessions into a rental truck and driving me out of town. We arrived at the antebellum two-story where I was to rent the upstairs. The charming owners lived downstairs and greeted us, asking, 'Would y'all care for a libation?' Until the day my husband proposed, that was the most welcome question of my life.*"

Offering drinks is often more about hospitality than about quenching thirst. Iced down in a cooler, piping hot from a thermos; refreshing on the patio, soothing by the fire; garnished with a sprig of mint or with a cinnamon stick, the "libation" can make or break any occasion. We have included a variety for the seasons, for casual or formal affairs.

Eggceptional Eggnog

6 whole eggs
3 eggs, separated
1½ cups sugar
2 cups heavy cream
1 teaspoon vanilla extract
3 cups whole milk
1½ cups dark rum (optional)
⅛ teaspoon ground nutmeg
⅛ teaspoon ground cinnamon
⅛ teaspoon ground cardamom
    additional nutmeg for garnish

- In a large bowl, using an electric mixer set on high speed, beat the whole eggs, yolks and sugar until frothy and light, about 5 minutes.
- Add the heavy cream and vanilla and beat until thick, another 5 minutes. Beat in the milk. Set aside.
- In a medium bowl, using an electric mixer or whisk, beat the egg whites until stiff.
- Stir the nutmeg, cinnamon and cardamom into the rum. Pour the spiced rum into the egg-cream mixture, stir, and then fold in half the egg whites.
- Pour the mixture into a large serving bowl. Dollop the remaining beaten egg whites on top and sprinkle with nutmeg.

Yield: 10 servings

Hot Buttered Rum

1   pound butter
1   (16-ounce) package brown sugar
1   (16-ounce) package powdered sugar
    cinnamon to taste
    nutmeg to taste
1   quart vanilla ice cream (good quality), softened slightly
    rum
    boiling water
1   pint heavy cream, whipped with 1 teaspoon vanilla extract

- Cream butter, brown sugar, powdered sugar, cinnamon and nutmeg until fluffy.
- Fold in ice cream.
- Freeze until ready to use, up to 6 months.
- Place 3 tablespoons mix in a mug with 1 jigger of rum.
- Fill with boiling water.
- Top with whipped cream.

Yield: 24 servings

Generate warmth for your wintertime party by making large quantities of Hot Buttered Rum. This recipe can be made and served hot in a coffee server or even a "well-dressed" crock pot. Serve whipped cream separately on the side.

Beach Bum Cooler

1   (750-milliliter) bottle inexpensive pink champagne
1   liter inexpensive white wine
4   ounces brandy
4   ounces triple sec
2   ounces Grand Marnier
½   (6-ounce) can orange juice concentrate
    juice of 1 lemon
2   (10-ounce) packages frozen strawberries with syrup
1   liter club soda
1   liter 7-up
    ice

- Mix and chill well before serving.

Yield: 24 servings

Fitzgerald's Irish Cream

1   cup vodka
1   tablespoon Kahlúa
1   (14-ounce) can sweetened condensed milk
2   tablespoons chocolate syrup
1½ cups heavy cream
2   teaspoons instant coffee
1   teaspoon vanilla extract
½   teaspoon almond extract

- Combine all ingredients in a blender. Blend until smooth.
- Store tightly covered in a refrigerator, up to 1 month.
- Shake well before serving.

Yield: 12 to 14 servings

Cran-Apple Bourbon Punch

1   (32-ounce) bottle cran-apple juice cocktail
1   (28-ounce) bottle ginger ale
1   (12-ounce) can frozen lemonade concentrate
1½ cups bourbon whiskey

- Mix all ingredients in an airtight 4-quart container and freeze overnight.
- Scrape and scoop into stemmed glasses.
- Serve immediately.

Yield: 16 servings

Champagne Brunch Punch

2   (12-ounce) cans frozen lemonade concentrate
2   (12-ounce) cans water
2   quarts champagne, chilled
2   quarts club soda, chilled
1   (10-ounce) bag frozen whole berries

- Gently mix liquids in a punch bowl.
- Add the frozen berries.
- Serve in champagne flutes with 1 to 2 berries floating in each glass.

Yield: 16 servings

Bright Beginnings Punch

1   (6-ounce) can frozen lemonade concentrate, thawed
1   (6-ounce) can frozen pineapple juice concentrate, thawed
1   (6-ounce) can frozen strawberry daiquiri mix, thawed
5   cups cold water/ice combined
1   cup fresh fruit (strawberries or bananas are best)

• Stir all ingredients and serve in a pitcher or punch bowl.

Note: Easy to double or triple.

Note: May make ahead and add fruit just before serving.

Yield: 12 servings

Lemon Tea Refresher

8   cups water
12 small tea bags
10 whole cloves
1½ cups sugar
1   (12-ounce) can lemonade concentrate

• Boil water. Steep tea bags for 5 minutes with cloves.
• Add sugar and lemonade.
• Mix together.
• Add enough water to make 1 gallon of iced tea.

Yield: 10 servings

Orange Scream!

1   (16-ounce) can orange juice concentrate, softened
½   cup instant nonfat dry milk
½   cup water
1   teaspoon vanilla extract
8 to 10 ice cubes

• Process all ingredients in a blender on low for 1 minute.
• Add a little more water if the mixture is too thick, and blend for another minute.

Yield: 4 servings

Watermelon Granita

5 to 6	cups watermelon cubes, seeded
2	teaspoons freshly squeezed lemon juice
1/4	cup sugar
10	ounces vodka or rum (optional)
	lemon slices or mint sprigs for garnish

- Place first three ingredients in a blender or food processor. Blend until smooth.
- Pour through a strainer or cheesecloth to remove pulp.
- Place strained liquid in a freezer-proof glass baking dish and freeze for 2 to 3 hours, stirring mixture with a fork at 1/2-hour intervals to break up ice crystal.
- Add vodka or rum if preparing an alcoholic beverage.
- Serve slushy mixture in wine or martini glasses, garnished with a lemon slice or a mint sprig.

Yield: 10 to 12 servings

Warm-n-Spicy Tea

1/2	gallon unsweetened tea
2	cups orange juice
6 to 8	ounces pineapple juice
1/4	cup freshly squeezed lemon juice
1/2	cup sugar
1	tablespoon honey
1/2	cup whole cloves, tied in cheesecloth
1	cinnamon stick

- In a large pot, heat tea to hot but not boiling. Add next 6 ingredients and stir.
- Continue to heat, and when tea mixture is again hot but not boiling, add cinnamon stick for only 60 seconds; then remove the cinnamon stick from the tea.
- Continue heating and serve warm.
- Remove cloves after approximately 20 minutes of heating.

Yield: 12 servings

Gambler's Slush

8   **lemons**
4   **cups bourbon whiskey**
4   **cups water**
1   **cup sugar**
    fresh mint to garnish

- Squeeze lemons, reserving rinds.
- Measure 1½ cups juice into large freezer-proof jar. Add bourbon, water and sugar and stir until sugar dissolves. Add lemon rinds.
- Cover and let stand at room temperature for 24 hours. Squeeze rinds into bourbon mixture, then discard. Strain bourbon mixture and return to jar.
- Cover jar and freeze 24 hours.
- Scoop slush into glasses. Garnish with mint sprigs and serve immediately.

Yield: 12 servings

Backyard Berry Delight

1   **cup strawberries**
1   **cup raspberries**
1   **cup blueberries**
1   **cup lowfat milk**
1   **cup apple juice**

- Chill all ingredients.
- Process in a blender.
- Serve in a tall glass.

Yield: 4 servings

Appetizers and Beverages

Smithfield Biscuits

Fresh out of the oven, split apart and slathered with butter, these biscuits are heavenly.

3	cups self-rising flour
2	teaspoons baking powder
3	teaspoons powdered sugar
½	cup shortening
1¼	cups buttermilk
2	tablespoons butter, melted

- Preheat oven to 450°F.
- Sift together flour, baking powder and powdered sugar. Cut in shortening until mixture resembles coarse crumbs. Stir in buttermilk until just moistened.
- Turn dough out onto a lightly floured surface. Sprinkle dough with just enough flour to handle. Gently knead dough 6 times or until no longer sticky. Lightly flour top of dough and fold in half. Pat or roll dough to ½-inch thickness. Cut dough with a floured biscuit cutter.
- Place biscuits on an ungreased baking sheet. For soft sides, place biscuits so they are touching each other. For crusty sides, place biscuits 1-inch apart. Brush tops of biscuits with melted butter.
- Bake for 12 minutes.

Yield: 18 biscuits

Sweet Potato Biscuits

Country ham was meant to land on a warm, sweet potato biscuit.

2 to 2¾	cups all-purpose flour, divided
5	teaspoons baking powder
1	teaspoon salt
¼	cup sugar
2	cups cooked, mashed sweet potatoes
½	cup shortening
¾	cup milk

- Preheat oven to 425°F.
- Sift together 2 cups flour, baking powder, salt and sugar. Make a well in center of flour mixture. Pour in sweet potatoes and mix well. Add shortening and mix well. Add milk and mix well.
- In bowl, gradually knead in additional flour until dough is no longer sticky.
- Turn dough out onto a lightly floured surface. Pat dough to ½-inch thickness. Cut dough with a floured, 2-inch biscuit cutter.
- Place biscuits on an ungreased baking sheet. For soft sides, place biscuits so they are touching each other. For crusty sides, place biscuits 1-inch apart.
- Bake for 10 to 15 minutes or until golden brown.

Yield: 30 biscuits

In a series of essays entitled *Growing Up In Raleigh,* Edgar M. Wyatt recalls being served big breakfasts at Oak View farm in the 1930s. The Wyatt family owned the property from 1886 until 1940, and a superintendent and his family lived on the premises.

"We ate with the family in the kitchen, which was several yards from the main house. I can taste those big, fat biscuits, red-eye gravy, ham and fresh vegetables cooked on a wood stove. There was no electricity, indoor plumbing, or phone service at the farm at that time. There was a hand pump at the end of the kitchen sink with a water bucket handy to prime the pump. There was always plenty of fresh milk."

Raleigh Times advertisement for A & P grocery store, April 4, 1928, the first year that the Junior League was active in Raleigh:

Red Circle coffee, 39¢ per pound

Large can sweet potatoes, 10¢

Finest compound lard, 2 pounds for 25¢

Quick and Incredible Cheese Biscuits
Bite-size, melt-in-your-mouth biscuits

2   cups (about 8 ounces) shredded sharp cheddar cheese
1   cup butter, melted
1   cup sour cream
2   cups self-rising flour

- Preheat oven to 350°F.
- Mix together cheese and melted butter. Cool for 2 minutes. Add sour cream and mix well. Stir in flour.
- Spoon batter into greased miniature muffin cups.
- Bake for 18 to 22 minutes.

Note: Batter can be stored overnight in the refrigerator.

Variations: Combine ½ teaspoon garlic powder or ½ teaspoon ground cayenne pepper with flour before adding to cheese mixture.

Variation: Combine butter and sour cream. Do not add cheese. Stir in flour that has been combined with 2 teaspoons dried dill seed. Immediately after baking, brush tops of muffins with 2 tablespoons melted butter and sprinkle with 1 teaspoon dried dill weed.

Yield: 48 biscuits

Herbed Carrot Biscuits
Carrots give these drop biscuits a slightly sweet taste, and cornmeal adds substance.

1¼ cups all-purpose flour
¾   cup cornmeal
3   teaspoons baking powder
½   teaspoon salt
¼   cup sugar
1   tablespoon minced fresh basil
1   tablespoon minced fresh parsley
¾   cup butter
½   cup shredded carrots
¾   cup milk
1   egg, lightly beaten

- Preheat oven to 400°F.
- Combine flour, cornmeal, baking powder, salt, sugar, basil and parsley. Cut in butter until mixture resembles coarse crumbs. Add carrots. Stir in milk and egg until just moistened.
- Drop dough by ¼ cup onto an ungreased baking sheet.
- Bake for 12 to 14 minutes or until light golden brown.

Yield: 12 biscuits

Marriott Little

Megg's Cups
watercolor, 1994

From the private collection of
The Honorable and Mrs. Robert B. Rader, Raleigh, NC.

Breads and Brunch

Savory Onion Scones

Caramelized onions give moist scones a unique flavor.

5   tablespoons butter, divided
¾   cup (about 1 large) chopped onion
2   cups all-purpose flour
3   teaspoons baking powder
2   tablespoons sugar
½   teaspoon salt
¾   teaspoon coarsely ground pepper
½   cup heavy cream
1   egg, lightly beaten

- Preheat oven to 400°F.
- Melt 4 tablespoons butter in a small skillet. Cook onion until crisp-tender. Set aside.
- Sift together flour, baking powder, sugar, salt and pepper. Add cream, egg and onion. Stir until just moistened.
- Turn dough out onto a lightly floured surface. Sprinkle dough with just enough flour to handle. Gently knead dough 5 or 6 times or until no longer sticky.
- Place dough on an ungreased baking sheet. Pat or roll dough into an 8-inch circle. Cut dough into 8 wedges and separate slightly.
- Bake for 12 to 16 minutes or until very light brown.
- Brush wedges with 1 tablespoon melted butter.

Yield: 8 scones

Southerners love their biscuits, but the Scottish scone has never fallen out of favor. Scones are traditionally sliced into wedges, baked and served warm. Sweet scones are often served at tea with jams, fresh whipped butter and clotted cream. Onion Scones are better served with main course dishes than at tea.

Carolina Cornbread

A moist cornbread full of whole kernels of corn

½   cup butter, softened
2   eggs
1   cup sour cream
1   (8½-ounce) can corn, drained
1   (8½-ounce) can creamed corn
1½ cups self-rising cornmeal

- Preheat oven to 350°F.
- Mix together butter, eggs, sour cream, corn, creamed corn and cornmeal.
- Spoon batter into a greased 13x9-inch baking pan.
- Bake for 50 to 55 minutes.

Yield: 20 servings

"True Southerners," wrote renowned chef Bill Neal, "hold historical and cultural ties close to heart, more than geography; they will always be Southern wherever they are—New York, Chicago, Paris, London—and food is an important part of cultural identity."

Good Old Grits
Bill Neal and David Perry

Cornbread makes good company in menus both spicy and sweet. Try these combinations:

- Serve chili over cornbread waffles and top with sour cream, chopped onions and grated cheddar cheese.
- Bury a thick slice of cornbread in a bowl of black bean soup.
- Split large corn muffins, spread the halves with grainy mustard and fill them with deli meats and slices of cheese.
- Serve warm cornbread with butter and real maple syrup.
- Add a teaspoon of jam to the center of corn muffins before baking.

Traditional Southern Cornbread

Many southern meals are not complete until a thick slice of cornbread has been added to the plate.

2	eggs, well beaten
½	cup vegetable oil
2	cups buttermilk
1½	cups white self-rising cornmeal
1	cup all-purpose flour
1	(¼-ounce) package active dry yeast
1½	teaspoons baking powder
½	teaspoon baking soda
1½	teaspoons salt
1	tablespoon sugar

- Preheat oven to 450°F.
- Mix together eggs, oil and buttermilk. Set aside.
- Combine cornmeal, flour, yeast, baking powder, baking soda, salt and sugar. Stir in egg mixture until batter is smooth.
- Spoon batter into a well-greased 10-inch cast iron skillet.
- Bake for 15 minutes.

Variations: Add one or more of the following to batter:

½	cup crumbled bacon
1	cup shredded cheddar or Monterey Jack cheese
1	cup canned, fresh, frozen or creamed corn
1	large onion, chopped
1	(4-ounce) can green chile peppers, drained and chopped
2	jalapeño peppers, seeded and chopped
½	cup diced sun-dried tomatoes

Variations: Spoon batter into greased cornstick pans and bake for 10-12 minutes or spoon batter into greased muffin cups and bake for 15 minutes.

Yield: 12 servings

Old-Fashioned Dinner Rolls

A little extra time and care will result in the softest, best-tasting rolls.

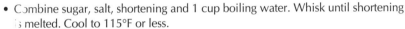

²/₃ **cup sugar**
1½ **teaspoons salt**
1 **cup shortening**
2 **cups water, divided**
2 **(¼-ounce) packages active dry yeast**
2 **eggs**
5 **cups (approximately) unbleached all-purpose flour**
3 **tablespoons butter, melted**

- Combine sugar, salt, shortening and 1 cup boiling water. Whisk until shortening is melted. Cool to 115°F or less.
- Dissolve yeast in 1 cup warm (110 to 115°F) water. Let stand 5 minutes.
- Pour yeast into shortening mixture. Add eggs and mix well. Gradually add flour until dough pulls cleanly away from sides of bowl.
- Place dough into a large greased bowl, turning to coat all surfaces. Cover bowl with plastic wrap held in place by a rubber band. Place in refrigerator and let rise overnight.
- Approximately 3½ hours before use, turn dough out onto a lightly floured surface and shape as desired.
- Place rolls on a greased baking sheet and let rise for 3 hours.
- Preheat oven to 375°F.
- Bake for 10 minutes.
- Brush rolls with melted butter.

Shaping Methods

- Bowknots: Shape dough into 2-inch balls. Roll each ball into a 10-inch rope. Tie rope in a loose knot, leaving 2 long ends.
- Cloverleaves: Shape dough into 1½-inch balls, pulling edges under to make smooth tops. Place 3 balls, smooth side up, in each cup of a greased muffin pan.
- Crescents: Divide dough into quarters and shape each into a ball. Roll each ball into a 12-inch circle. Cut each circle into 12 wedges. Roll wedges toward point beginning at wide end of wedge. Place rolls on baking sheet, point side down, curving ends to form a crescent.
- Flowers: Shape dough into 2-inch balls, pulling edges under to make smooth tops. Using kitchen shears, make 5 snips, cutting completely through dough, from edge almost to center.
- Rosettes: Shape dough into 2-inch balls. Roll each ball into a 12-inch rope. Tie rope in a loose knot, leaving 2 long ends. Tuck top end under roll. Bring bottom end up and tuck it into center of roll.
- Swirls: Shape dough into 2-inch balls. Roll each ball into an 8-inch rope. Beginning at center, make a loose coil with each rope and tuck end under.

Yield: Varies depending on shaping method

Dough needs a warm spot in which to rise. Temperatures between 80° and 85° are best. Place the bowl of dough on a wire rack over a pan of hot water. Or, warm the oven for one minute then turn it off and set the bowl of dough inside and close the door. Need something to do while the dough rises? Turn on the television and place the bowl, covered with a towel, on top of the set.

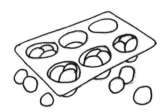

Give oats a toasty flavor by roasting them in a dry skillet over medium-high heat until lightly browned. Once they've cooled, add toasted oats in place of plain ones to your favorite bread and cookie recipes.

Oatmeal Rolls with Herb Butter

A panful of hearty rolls brushed with butter and topped with herbs

2	cups water, boiling
1	cup rolled oats
9	tablespoons butter, divided
3¾ to 4¾	cups all-purpose flour, divided
¼	cup sugar
2	teaspoons salt
2	(¼-ounce) packages active dry yeast
1	egg
1	tablespoon grated Parmesan cheese
1½	teaspoons minced fresh basil
¾	teaspoon minced fresh oregano
2	cloves garlic, minced

- Add boiling water to oats. Mix well. Stir in 3 tablespoons butter. Cool to 120° to 130°F.
- In a large bowl, combine 1½ cups flour, sugar, salt and yeast. Add oat mixture and egg. Beat with mixer at low speed until just moistened. Beat for 3 minutes at medium speed. Stir in an additional 1¾ to 2½ cups flour to form a stiff dough.
- Turn dough out onto a lightly floured surface. Knead in ½ to ¾ cup flour until dough is smooth and elastic, about 5 minutes. Shape dough into a ball. Cover with a large bowl and let rest for 15 minutes.
- Punch dough down in center with a fist and fold the edges to the center. Repeat.
- Press dough evenly into a greased 13x9-inch baking pan. Cut dough into 2-inch square rolls, using a very sharp knife to cut completely through dough. Cover pan with greased plastic wrap and a cloth towel. Let rise until doubled in bulk or until an indentation remains when you lightly press a finger against the edge of the rolls, about 45 minutes.
- Preheat oven to 375°F.
- Redefine cuts by poking tip of knife into cuts until knife hits bottom of pan; do not pull knife through dough. Spoon 4 tablespoons melted butter over rolls.
- Bake for 15 minutes.
- Brush remaining 2 tablespoons melted butter over rolls. Combine Parmesan cheese, basil, oregano and garlic. Sprinkle on top of rolls.

Yield: 24 rolls

Quick Herbed Focaccia

The whole family can pitch in to create pizza-wedge quick bread.

1   (12-inch) partially baked pizza crust
2   cloves garlic, minced
2   tablespoons olive oil
1   teaspoon dried Italian seasoning
1   tablespoon grated Parmesan cheese

- Preheat oven to 350°F.
- Place pizza crust on an ungreased baking sheet.
- Combine garlic and olive oil. Brush on pizza crust. Sprinkle Italian seasoning and Parmesan cheese over pizza crust.
- Bake for 8 minutes or until golden brown.
- Cut into wedges prior to serving.

Yield: 8 servings

Parmesan Twists

Serve these versatile twists with soup at lunch or alongside an Italian entrée at dinner.

1   cup all-purpose flour
½   teaspoon dried Italian seasoning
¼   cup butter, softened
1   cup grated Parmesan cheese
½   cup sour cream
1   egg yolk, slightly beaten
1   tablespoon water
       Poppy seeds

- Preheat oven to 350°F.
- Combine flour and Italian seasoning. Set aside.
- Cream butter. Add Parmesan cheese and sour cream. Beat well with mixer at medium speed. Gradually add flour mixture, blending until smooth.
- Turn dough out onto a lightly floured surface and divide in half. Lightly flour top of dough and roll each half into a 12x7-inch rectangle. Cut into 6x1-inch strips. Twist each strip 3 times.
- Place on a greased baking sheet. Combine egg yolk and water. Brush on twists. Sprinkle twists with poppy seeds.
- Bake for 10 to 12 minutes or until lightly browned.

Yield: 30 twists

Add Quick Herbed Focaccia to a picnic basket and relax in one of Raleigh's many picnicking spots. Find shade under the oaks at Pullen Park. Or glide across Shelley Lake in a rented boat and open your basket under the lakeside pines. In summer enjoy a movie under the stars and a romantic picnic for two at the North Carolina Museum of Art. Fireworks and a North Carolina Symphony performance round out the season on the vast lawn at Meredith College where picnickers gather by the thousands on Labor Day weekend.

Parmesan Twists are outstanding appetizers as well. Arrange them in a large napkin-lined basket and surround it with bowls of dips, such as marinara sauce, melted fondue-style cheese or hummus.

Quick breads are so named because they do not use yeast and therefore do not have to rise before baking. Other leavenings, baking soda and baking powder, are used in place of yeast. Baking soda reacts quickly with liquids and acidic ingredients such as buttermilk and sour cream. For best results put bread containing baking soda in the oven as soon as the liquid has been added. Baking powder reacts with liquids and with heat during baking. To determine if baking powder is active, add one teaspoon to a ½ cup of warm water. Vigorous bubbles indicate the powder is still active.

Sun-dried Tomato Quick Bread

Flavors of the Mediterranean in an herb-infused quick bread

2	cloves garlic, minced
1	teaspoon dried rosemary
1	teaspoon coarsely ground pepper
½	cup sun-dried tomatoes packed in oil, chopped and drained, reserving 2 tablespoons oil
3	cups all-purpose flour
2	teaspoons baking powder
1	teaspoon baking soda
1	teaspoon salt
2	tablespoons sugar
2	eggs
1½	cups milk
3	tablespoons shortening, melted and cooled
½	cup pitted and chopped kalamata or other brine-cured black olives
2	tablespoons drained and minced bottled capers
½	cup minced fresh flat-leafed parsley
1	cup grated Parmesan cheese

- Preheat oven to 350°F.
- In a small skillet over medium-low heat, cook garlic, rosemary and pepper in reserved oil from sun-dried tomatoes. Stir constantly until garlic is softened and fragrant but not browned.
- Sift together flour, baking powder, baking soda, salt and sugar. Set aside.
- Whisk together eggs, milk and shortening. Add garlic mixture. Stir in flour mixture until just combined. Fold in sun-dried tomatoes, olives, capers, parsley and Parmesan cheese.
- Spoon batter into 4 greased and floured 5½x3½-inch loaf pans.
- Bake for 35 to 40 minutes or until a wooden pick inserted in center of loaf comes out clean.
- Cool in pan for 10 minutes. Remove to wire rack and cool completely.

Yield: 4 loaves

Master Pizza Dough

Basic Recipe

3 to 3½ cups all-purpose flour
1   package quick-rising yeast
¾   teaspoon salt
1   cup very warm water (120 to 130°F)
2   tablespoons olive oil or vegetable oil
**   cornmeal**

- In large bowl, combine 2 cups flour, undissolved yeast and salt.
- Stir very warm water and olive oil into dry ingredients.
- Stir in enough remaining flour to make soft dough.
- Knead on lightly floured surface until smooth and elastic, about 4 to 6 minutes.
- Cover and let rest on flour surface 10 minutes.
- Lightly oil 1 (14-inch) or 2 (12-inch) round pizza pans. Sprinkle with cornmeal.
- Shape dough into smooth ball.
- Divide and roll dough to fit desired pans.
- Top pizza as desired.
- Bake at 400°F for 20 to 30 minutes or until done. Baking time depends on size and thickness of crust and selected toppings.

Variation: Garlic and Herb Pizza Dough
- Add 2 teaspoons dried basil, oregano or rosemary leaves and 1 clove garlic, finely minced, along with dry ingredients.

Food Processor Pizza Dough

3 cups all-purpose flour
1 package quick-rising yeast
¾ teaspoon salt
2 tablespoons olive oil or vegetable oil
¾-1 cup warm water (105° to 115°F)

- **Insert metal blade in food processor bowl.**
- **Add flour, undissolved yeast and salt. Process about 5 to 10 seconds to combine.**
- **Add oil and water. Begin processing until ball forms, about 10 to 15 seconds. (All the water may not be needed.)**
- **Continue processing 60 seconds to knead dough.**
- **Shape into ball.**
- **Cover and let rest on floured surface 10 minutes.**
- **Shape, top and bake as directed in Basic Recipe.**

Flavored butters add an extra sweet or zesty taste to freshly baked bread. Cream ½ cup butter until light and fluffy. Blend in any of the following:

- ½ cup preserves
- 1 teaspoon lemon or orange juice, 1 table-spoon powdered sugar, and ½ teaspoon lemon or orange zest
- ¼ cup honey, 1 table-spoon minced fresh parsley and a dash of white pepper
- 2 cloves garlic, minced
- 2 tablespoons minced fresh herbs
- 1 teaspoon lemon juice, 1 tablespoon minced fresh parsley, ¼ teaspoon dried savory, ⅛ teaspoon salt, and a dash of pepper

Rustic Honey Wheat Bread

Full of good-for-you grain, a substantial bread to serve with flavored butters

2	cups hot water
½	cup honey or molasses
2	(¼-ounce) packages active dry yeast
2	eggs
⅓	cup vegetable oil
½	cup rolled oats
½	cup yellow cornmeal
½	cup wheat germ
2	teaspoons salt
3	cups whole wheat flour
3	cups (approximately) unbleached all-purpose flour

- Stir together water and honey or molasses. Cool to 110°–115°F. Add yeast and stir until dissolved. Let stand 5 minutes.
- Add eggs, oil, oats, cornmeal, wheat germ and salt. Beat until well blended. Add wheat flour and enough unbleached all-purpose flour to make a stiff dough.
- Turn dough out onto a lightly floured surface and knead until dough is smooth and elastic. Shape dough into a ball and place it into a large greased bowl, turning to coat all surfaces. Cover bowl with a cloth towel and allow dough to rise until doubled in bulk or until an indentation remains when you lightly press a finger ½-inch into the dough, one to two hours.
- Punch dough down in center with a fist and fold the edges to the center.
- Turn dough out onto a lightly floured surface. Divide into thirds. Roll dough into a rectangle. Roll dough up jelly-roll style, starting from the short side. Seal seam and ends and place seam side down in a greased loaf pan. Repeat with remaining parts. Let rise until doubled in bulk or until an indentation remains when you lightly press a finger against the edge of the loaf, about one hour.
- Preheat oven to 375°F.
- Bake for 20 minutes. Lower oven temperature to 350°F and continue baking for 20 more minutes.
- Cool in pan for 5 minutes. Loosen edges and remove loaves to wire rack to cool completely.

Yield: 3 loaves

Orange Glazed Poppy Seed Bread

A quick sweet bread that disappears as soon as it comes to the table

3	cups all-purpose flour
1½	teaspoons baking powder
1½	teaspoons salt
2½	cups sugar
1½	tablespoons poppy seeds
1½	teaspoons butter flavoring
2	teaspoons vanilla extract
3	eggs
1½	cups vegetable oil
1½	cups milk
	Glaze (recipe follows)

- Preheat oven to 350°F.
- Combine flour, baking powder, salt, sugar, poppy seeds, butter flavoring, vanilla, eggs, oil and milk. Beat for 2 minutes with mixer at medium speed.
- Spoon batter into 2 greased and floured 9x5-inch loaf pans.
- Bake for 35 minutes. Cover loaves with foil and bake for 25 more minutes or until a wooden pick inserted in center of loaf comes out clean.
- Cool in pan for 10 minutes. Remove loaves to wire rack and prick the tops a number of times with a wooden pick.

Glaze

¾	cup sugar
½	teaspoon butter flavoring
½	teaspoon vanilla extract
¼	cup orange juice

- Combine sugar, butter flavoring, vanilla and orange juice. Drizzle atop warm bread.

Variation: Fill greased muffin cups ⅔ full. Bake for 14 minutes. Prick tops of muffins a number of times with a wooden pick. Dip immediately in glaze.

Yield: 2 loaves

In preparation for a busy morning, ready ingredients the night before. Mix dry and wet ingredients separately, cover them and store in the refrigerator. Grease loaf pans or muffin tins and set the temperature on the oven gauge. Attach notes about baking times or menu reminders to the hood over the stove. Fill the coffee maker or teapot with water and set your table. When you walk into the kitchen the next morning, you will feel ready to host an army.

Are copper molds languishing on the walls or in the cabinet recesses of your kitchen? Bring them out as colorful serving dishes for brunchtime breads. Line copper molds with cloth napkins or linen dish towels and fill them with bread slices, muffins or scones.

Lemon Glazed Pumpkin Bread

A spicy bread that tastes best on cool autumn mornings

1	cup butter, softened
2	cups sugar
4	eggs
1	(15-ounce) can pumpkin
3¾	cups all-purpose flour
2	teaspoons baking soda
1	teaspoon salt
2	teaspoons ground cinnamon
1	teaspoon ground nutmeg
½	teaspoon ground cloves
½	teaspoon ground ginger
2	cups (about 12 ounces) semisweet chocolate chips
1½	cups chopped nuts
	Glaze (recipe follows)

- Preheat oven to 350°F.
- Cream butter, sugar and eggs. Blend in pumpkin. Add flour, baking soda, salt, cinnamon, nutmeg, cloves and ginger. Mix well. Fold in chocolate chips and nuts.
- Spoon batter into 4 greased and floured 5½x3½-inch loaf pans.
- Bake for 40 to 50 minutes or until a wooden pick inserted in center of loaf comes out clean.
- Cool in pan for 10 minutes. Remove loaves to wire rack and prick the tops a number of times with a wooden pick.

Glaze

1	cup powdered sugar
¼	teaspoon ground cinnamon
¼	teaspoon ground nutmeg
3 to 4	tablespoons lemon juice

- Sift together powdered sugar, cinnamon and nutmeg. Stir in 3 tablespoons lemon juice. If necessary, stir in additional lemon juice, 1 teaspoon at a time, until drizzling consistency. Drizzle atop warm bread.

Note: Use a very sharp knife to cut this bread.

Yield: 4 loaves

Moravian Sugar Cake

A cherished recipe directly from a Raleigh Moravian Church charter member

½   cup water, 110° to 115°F
½   cup plus ½ teaspoon sugar, divided
1   (¼-ounce) package active dry yeast
1   cup butter, divided
½   cup hot mashed potatoes
1   teaspoon salt
¼   cup milk, 110° to 115°F
¼   cup potato water, cooled to 110° to 115°F
1   egg, beaten
3   cups all-purpose flour
1   teaspoon ground cinnamon, divided
1   cup brown sugar, divided

- Stir together water and ½ teaspoon sugar. Add yeast and stir until dissolved. Let stand 5 minutes.
- Cream ½ cup softened butter and ½ cup sugar. Mix in mashed potatoes and salt. Add milk and potato water and beat well. Mix in yeast mixture. Add egg. Add flour, 1 cup at a time, mixing well after each addition.
- Cover bowl with a cloth towel. Let dough rise until doubled in bulk, about 1 hour.
- Stir dough and divide between two 9-inch cake pans. Let rise until doubled in bulk, about one hour.
- Preheat oven to 350°F.
- Sprinkle top of each cake with ½ teaspoon cinnamon and ½ cup brown sugar. Cut ½ cup butter into thin slices. Divide equally and place on top of each cake.
- Bake for 20 minutes or until a wooden pick inserted in center of cake comes out clean.
- Cool in pan for 10 minutes. Remove to wire rack and cool completely

Yield: 16 servings

In 1953 the Raleigh Moravian Church was organized, a sister to the famous church and community in Winston-Salem, NC. The founding members brought traditions with them that guided the Salem congregation, among them the Christmas Candle Tea. On the first Saturday of December, members of the Raleigh Moravian Women's Fellowship, attired in mid-18th century costumes, gather to bake and serve sugar cakes, cookies and creamed and sugared coffee to the crowd assembled for the warmth and fellowship inside the church.

In the heart of Raleigh's Historic Oakwood, the Oakwood Inn opened its doors to guests in 1984. The Inn, formerly the 1871 Raynor-Stronach House, is decorated in classic Victorian style with period antiques and working fireplaces. Here guests are pampered with afternoon tea, full breakfasts and concierge advice.

Greet guests in your home as they are greeted at the Oakwood Inn: with the aroma of freshly baked cookies. Other bed and breakfast hints: plan off-the-griddle breakfasts to accommodate varied breakfast serving times. Or serve a breakfast casserole that can be kept warm in a 250° oven with a glass of water inside to prevent drying.

Cream Cheese Coffee Cake with Raspberries and Almonds

Other fruits to try in this bread are apricots, blueberries, apples, strawberries or cherries.

$2\frac{3}{4}$ cups plus 2 tablespoons all-purpose flour
1   cup brown sugar
1   cup butter, softened
$\frac{1}{2}$ teaspoon baking powder
$\frac{1}{2}$ teaspoon baking soda
$\frac{1}{4}$ teaspoon salt
$\frac{3}{4}$ cup sour cream
3   eggs, divided
2   teaspoons almond extract, divided
2   (8-ounce) packages cream cheese, softened
$\frac{1}{2}$ cup sugar
$\frac{1}{2}$ cup raspberry preserves
1   cup raspberries
$\frac{1}{4}$ teaspoon ground cinnamon
$\frac{1}{2}$ cup sliced almonds
    Glaze, optional (recipe follows)

- Preheat oven to 350°F.
- Combine flour and brown sugar. Cut in butter until mixture resembles coarse crumbs. Reserve 2 cups crumb mixture. To remaining crumb mixture, add baking powder, baking soda, salt, sour cream, 1 egg and 1 teaspoon almond extract. Blend well.
- Spread batter over bottom and halfway up sides of a greased and floured 10-inch springform pan.
- Combine cream cheese, sugar, 1 teaspoon almond extract and 2 eggs. Pour over batter in pan.
- Carefully spoon preserves and raspberries over cream cheese filling.
- Combine reserved crumb mixture, cinnamon and almonds. Sprinkle over top of raspberries.
- Bake for 45 to 50 minutes or until cream cheese filling is set and crust is deep golden brown.
- Cool in pan for 15 minutes. Remove sides of pan and cool completely.

Glaze

$\frac{1}{2}$ cup (about 3 ounces) semisweet chocolate chips
1   tablespoon shortening

- Melt chocolate chips and shortening in microwave oven. Mix well. Drizzle over top of cake.

Yield: 16 servings

Key Lime Muffins

Key lime glaze adds a tart topping to moist muffins.

2	cups all-purpose flour
1	tablespoon baking powder
½	teaspoon salt
1	cup sugar
1	teaspoon grated lime zest
2	eggs
¼	cup vegetable oil
⅓	cup milk
¼	cup key lime juice
	Glaze (recipe follows)

- Preheat oven to 400°F.
- Combine flour, baking powder, salt, sugar and lime zest. Add eggs, oil, milk and lime juice. Stir until just moistened.
- Fill greased muffin cups ¾ full.
- Bake for 15 to 18 minutes or until lightly browned.

Glaze

1	cup powdered sugar
2 to 3	tablespoons key lime juice

- Blend powdered sugar and 2 tablespoons lime juice. If necessary, stir in additional lime juice, 1 teaspoon at a time, until drizzling consistency. Drizzle atop warm muffins.

Yield: 12 muffins

Look for bottled Key lime juice in the baking section of the grocery store. Uniquely tart Key limes are grown in the Florida Keys. They are yellow when ripe and measure about 2 inches in diameter.

Lunch from a box every day becomes monotonous. Put a midday smile on your child's face with these ideas:

- **Create a theme using leftover napkins from birthday parties and foods to match. For an under-the-sea lunch, provide a tuna salad sandwich, fish-shaped crackers and oyster cracker "bubbles" mixed together, tropical fruit, and cookies decorated in sea shapes (see Sugar Cookies with Painted Glaze on page 273).**

- **Put a colorful new pencil, a set of stickers or a self-inking stamp in the lunchbox with a note of encouragement and love.**

- **Make foods in one shape. Include square cheese crackers, a sandwich cut into squares, cubes of fruit and graham cracker squares spread with chocolate-hazelnut spread for dessert. Do the same with triangles or circles.**

- **Vary the type of bread used to make sandwiches. Use miniature pitas or bagels, savory muffins, pumpernickel swirl slices from the deli, or tortilla wraps.**

Gingersnap Muffins

Add a surprise to your child's lunchbox with the taste of gingersnaps baked into a muffin.

2	cups water, divided
1	cup raisins
1	cup all-purpose flour
1	teaspoon baking soda
1/4	teaspoon salt
1/2	teaspoon ground cinnamon
1/2	teaspoon ground ginger
1/4	teaspoon ground cloves
1/4	cup butter, softened
1/4	cup sugar
1	egg
1/2	cup molasses

- Preheat oven to 375°F.
- Pour 1½ cups boiling water over raisins. Let stand for 5 minutes. Drain well.
- Sift together flour, baking soda, salt, cinnamon, ginger and cloves. Set aside.
- Cream butter and sugar. Beat in egg and molasses. Stir in flour mixture. Gradually add ½ cup hot water, stirring until smooth. Fold in raisins.
- Fill well-greased muffin cups ⅔ full.
- Bake for 18 to 20 minutes.

Yield: 12 muffins

Currant Scones

1	cup currants
3	tablespoons sherry
4½	cups all-purpose flour
2	teaspoons baking powder
½	teaspoon baking soda
2	tablespoons sugar
	Pinch of salt
1	cup unsalted butter, cut into small pieces
1¼	cups heavy cream, divided
1	egg
¼	cup half-and-half

- Soak currants in sherry. Set aside.
- Sift together flour, baking powder, baking soda, sugar and salt. Cut in butter until mixture resembles coarse crumbs. Add currants. Stir in 1 cup cream.
- In bowl, knead in additional cream until dough just holds together.
- Wrap dough in wax paper and chill for 30 minutes.
- Preheat oven to 375°F.
- Turn dough out onto a lightly floured surface. Roll dough to ¾-inch thickness. Cut dough with a 2-inch scalloped biscuit cutter.
- Place scones so they are touching each other on a greased baking sheet.
- Combine egg and half-and-half and brush on tops of scones.
- Bake for 13 to 15 minutes or until golden brown and puffed.

Yield: 20 scones

Although the tradition of afternoon tea seldom stops our busy schedules in Raleigh, there was a time when tea was important enough to cause a stir among North Carolinians. On October 25, 1774, before the Boston Tea Party, a group of 51 like-minded ladies in Edenton, North Carolina, held their own boycott of the heavily taxed goods arriving from England. They proclaimed: "We, the Ladys of Edenton, do hereby solemnly engage not to conform to the Pernicious Custom of Drinking Tea...will not promote ye wear of any manufacturer from England until such time that all acts which tend to enslave our Native Country shall be repealed."

Today we can honor their sacrifice by allotting a few minutes in the mid-afternoon to savor a cup of hot tea and a bite of something sweet. Whether at our office desks or doing homework with the children, a moment of indulgence makes for a peaceful day's end.

Kneading Dough

Kneading dough distributes ingredients evenly throughout, creating strength, elasticity and structure necessary for good bread.

Use a press, fold and turn motion to knead dough by hand. You may also knead dough using a mixer fitted with a dough hook or a food processor fitted with a steel or dough blade.

Tips:

- **If dough is not kneaded enough, the bread will be dry and heavy with a crumbly texture.**
- **If dough is kneaded too much (more than 10 minutes), it can become dry and coarse.**
- **Add flour gradually when kneading dough, in small amounts just so that dough is no longer sticky.**
- **Too much flour added during kneading may produce streaks and uneven grain.**

Apple Raisin Cinnamon Rolls

Take some time to create rolls that taste like they came from your grandmother's kitchen.

1	(¼-ounce) package active dry yeast
1¼	cups milk, 100°F
5	cups all-purpose flour, divided
1¾	cups sugar, divided
1	teaspoon salt
2	eggs, lightly beaten
½	cup plus 2 tablespoons unsalted butter, divided
3	tablespoons ground cinnamon
2	cups (about 2 medium) chopped cooking apples
½	cup raisins
	Glaze (recipe follows)

- Dissolve yeast in warm milk. Let stand 5 minutes.
- Sift together 3½ cups flour, ¾ cup sugar and salt. Add yeast mixture, eggs and 2 tablespoons melted butter. Stir until well blended. Add 1 cup flour and stir until dough pulls cleanly away from sides of bowl.
- Turn dough out onto a lightly floured surface. Knead in remaining ½ cup flour until dough is smooth and elastic, about 8 minutes.
- Place dough into a large greased bowl, turning to coat all surfaces. Cover bowl with plastic wrap. Let rise until doubled in bulk, about 2 hours.
- Turn dough out onto a lightly floured surface. Roll dough into an 18x14-inch rectangle.
- Mix together ½ cup softened butter, 1 cup sugar and cinnamon until smooth and spreadable. With a spatula, spread filling evenly over dough to within ½-inch of edge. Sprinkle apples and raisins over filling.
- Using a dough scraper, tightly roll dough, starting from the long side. Seal roll by pinching dough together at the seam.
- Using a ruler and a knife, mark dough at 1¼-inch intervals. Cut rolls by pressing knife down sharply through dough.
- Place rolls in 2 greased 8-inch square baking pans. Cover with plastic wrap. Let rise until doubled in bulk, about 2 hours.
- Preheat oven to 350°F.
- Bake for 20 to 25 minutes or until golden brown.
- Loosen edges. Hold a platter against pan and flip upside down. Repeat onto serving platter so that rolls are upright.

(continued on next page)

Apple Raisin Cinnamon Rolls *continued*

Glaze

4	cups powdered sugar
4	tablespoons butter, melted
1	teaspoon vanilla extract
8 to 10	tablespoons milk

- Combine powdered sugar, melted butter and vanilla. Stir in milk, 1 tablespoon at a time, until consistency of maple syrup. Drizzle atop warm rolls.

Note: Panned rolls may be placed in the refrigerator to rise overnight. Let sit at room temperature for 1 hour prior to baking.

Yield: 18 rolls

Banana Pecan Waffles

Waffles become something special when flavors of banana and buttery pecans are mixed in.

1¾	cups all-purpose flour
1	tablespoon baking powder
½	teaspoon salt
1	tablespoon sugar
¼	cup butter, melted
1½	cups milk
3	eggs, separated
½	banana, mashed
½	cup finely chopped pecans
	maple syrup

- Sift together flour, baking powder, salt and sugar. Mix in melted butter, milk and egg yolks.
- Beat egg whites until peaks are stiff but not dry. Gently fold into batter.
- Fold in banana and pecans.
- Spoon ½ cup batter onto a hot, well-greased waffle iron. Spread batter to within ¼-inch of edge of grids.
- Bake until waffle is golden brown.
- Repeat with remaining batter.
- Serve with maple syrup

Yield: 6 servings

Instead of throwing away overripe bananas, freeze them in a plastic zippered bag. Use them slightly thawed in baking recipes or as a base for healthy milkshakes by blending them with milk and a small amount of sugar or chocolate syrup.

"My grandmother makes the best biscuits in the world. She just throws the ingredients together and they are perfect. She had sixteen grandchildren and she kept a child-sized rolling pin marked with the name of each one in her kitchen. When we went to visit, we could get out our own little rolling pins and help her roll out the biscuits. Now that I have children of my own, she has added their names to her rolling pin collection."

Sunday Morning Cinnamon Orange Biscuits

Wake up your family with light, cinnamon-swirled biscuits topped with orange sauce.

2   cups all-purpose flour
1   tablespoon baking powder
½   teaspoon salt
3   tablespoons shortening
¾   cup milk
5   tablespoons butter, divided
¾   cup sugar, divided
1   teaspoon ground cinnamon
½   cup orange juice
2   teaspoons grated orange peel

- Preheat oven to 450°F.
- Sift together flour, baking powder and salt. Cut in shortening until mixture resembles coarse crumbs. Stir in milk until just moistened.
- Turn dough out onto a lightly floured surface. Sprinkle dough with just enough flour to handle. Gently knead dough 10 to 12 times or until no longer sticky. Roll dough into a 15x12-inch rectangle.
- Spread 2 tablespoons softened butter on dough. Combine ¼ cup sugar with cinnamon and sprinkle over butter. Roll dough up jelly-roll style, starting from the short side. Cut into 12 equal slices.
- Place biscuits in a well-greased 9-inch round baking pan.
- Combine ½ cup sugar, orange juice, 3 tablespoons melted butter and orange peel. Pour over biscuits.
- Bake for 20 to 25 minutes or until lightly browned.
- Cool in pan for 5 minutes prior to serving.

Yield: 12 biscuits

Praline French Toast

A golden praline topping adds a grand finish to overnight French toast. Great for company!

1	(13 to 16-ounce) loaf French bread, sliced into 1-inch slices
8	eggs
2	cups half-and-half
1	cup milk
1	teaspoon vanilla extract
2	tablespoons sugar
¼	teaspoon ground cinnamon
¼	teaspoon ground nutmeg
	dash of salt
	Praline Topping (recipe follows)

- In a greased 13x9-inch baking dish, arrange bread slices in two rows with slices overlapping.
- Combine eggs, half-and-half, milk, vanilla, sugar, cinnamon, nutmeg and salt.
- Pour mixture over bread slices. Cover with foil and refrigerate overnight.

Praline Topping

1	cup butter
1	cup brown sugar
2	tablespoons light corn syrup
½	teaspoon ground cinnamon
½	teaspoon ground nutmeg
1	cup chopped pecans
	maple syrup

- Prior to serving, preheat oven to 350°F.
- Melt butter in a small saucepan over medium heat. Add brown sugar, corn syrup, cinnamon, nutmeg and pecans. Stir constantly until smooth.
- Spread topping evenly over bread slices.
- Bake uncovered for 40 minutes or until puffed and golden brown.
- Serve with maple syrup.

Yield: 10 servings

During the late 19th century, Blount Street in downtown Raleigh was lined with the city's finest homes, including the governor's mansion. Over time the large homes were purchased by the state government for use as office space. The transformation of an 1881 former residence to the William Thomas House Bed and Breakfast brought some of the charms of home back to the busy avenue. The proprietors ensure the comfort of their guests by giving them the grand tour when they arrive and by arranging dinner reservations or ordering play tickets. Their motto is, "The best way to make guests feel at home is to enjoy taking care of them." By sharing what you know and what you have, you guarantee a memorable stay for your guests, too.

Raleigh's City Market is a mission-style marketplace that served as the farmers' market until the 1950s. It has since been restyled as a market of boutiques, restaurants, shops and art galleries. The City Market's revitalization has inspired expansion beyond its borders as well. Exploris, a unique children's museum highlighting world cultures and economies, has risen nearby, across Moore Square.

Moore Square's most distinctive feature is a giant copper acorn that sits directly across the street from the City Market. A creation of local artist David Benson, the acorn is hoisted by a crane each year above New Year's eve revelers. It drops at midnight as part of Raleigh's family-oriented First Night celebration of the new year. The Artsplosure Festival and the annual St. Patrick's Day Parade are two other events that culminate at Moore Square.

Irish Potato Pancakes with Savory Fillings

Tír na nÓg, an Irish pub and restaurant near Raleigh's historic City Market, thrills patrons with this recipe for crepe-like potato pancakes folded over herbed cream cheese with Roasted Red Pepper and Portobello Mushroom or Salmon Filling. As in Ireland, at the restaurant they call it boxty.

1 **cup whole milk**
1 **cup heavy cream**
2 **eggs**
1 **tablespoon cornstarch**
1½ **cups all-purpose flour**
1 **pound potatoes, finely shredded**
   salt and pepper to taste
   Roasted Red Pepper and Portobello Mushroom Filling or Salmon Filling (recipes follow)

- Mix together milk, cream and eggs. Stir in cornstarch and flour. Fold in potatoes. Add salt and pepper to taste.
- Drop ½ cup of batter into a greased nonstick skillet. Tilt pan to spread batter out thinly. Cook over medium-high heat. When bubbles form on edge, flip pancake and cook on other side until done.

Roasted Red Pepper and Portobello Mushroom Filling

3 **large portobello mushrooms**
½ **cup plus 2 tablespoons balsamic vinegar, divided**
¼ **cup olive oil**
2 **red bell peppers**
1 **small red onion**
1 **(8-ounce) package herbed cream cheese spread**

- Marinate mushrooms in ½ cup balsamic vinegar and olive oil for at least one hour.
- Grill mushrooms until tender. Julienne and cool.
- Grill peppers until skin blisters and separates. Clean skin under running water. Seed, julienne and cool.
- Julienne onion. In a small skillet over medium-high heat, sauté with 2 tablespoons balsamic vinegar. Cool.
- Mix together mushrooms, peppers and onion.
- To assemble, spread half of pancake with cream cheese. Top with vegetable mixture. Fold pancake over and microwave for 30 to 45 seconds. Serve hot.

(continued on next page)

(Irish Potato Pancakes *continued*)

Salmon Filling

1   pound salmon fillets
1   tablespoon freshly squeezed lemon juice
1   tablespoon white wine
    salt and pepper to taste
1   (8-ounce) package herbed cream cheese spread
2   tomatoes, seeded and diced

- Preheat oven to 350°F.
- Place salmon on a greased, foil-covered baking sheet. Season with lemon juice, wine, salt and pepper.
- Bake for 30 minutes or until cooked through.
- Cool and flake with fork.
- To assemble, spread half of pancake with cream cheese. Top with salmon and diced tomatoes. Fold pancake over and microwave for 30 to 45 seconds. Serve hot.

Yield: 4 to 5 servings

Front Porch Frittata

Toss together a flavorful frittata for a change of pace.

8   slices bacon, chopped
1   tablespoon olive oil
1   medium onion, thinly sliced
2   medium tomatoes, peeled, seeded and chopped
10 eggs
½   cup chopped fresh basil
    salt and pepper to taste
¾   cup grated Parmesan cheese

- In a medium nonstick skillet, cook bacon over medium-high heat until crisp. Remove bacon to paper towels. Drain all except 1 tablespoon drippings. Add olive oil to pan. Add onions and cook over medium-high heat until golden brown. Reduce heat to medium and add tomatoes. Stirring often, cook until liquid evaporates.
- Preheat broiler.
- Whisk together eggs, basil, salt and pepper. Pour into skillet. Sprinkle bacon over top of egg mixture. Cook, lifting edges of frittata to let egg run underneath, for 10 minutes or until bottom is golden and top is not set.
- Sprinkle Parmesan cheese over top of frittata.
- Broil for 3 to 5 minutes or until top puffs and turns golden.
- Slide frittata onto platter. Cut into wedges and serve immediately.

Yield: 6 servings

To fully enjoy a pleasant outdoor meal, keep annoyances to a minimum by:

- bringing everything you need outside, eliminating repeat trips into the house. Use baskets as caddies for silverware, condiments and table linens. Keep a full carafe of your beverage in a tableside champagne cooler.
- positioning your table in shade that will follow you as the sun moves.
- sewing substantial, decorative buttons to the corners of the cloth as ballast to keep breezes from sending the tablecloth flying into everyone's food.

Crab Benedict with Basil Hollandaise Sauce

Extra special occasions call for an extravagant brunch dish, like this updated Eggs Benedict.

6	slices bacon
2	tablespoons olive oil
2	pounds (about 3 bunches) spinach, stems discarded and leaves washed and spun dry
	salt and pepper to taste
2	tablespoons butter
1	pound fresh jumbo lump crabmeat, picked free of shell and cartilage
2	teaspoons white vinegar
6	eggs
6	puff pastry shells, baked according to package directions
	Basil Hollandaise Sauce (recipe follows)
1	cup chopped tomatoes (optional)

- In a medium skillet, cook bacon over medium-high heat until crisp. Remove bacon to paper towels. Crumble and set aside.
- Drain all except 1 tablespoon drippings. Add olive oil to pan. Add spinach and cook over medium-high heat for 3 minutes or until wilted. Add salt and pepper to taste. Keep warm.
- In a separate skillet, melt butter over medium-low heat. Add crabmeat and toss for 3 to 4 minutes until heated through. Keep warm.
- Fill a large skillet with 2 inches of water. Add vinegar. Bring to a boil, then reduce heat to simmer. Poach 3 eggs at a time by breaking each egg into a saucer and sliding it into the water. Using a slotted spoon, immediately push white back toward yolk. Simmer 3 minutes for soft eggs, 5 minutes for firm eggs.
- While eggs are poaching, arrange pastry shells on a platter or individual plates. Divide spinach and then crabmeat evenly among pastry shells. Place an egg in each pastry shell. Top with Basil Hollandaise Sauce, crumbled bacon and chopped tomatoes.

Basil Hollandaise Sauce

3	egg yolks, lightly beaten
1	tablespoon freshly squeezed lemon juice
1	tablespoon chopped fresh basil
¼	teaspoon salt
	pinch of white pepper
½	cup unsalted butter, melted

- In a blender, combine egg yolks, lemon juice, basil, salt and white pepper. Blending at high speed, add butter, a few drops at a time, until mixture is smooth.

Yield: 6 servings

Country Ham with Red-Eye Gravy

An old southern favorite that can serve as the centerpiece for a big country breakfast

6   **slices country ham, ¼-inch thick**
2   **tablespoons butter**
2   **tablespoons brown sugar**
½   **cup strong black coffee**

- Cut gashes in fat around edges of ham slices.
- In a heavy skillet, melt butter over low heat. Sauté ham until lightly browned, turning several times.
- Remove ham from skillet and keep warm.
- Stir sugar into pan drippings. Stirring constantly, cook over low heat until sugar dissolves. Add coffee and mix well. Simmer for 5 minutes.
- Spoon Red-Eye Gravy over ham prior to serving.

Yield: 6 servings

Charles Kuralt, Emmy Award-winning journalist from North Carolina, traveled throughout America for more than 25 years. Despite his many adventures and dining experiences, his heart never left North Carolina and the foods he enjoyed while growing up. In an interview with *Bon Appétit* magazine, he fondly reminisced about his favorite foods. "Grits and eggs and country ham. The ham was salt-cured and so thick and hard that you practically needed a hacksaw to cut it. And buttermilk biscuits. Oh my, what wonderful breakfasts."

Gruyère Cheese Grits

Everyday grits get a kick from sharp Gruyère and garlic.

4   **cups water**
1   **teaspoon salt**
1   **clove garlic, minced**
1   **cup quick-cooking grits**
½   **cup unsalted butter**
1   **cup (about 4 ounces) shredded cheddar cheese**
½   **cup (about 2 ounces) shredded Gruyère cheese**
½   **cup milk**
    hot pepper sauce to taste
    salt and white pepper to taste
2   **eggs, well beaten**

- Preheat oven to 325°F.
- In large saucepan, combine water, salt and garlic. Bring to a boil and add grits. Stirring constantly, cook over medium heat until grits thicken.
- Remove from heat and stir in butter, cheddar cheese, Gruyère and milk. Add hot pepper sauce, salt and pepper to taste. Quickly stir in eggs.
- Pour grits into a greased 2-quart baking pan.
- Bake for one hour.

Yield: 8 servings

"Ode to Grits":

"True grits, more grits, fish, grits, and collards. Life is good where grits are swallowed."

Roy Blount, Summer 1986

Italian Egg Bake

A rich egg casserole to feed a crowd

16	**ounces sweet Italian sausage**
1	**teaspoon butter**
½	**medium red onion, chopped**
8	**ounces mushrooms, sliced**
12	**eggs, beaten**
1	**cup milk**
½	**teaspoon salt**
½	**teaspoon pepper**
½	**teaspoon seasoned salt**
8	**ounces mozzarella cheese**
2	**medium tomatoes, peeled and chopped**

- Preheat oven to 400°F.
- Peel casing from sausage and cut into bite-sized pieces.
- In a medium skillet, sauté sausage over medium-high heat until crumbly. Drain and set aside.
- Wipe skillet clean, then melt butter over medium-high heat. Add onion and mushrooms and cook until tender.
- In a large bowl, whisk together eggs, milk, salt, pepper and seasoned salt. Stir in mozzarella and tomatoes. Add sausage, onions and mushrooms.
- Pour egg mixture into a greased 13x9-inch baking pan.
- Bake for 30 to 40 minutes.

Note: May be prepared the night before, refrigerated, and baked the next morning.

Yield: 10 servings

Center a platter of Brunch Mixed Grill on the buffet table to please a variety of tastes. Pile the platter with country sausage patties and links, bacon, and cooled leftover slices of meat (such as steak or leg of lamb) tossed with bottled Italian dressing. Stand a bunch of fresh rosemary, lavender and chive blossoms tied with a ribbon in the middle of the platter.

Scrambled Eggs with Chèvre and Chives

Everyone will scramble for seconds of these!

3	**tablespoons butter**
12	**eggs, beaten**
5	**ounces chèvre or Montrachet without ash, cut into small cubes**
3	**tablespoons chopped fresh chives**
	salt and pepper to taste.

- In a large skillet, melt butter over medium heat. Do not allow butter to brown. Add eggs and stir often. When eggs are half done, add chèvre and chives. Continue to cook until eggs are done and chèvre is incorporated. Add salt and pepper to taste.

Note: The secret to the creaminess of these eggs is to cook them very slowly.

Variation: Substitute 5 ounces cream cheese for chèvre.

Yield: 6 servings

Mimosa Compote

Warm champagne sauce heightens the citrus flavor of oranges and grapefruits.

3   **oranges, peeled**
2   **grapefruits, peeled**
⅓   **cup champagne**
¼   **cup freshly squeezed orange juice**
¼   **cup honey**
¼   **teaspoon ground cinnamon**
¼   **cup finely chopped almonds, toasted**

- Section oranges and grapefruits. Remove remaining white membrane.
- In a medium saucepan, combine champagne, orange juice, honey and cinnamon. Cook over medium heat until honey dissolves. Add fruit sections and cook for 1 minute.
- Pour compote into a serving dish. Sprinkle with almonds. Serve hot or cold.

Yield: 4 servings

Glazed Mixed Berries and Bananas

For a fun presentation, serve in a pineapple boat or melon bowl.

½   **pound strawberries, sliced**
½   **pound blueberries**
2   **bananas, sliced**
¾   **cup powdered sugar**
    juice of 1 orange
    juice of ½ lemon

- Toss together strawberries, blueberries and bananas. Divide equally among 4 ramekins.
- Combine powdered sugar, orange juice and lemon juice. Stir until powdered sugar dissolves. Pour over fruit.

Yield: 4 servings

Fruit salads gain elegance from fine containers. Use silver spoons to serve fruit from large wine goblets, crystal or silver bowls, decorative glass flower vases or Depression glass pedestal dishes in a rainbow of pastel colors.

Cranapple Bake is a warm treat at brunch, but it also complements pork or poultry at a holiday meal. Serve leftovers warmed and topped with vanilla yogurt for a complete breakfast by the bowlful.

Cranapple Bake

Baked apples over a bed of sweetened cranberries make brunch a comforting treat on a cold morning.

3	cups (about 12 ounces) fresh or frozen cranberries
1½	cups sugar
4	tablespoons cornstarch
6 to 8	medium Golden Delicious apples, peeled and halved
½	cup apple juice
½	cup cognac or apple brandy
1	cup rolled oats
¼	cup all-purpose flour
1	cup sugar
1	cup chopped pecans or walnuts
½	cup butter, melted
1	teaspoon vanilla extract

- Preheat oven to 350°F.
- Spread cranberries in a greased 13x9-inch baking pan.
- Combine sugar and cornstarch and sprinkle over cranberries.
- Make three vertical slashes in each apple half. Do not slice all the way through. Arrange apple halves on top of cranberries.
- Pour apple juice and cognac or apple brandy over apples.
- Combine oats, flour, sugar and pecans. Add melted butter and vanilla, mixing well. Press topping evenly over apples.
- Bake for one hour and 20 minutes.

Yield: 10 servings

Margaret Hill
Still Life With Peaches And Melons
oil on canvas, 1997

Soups and Salads

Cream of Six Onion Soup

Delicious hot or cold

3	tablespoons butter
3	leeks, chopped (white part only)
1	yellow onion, chopped
1	white onion, chopped
4	shallots, chopped
2	cloves garlic, chopped
4	cups chicken stock or broth
2	cups heavy cream
1	bunch chives, chopped
	salt and pepper

Garnish this simple, rich soup with freshly grated Parmesan, chopped toasted pecans, steamed whole shrimp, a dash of sherry or a dollop of sour cream.

- Melt butter in 6-quart saucepan. Add leeks, onions, shallots and garlic. Sauté until soft but not brown.
- Add stock and bring to boil. Cover, lower heat and simmer 30 to 40 minutes.
- Purée (a blender works perfectly).
- Return to pan and stir in cream and chives. (Save a few chives for garnish.)
- Season to taste with salt and pepper.

Yield: 8 servings

Cheddar Cheese Soup

A hearty alternative to chili for a Sunday night supper

½	cup butter
1	cup finely chopped onions
1	cup finely chopped carrots
1	cup all-purpose flour
1	quart chicken stock
3	cups grated cheddar cheese
1	quart milk
1	teaspoon salt
½	teaspoon white pepper

Use individual round loaves of country bread as soup bowls. Cut the top quarter off and hollow out to make a bowl, being careful not to cut through the bottom. Then, brush the insides with olive oil and toast the "bowls" and "lids" at 350° for 10 minutes until crusty. Serve immediately using plate liners.

- Melt butter in soup pot. Sauté onions and carrots in butter until soft.
- Add flour and mix until smooth.
- Add chicken stock slowly to prevent lumping. Bring to a boil, reduce heat, and simmer for 15 minutes.
- Add cheese; cook 10 minutes longer.
- Add milk, salt and pepper.
- Heat to serving temperature.

Yield: 12 servings

Roasting is the key to capturing the fullest flavor of the yellow peppers.

Substitute red or orange peppers for subtle flavor variations.

When puréeing, add stock in small batches so blender will not overflow.

Yellow Pepper and White Bean Soup

An exceptional first course for lamb dishes

3	yellow bell peppers
1	tablespoon olive oil
1	small onion, chopped
⅛	teaspoon dried crushed cayenne pepper
4	cups chicken stock or broth
1	(16-ounce) can cannellini (white beans), rinsed and drained
	salt and pepper

- Char bell peppers under broiler or over gas flame. Place in paper bag and let stand 6 minutes.
- Peel, seed and chop peppers.
- Heat oil in medium saucepan. Add onion and sauté until tender, about 10 minutes.
- Add peppers and crushed cayenne pepper and sauté 1 minute.
- Add stock and cannellini. Bring to a boil. Reduce heat, cover and simmer 15 minutes.
- Purée.
- Season to taste with salt and pepper.
- Can be served hot or chilled.

Yield: 4 servings

Perfect for fall and winter meat dishes, the colors here are symbolic of autumn in North Carolina.

Sweet Potato and Carrot Soup

Cheese muffins make the perfect companion to this nutritious soup.

4	tablespoons butter
1	large onion, finely chopped
2	large sweet potatoes, peeled and diced
5	large carrots, peeled and diced
3	tablespoons chopped fresh cilantro
	juice of 1 lemon
3¾	cups stock (vegetable, chicken or beef)
1	teaspoon salt
½	teaspoon white pepper
	sour cream for garnish

- Melt butter in skillet. Sauté onion until transparent.
- Add sweet potatoes and carrots. Reduce heat to very low and cook 20 to 25 minutes, stirring occasionally, until vegetables are tender.
- Add cilantro, lemon juice, stock, salt and pepper.
- Allow to cool slightly. Pour into blender or food processor. Blend until soup is fairly smooth but retains some texture.
- Return to pan and reheat over very low until piping hot.
- Serve with dollop of sour cream.

Yield: 6 servings

Carrot Ginger Soup

2	tablespoons butter
1½	cups chopped onion
10 to 12	peeled carrots, sliced (approximately 4 cups)
1½	tablespoons grated fresh ginger
4	cups chicken stock
¼	cup orange juice
1½	cups milk
1½	cups heavy cream
	salt and pepper
	paprika for garnish
	sour cream for garnish
	parsley or chives for garnish

- Melt butter in soup pot and sauté onion until transparent.
- Add carrots, ginger and broth. Cover and simmer 25 to 30 minutes, until carrots are tender.
- Strain mixture and reserve liquid.
- Purée vegetables in a food processor or blender.
- Return vegetables to broth and add orange juice, milk and cream. Salt and pepper to taste.
- Heat through but do not boil.
- Garnish with paprika, sour cream and parsley or chives.

Yield: 6 to 8 servings

Homemade chicken stock is indispensable to the cook who desires truly rich, fresh-tasting soups and sauces. Stock will keep in the refrigerator 3-4 days or in the freezer 3-4 months. Select different size containers (ice cube trays, ½ cup plastic tubs, quart containers) for freezing.

Homemade Chicken Stock

about 1½ pounds chicken
   bones and carcass
about 2 cups mixed onion,
   celery and carrot,
   roughly chopped
1 clove
1 bouquet garni
2 garlic cloves, chopped
6 peppercorns
2 quarts water

- Add bones to vegetables in heavy pan, cover with water and bring to a boil.
- Simmer 2-3 hours, skimming often.
- Ladle into a chinois set over a bowl. Press the solids with the ladle to extract all of the liquid.
- Cover and refrigerate until fat hardens enough for easy removal. Transfer defatted stock to storage containers.

Cookie Cutter Toppings

Add interest and texture to soups by using puff pastry dough (purchased or homemade) and small cookie cutters to create decorative toppings. After cutting the pastry into festive shapes, bake until slightly golden. You may wish to flavor the pastry with grated cheeses or spices before baking, but be certain the extra flavor will enhance and not overpower your soup.

Garlic Soup

Sautéing the garlic brings out the sweet, nutty flavor, quite a contrast from the pungency of fresh garlic.

2	tablespoons olive oil
1½	cups sliced onions
⅓	cup peeled garlic cloves (12 to 14), plus 1 tablespoon minced garlic
3	bay leaves
1	teaspoon salt
½	teaspoon pepper
8	cups chicken stock
1	teaspoon chopped fresh basil
1	teaspoon chopped fresh thyme
2	cups diced French bread
½	cup heavy cream
⅓	cup grated Parmesan cheese
	croutons for garnish

- Heat oil in soup pot over medium-high heat.
- Add onions, garlic cloves, bay leaves, salt and pepper. Sauté until caramelized, about 7 minutes.
- Stir in stock, minced garlic, basil and thyme and bring to a boil.
- Reduce heat and simmer 40 minutes.
- Turn heat up to high and whisk in bread and cream until dissolved.
- Whisk in Parmesan cheese and remove from heat.
- Serve sprinkled with croutons.

Yield: 8 servings

To remove corn kernels from the cob, hold the cob vertically over a baking pan. Carefully slice straight down using a very sharp knife. (If you want more cream from the corn than crunchy kernels, score the kernels before cutting.) When you have removed all of the kernels from the cob, use the dull side of the knife and scrape the cob on all sides to extract the milk.

Corn Chowder

When fresh summer corn is abundant, substitute it here.

6	slices bacon, chopped
1	cup chopped onion
2	cups boiling water
1	cup potatoes, cut into ½-inch dice
½	teaspoon salt
	dash pepper
4	tablespoons butter
1	(16-ounce) can cream-style corn
1	(16-ounce) can whole kernel corn
1 to 2	cups milk or half-and-half
	snipped fresh parsley

(continued on next page)

Corn Chowder *continued*

- In soup pot, cook bacon until crisp. Drain on paper towels.
- In 1½ tablespoons bacon fat, cook onion until tender and translucent.
- Add bacon and boiling water; simmer 3 to 5 minutes.
- Add diced potatoes, salt and pepper. Make sure amount of water barely covers potatoes. Simmer potatoes 10 minutes and add butter.
- When potatoes are tender, stir in cream-style corn and whole kernel corn, undrained. Add milk or half-and-half.
- Taste and adjust seasonings if necessary.
- Heat to serving temperature.
- Sprinkle with snipped parsley.

Yield: 4 to 6 servings

Red and White Chicken Chili

Control the heat with your picante sauce choice.

6	chicken breasts, halved, skinned and boned
1	medium onion, chopped
1	medium green bell pepper, chopped
2	cloves garlic, minced
1	tablespoon vegetable oil
2	(14½-ounce) cans stewed tomatoes, undrained and chopped
1	(15-ounce) can pinto beans, drained
⅔	cup picante sauce
1	teaspoon chili powder
1	teaspoon ground cumin
½	teaspoon salt
	shredded cheddar cheese
	sour cream
	sliced green onions

- Cut chicken into 1-inch cubes.
- Cook chicken, onion, pepper and garlic in hot oil in a Dutch oven until browned.
- Add tomatoes, beans, picante sauce and spices.
- Cover, reduce heat, and simmer for 20 minutes.
- To serve, top with cheese, sour cream and green onions.

Yield: 10 to 12 servings

Stilton Soup with Miniature Ham Biscuits

Many cheese enthusiasts consider the blue cheeses their favorites. The blue-green veins which distinguish these cheeses are created from flavor-producing molds which are injected during the curing process. Stilton, a blue cheese from England, is often referred to as the "King of Cheeses." It has a distinctive cheddar flavor.

1	cup whole milk
½	cup half-and-half
½	cup coarsely chopped onions
12	whole white peppercorns
	pinch dry mustard
1	bay leaf
2	tablespoons unsalted butter
2	tablespoons all-purpose flour
2 to 3	cups chicken broth
6	ounces Stilton cheese
	salt and pepper to taste
	chopped parsley
	Miniature Ham Biscuits (recipe follows)

- Bring the milk, half-and-half, onion, peppercorns, mustard and bay leaf to a boil in a heavy-bottomed saucepan.
- Remove from heat and let stand for 15 to 20 minutes to allow flavors to meld. Strain the mixture, discarding solids, and set aside to cool.
- In a large saucepan, melt 2 tablespoons butter over medium heat. Add the flour and cook, stirring constantly, for 2 to 3 minutes. Do not brown.
- Remove the flour-butter mixture from heat. Gradually pour in the milk mixture. Return to heat, still stirring, and add chicken broth.
- Bring soup to boil, then reduce heat to medium and simmer 5 to 7 minutes.
- Remove the saucepan from heat and add the crumbled Stilton, stirring until all the cheese is melted.
- Season to taste with salt and pepper, and thin as necessary with additional broth.
- Serve soup immediately, sprinkling with parsley and placing ham biscuit on the side.

Miniature Ham Biscuits

6	small soft dinner rolls
¼	cup butter, melted
6	pieces prosciutto or Smithfield ham

- Split rolls in two and dip each half in melted butter, just coating the face of the roll. Place ham inside, and wrap biscuits in foil. Heat at 350°F for 10 minutes.

Yield: 4 to 6 servings

Crab Bisque

3   tablespoons butter
¼   cup chopped mushrooms
2   tablespoons chopped onions
2   tablespoons chopped carrots
1   (14½-ounce) can chicken broth
⅛   teaspoon salt
⅛   teaspoon cayenne pepper
1½ cups half-and-half
½   cup white wine
½   pound crabmeat, picked free of shell
    tomato paste
¼   cup sherry
    parsley to garnish

- Melt butter in a large saucepan over low heat. Sauté mushrooms, onions and carrots until tender.
- Add chicken broth, salt and cayenne pepper. Bring mixture to a boil, reduce heat, and simmer 10 minutes.
- Pour half of vegetable mixture into blender and process until smooth, being careful not to burn yourself. Repeat with second half of vegetable mixture.
- Combine vegetable purée, half-and-half, wine and crabmeat in the saucepan.
- Add tomato paste until bisque is desired color.
- Add sherry and cook until thoroughly heated.
- Sprinkle with parsley to garnish.

Yield: 6 to 8 servings

Although you can usually purchase crabmeat, preparing your own from fresh Atlantic Blue crabs significantly enhances the flavor of this wonderful bisque. To prepare crabmeat for bisque, follow these steps:

- Cook four to six crabs in boiling water (flavored with crab boil spices and beer) until bright red, about 30 minutes.
- Turn crab on its back and break off legs and claws.
- Pull off apron (underside shell) from the scalloped edge to the back.
- Remove top shell by using thumb to lift away shell from apron hinge.
- Remove and discard gills and stomach sac.
- Break remaining crab in half lengthwise and pick out crabmeat.

When steaming your own
shrimp add ¼ cup sherry
to the liquid for flavor.
Steam with heads and
shells intact to extract the
fullest flavor.

North Carolina Shrimp Bisque

½   cup butter
½   cup plus two tablespoons all-purpose flour
1   cup finely chopped celery
1   medium onion, finely chopped
1   cup water or broth from steaming shrimp
2¼ cups milk
1½ teaspoons Worcestershire sauce
1   cup marinara sauce
1   bay leaf
½   cube fish-flavored bouillon or 1 teaspoon lobster base
2   cups steamed shrimp, finely chopped
    hot pepper sauce to taste
1   pint heavy cream

- In a large soup pot, combine butter and flour over medium heat. After butter melts, cook for 2 minutes, stirring constantly, to form a light roux.
- Add celery and onions and cook until onions are tender, about 3 minutes.
- Slowly add water or broth from steamed shrimp and milk. Stir until no lumps are apparent.
- Add Worcestershire sauce, marinara sauce, bay leaf and bouillon.
- Add shrimp and stir to incorporate.
- Add hot pepper sauce to taste.
- Cover and simmer over very low heat for 1 to 2 hours. Stir occasionally to prevent sticking.
- Add cream and turn up heat to medium. Cook until heated through.

Note: Use crab rather than shrimp for a bisque that is equally divine.

Yield: 6 servings

If using frozen corn, add
1 (10-ounce) box of frozen
corn kernels during the
last 5 minutes of cooking.
If using frozen lobster
meat, thicken the chowder
by adding a tablespoon of
cornstarch dissolved in
2 tablespoons water.

Lobster and Corn Chowder

The delicacy of lobster with a down-home style.

3   ears fresh corn
½   large yellow onion, finely chopped
1   tablespoon unsalted butter
5   cups whole milk
2   cups heavy cream
½   pound (2 small) unpeeled potatoes, in ½-inch dice
1   ounce lobster paste
1½ cups water
¾   teaspoon salt
1½ teaspoons white pepper
½   pound cooked fresh lobster meat
½   tablespoon garlic powder
½   cup sherry

(continued on next page)

Lobster and Corn Chowder *(continued)*

- Shuck corn and cut kernels from cob.
- Sauté onions in butter until translucent, then combine with milk, cream and potatoes in a heavy-bottomed pot and bring to simmer.
- Dissolve lobster paste in water and add to milk mixture. Simmer for 20 minutes.
- Add corn and continue simmering 10 minutes.
- Season with salt and pepper.
- Add lobster meat, garlic powder and sherry.
- Heat through and serve.

Yield: 8 servings

Spicy Chicken Chili

1	pound boneless, skinless chicken cut into ½-inch cubes
2	tablespoons vegetable oil
1	medium onion, chopped
4	cloves garlic, minced
1	(6-ounce) can chopped green chiles, drained
1	cup chicken stock
1	teaspoon salt
½	teaspoon pepper
¼	teaspoon cayenne pepper
½	bunch cilantro, chopped
1	(14½-ounce) can Mexican tomatoes
1	(14½-ounce) can white beans, drained
2	tablespoons chili powder
1	tablespoon cumin
½	teaspoon oregano
½	cup sun-dried tomatoes, chopped
1	cup grated cheddar cheese
	Sour cream

- In a large Dutch oven, sauté chicken in oil for 5 minutes.
- Add onion and garlic and continue to cook until chicken is lightly browned.
- Add remaining ingredients in the order given, excluding cheese and sour cream. Bring to boil. Reduce heat and simmer 30 minutes.
- Serve with cheddar cheese and sour cream to garnish.

Yield: 6 servings

For those who prefer a less spicy dish, put out a variety of condiments that will help to check the heat. Sour cream is always a favorite, as are grated cheddar and Monterey Jack cheeses. For more variation, prepare a platter of raw celery and carrot sticks, chopped onions and soft tortillas cut into bite-size pieces. This chili is also delicious when served over stewed beans, rice or cheese grits.

Chicken Barley Soup

Make extra for your freezer or to share with family and friends.

Although one of our most important crops, 90% of the barley grown in America is fermented to make beer or is used as food for animals. Barley is a nutritious grain rich in protein and dietary fiber. It has been used by ancient civilizations as currency, as a measuring system, and for medicinal purposes—even for diagnosing pregnancy!

10	cups chicken broth
6	large carrots, chopped
3	large stalks celery, chopped
1	pound mushrooms, sliced
¾	cup barley
	juice of 1 lemon
	freshly ground pepper to taste
1	tablespoon dill
2½	cups cooked chicken, shredded (3 to 4 breasts)

- Bring chicken broth to boil over medium-high heat.
- Add carrots, celery, mushrooms and barley. Simmer until barley is soft, about 45 minutes.
- Add lemon juice, pepper, dill and chicken.
- Heat an additional 5 to 10 minutes.

Yield: 8 servings

Vegetarian Chili with Rice

A simple recipe for today's busy lifestyle

Our testers found this to be an amazingly good, healthy and satisfying dish.

1	(15½-ounce) can red kidney beans, drained
1	(15-ounce) can Great Northern beans, drained
1	(14½-ounce) can chopped tomatoes, undrained
1	(8-ounce) can tomato sauce
¾	cup chopped green bell pepper
½	cup chopped white onion
1	tablespoon chili powder
1	teaspoon sugar
½	teaspoon dried basil
2	cloves garlic, minced
1	cup water
1	teaspoon cumin
1	teaspoon cayenne pepper
2	cups hot cooked rice

- In a large saucepan, combine all ingredients except rice.
- Bring to a boil, reduce heat and simmer for 15 minutes, stirring occasionally.
- Serve over ½ cup cooked rice.

Yield: 4 servings

Chicken Tortilla Soup

Spicy and satisfying, top-rated by our testers

1	tablespoon olive oil
1	large onion, chopped
6	cups chicken stock
4	ounces green chiles, diced
1	teaspoon chili powder
1	teaspoon cumin
1	large clove garlic, crushed
½	teaspoon dried oregano
¼	teaspoon cayenne pepper
1	(16-ounce) can crushed tomatoes
1	pound boneless, skinless chicken breasts
⅓	cup chopped fresh cilantro
1	teaspoon salt (omit if using canned chicken broth)
1	teaspoon ground black pepper
1	cup corn, fresh, frozen or canned
	tortilla chips
	grated sharp cheddar or Monterey jack cheese

- Sauté onion in olive oil until clear.
- Bring chicken stock or broth to a boil. Add onion, green chiles, chili powder, cumin, garlic, oregano, cayenne pepper and tomatoes.
- Cut chicken into bite-sized pieces and add uncooked to soup mixture.
- Add cilantro, salt and black pepper to taste.
- Simmer approximately one hour.
- Add corn and cook 10 minutes more.
- Serve topped with crumbled tortilla chips and grated cheese.
- May cool to room temperature, then freeze for later use.

Yield: 8 servings

This soup was enjoyed "to the last drop" by photographers and journalists from *The Triangle Lifestyle Magazine* (January/February 1998). The magazine featured Chicken Tortilla Soup, Fireside Fondue and Million Dollar Cake as a warm winter menu that bolsters comradery.

Minestrone Soup

Instead of topping with grated cheese, serve with Cheese Biscuits on the side. Add strips of prosciutto to make this soup even heartier.

3	tablespoons olive oil
1	cup chopped onion
4 to 5	cloves garlic, crushed
1	teaspoon salt, divided
1	cup minced celery
1	cup cubed carrot
1	teaspoon dried oregano
1/4	teaspoon black pepper
1	teaspoon chopped fresh basil (or 1/2 teaspoon dried)
1	cup cubed zucchini
3/4	cup chopped green bell pepper
3 1/2	cups water or chicken stock (use stock for heartiness)
16	ounces tomato purée
1	(15-ounce) can pinto beans
3	tablespoons dry red wine
1	cup fresh chopped tomatoes
3/4	cup pasta (small shells, maruzzine)
	grated cheddar or Parmesan cheese
	sour cream

- Prepare all vegetables.
- Drain pinto beans, reserving liquid. Use liquid as part of the 3 1/2 cups water or stock.
- In a soup kettle, sauté onions and garlic in olive oil until they are soft and translucent.
- Add 1/2 teaspoon salt, carrot and celery. Mix well.
- Add oregano, black pepper and basil.
- Cover and cook over low heat 5 to 8 minutes.
- Add zucchini, green pepper, stock, purée, pinto beans and wine.
- Cover and simmer 15 minutes.
- Add tomatoes and 1/2 teaspoon salt.
- Keep at lowest heat until 10 minutes before serving. Then heat soup to slow boiling and add pasta. Boil gently until pasta is tender. Serve hot.
- Garnish with grated cheddar or Parmesan cheese and a dollop of sour cream.

Yield: 8 cups

Wild Rice Soup

Nutty wild rice adds texture to a thick cream soup.

6	tablespoons butter or margarine
1	tablespoon minced onion
½	cup all-purpose flour
3	cups chicken broth
2	cups cooked wild rice
⅓	cup minced ham
⅓	cup finely shredded carrots
3	tablespoons chopped slivered almonds
½	teaspoon salt
1	cup half-and-half
2	tablespoons dry sherry
	snipped parsley or chives

- Melt butter in saucepan; sauté onion until tender.
- Blend in flour; gradually stir in broth.
- Cook, stirring constantly, until mixture comes to a boil. Boil and stir 1 minute.
- Stir in rice, ham, carrots, almonds and salt. Simmer about 5 minutes.
- Blend in half-and-half and sherry; heat to serving temperature.
- Garnish with parsley or chives.

Note: ½ cup dry wild rice yields approximately 2 cups cooked.

Yield: 4 to 6 servings

"Wild rice" isn't rice at all but the seed of a native marsh grass. Extremely difficult to grow, wild rice is relatively expensive; however, it expands threefold when cooked. To precook the rice for soup, first rinse it well by covering with water in a bowl and discarding any debris that rises to the top; drain. Put 4 ounces of rice and 2¼ cups water in a large saucepan; bring to a boil. Lower the heat to simmer, cover the pot and cook for 45 minutes to 1 hour.

Madeira Mushroom Soup

A pleasant way to begin Thanksgiving

Madeira wine is produced only on the small island of Madeira off the Moroccan coast. When selecting a Madeira to use in soups and sauces, Verdelho Madeira is usually the wine of choice. This variety has a smoky, gentle fruit flavor.

6	tablespoons butter
1	medium onion, finely chopped
1	pound mushrooms, finely chopped
3	tablespoons all-purpose flour
3	cups chicken stock
³/₄	teaspoon salt
½	teaspoon pepper
½	cup Madeira
²/₃	cup heavy cream
	chopped parsley for garnish

- Melt butter in large saucepan.
- Add onion and sauté for 10 minutes or until evenly browned.
- Add mushrooms and cook for 2 minutes.
- Sprinkle in flour and cook until bubbly.
- Gradually stir in stock and season with salt and pepper. Bring to a boil, then cover and simmer for 10 minutes.
- Stir in Madeira and heavy cream. Heat through, but do not boil.
- Serve immediately garnished with snipped parsley.

Yield: 6 to 8 servings

Hearty Mushroom-Barley Soup

This vegetarian soup is substantial enough to serve as the main dish for a simple evening meal. Add warm, crusty bread, a fresh green salad and a glass of wine.

½	cup pearl (small) barley, uncooked
6½	cups water, divided
1 to 2	tablespoons butter
1	medium onion, chopped (about 1½ cups)
2	medium cloves garlic, minced
1	pound mushrooms, sliced
½	teaspoon salt
3	tablespoons soy sauce
3	tablespoons dry sherry
	Freshly ground black pepper

- Place the barley and 1½ cups of the water in a large saucepan or Dutch oven. Bring to a boil, cover and simmer until the barley is tender, 20 to 30 minutes.

(continued on next page)

Hearty Mushroom-Barley Soup *(continued)*

- Meanwhile, melt the butter in a skillet. Add the onion and sauté for about 5 minutes over medium heat.
- Add garlic, mushrooms and salt. Cover and cook, stirring occasionally, until everything is very tender, about 10 to 12 minutes.
- Stir in soy sauce and sherry.
- Add the sauté with its liquids to the cooked barley, along with the remaining 5 cups of water.
- Add a generous amount of freshly ground black pepper and simmer, partially covered, another 20 minutes over very low heat.
- Taste to correct seasonings and serve.

Yield: 8 servings

Tomato Bisque

A rich and nourishing soup to comfort tomato soup fans on winter days

½   **cup chopped onions**
½   **cup unsalted butter, divided**
1   **teaspoon dill seed**
1½ **teaspoons dill weed**
1½ **teaspoons dried oregano**
5   **cups tomatoes (preferably canned, crushed whole tomatoes)**
4   **cups chicken stock**
2   **tablespoons all-purpose flour**
2   **teaspoons salt**
½   **teaspoon white pepper**
¼   **cup chopped fresh parsley**
4   **teaspoons honey**
1¼ **cups heavy cream**
⅔   **cup half-and-half**
    sour cream

- In a large pot, sauté onions in 6 tablespoons butter along with dill seed, dill weed and oregano for 5 minutes, or until onions are translucent.
- Add tomatoes and chicken stock and heat.
- Make a roux by blending 2 tablespoons butter and 2 tablespoons flour, whisking constantly over medium heat for 3 minutes, without browning.
- Add roux to stock and whisk to blend. Add salt and pepper.
- Bring to a boil, stirring occasionally. Reduce heat and simmer for 15 minutes.
- Add chopped parsley, honey, cream and half-and-half.
- Remove from heat and purée. Strain.
- When ready to serve, reheat and serve with a dollop of sour cream.

Yield: 6 servings

For a more substantial version, omit straining step and garnish with cheddar cheese and fresh bacon bits instead of sour cream. Reduce or eliminate the salt if using canned chicken broth. Ladle into warmed mugs and serve with toast points.

Gazpacho

A chilled, refreshing, lowfat soup

1	cup finely chopped, peeled tomato (canned suitable)
½	cup finely chopped green bell pepper
½	cup finely chopped celery
½	cup finely chopped cucumber
¼	cup finely chopped onion
2	teaspoons snipped fresh parsley
1	teaspoon snipped fresh chives
1	small clove garlic, minced
2 to 3	tablespoons tarragon wine vinegar
2	tablespoons olive oil
1	tablespoon salt
¼	teaspoon pepper
½	teaspoon Worcestershire sauce
2	cups tomato juice
	croutons to garnish

Gazpacho is the ideal beginning for a summertime grilled menu. Serve in chilled soup bowls or mugs to retain the cool, brisk flavor.

- Combine all ingredients in stainless steel or glass bowl.
- Chill at least 4 hours.
- Serve with crisp croutons.

Yield: 6 servings

Tropical Fruit Gazpacho

1	cup tomato juice
1	cup pineapple juice
½	peeled, chopped mango
½	cup peeled, chopped papaya
½	cup chopped fresh pineapple
½	cup peeled, seeded and chopped cucumber
¼	cup chopped green bell pepper
¼	cup chopped red bell pepper
2	tablespoons minced fresh cilantro
¼	teaspoon salt
½ to 1	teaspoon hot sauce

- Combine all ingredients in a blender and pulse four times or until combined but not smooth.
- Cover and chill well.

Yield: 6 servings

Frosty Strawberry Soup

A whimsical presentation in pastels

1	quart fresh strawberries or 10 ounces frozen strawberries, thawed
1	teaspoon grated lemon peel
1	cup orange juice
1½	tablespoons instant tapioca
1	cup buttermilk
⅛	teaspoon ground allspice (or more to taste)
⅛	teaspoon ground cinnamon (or more to taste)
½	cup sugar
1	tablespoon lemon juice
2	lemon slices, halved
2	cantaloupes

- Reserve some berries for a garnish. Place remaining berries in blender with lemon peel and orange juice. Blend until smooth. Strain into a saucepan.
- Mix tapioca with a little strawberry purée and add to the remaining mixture in saucepan. Heat, stirring constantly, until mixture comes to full boil. Cook 1 minute or until mixture thickens.
- Remove from heat and add remaining ingredients except lemon slices and cantaloupes.
- Chill thoroughly.
- Cut cantaloupes in half making a decorative saw-tooth edge. Scoop out seeds. Turn upside down on paper towels. Refrigerate until ready to serve.
- Pour well-chilled soup into cantaloupe halves and garnish with lemon slices and reserved berries.

Yield: 4 servings

In May and June, strawberry farms boasting "U Pick" signs are all over eastern North Carolina. If picking your own is not an option, try the local farmer's market or a roadside stand.

"It is hot here in the summertime, but that never stopped Mother from taking us children to pick strawberries at local farms. We would each get a basket and, under Mother's watchful gaze, would fill the baskets and ourselves with ripe, juicy berries. Nothing tastes more like early summer than fresh strawberries..."

Refresh your luncheon
table with an asparagus
vase centerpiece. You will
need a large bunch of
fresh asparagus spears,
decorative ribbon, double-
sided tape and a clear
cylindrical vase measuring
10 to 12 inches high and 3
to 4 inches in diameter.
First, measure the asparagus by standing one spear
next to the vase and
trimming off the end so the
spear does not extend past
the top of the vase. Trim
the remaining spears to
conforming length. Affix a
piece of double-sided tape
around the diameter of the
vase. Stand the spears
around the vase to cover it
completely. Wrap a ribbon
around the spears and fill
the vase with yellow tulips,
daffodils or daisies.

Asparagus and Couscous Salad

Grains and vegetables, fruits and nuts

1	cup orange juice
1	cup water
3	teaspoons olive oil, divided
2	teaspoons salt, divided
2	teaspoons grated fresh ginger
1	cup couscous
18	asparagus spears cut into 1-inch lengths
1	red bell pepper, seeded and diced
½	cup frozen peas
1	(15-ounce) can mandarin oranges, drained
2	scallions, minced
½	teaspoon cayenne pepper
¼	cup toasted walnuts, chopped (see Note)

- In a saucepan, bring orange juice, water, 2 teaspoons olive oil, 1 teaspoon salt and ginger to a boil over high heat.
- Place couscous in a large bowl and pour orange juice mixture over. Cover tightly and allow to stand 20 minutes.
- In the meantime, heat 1 teaspoon olive oil in a nonstick skillet and sauté the asparagus 2 minutes. Add the red peppers and peas; sauté 1 minute.
- Add to the couscous along with the oranges, scallions, 1 teaspoon salt, cayenne pepper and nuts; combine well.
- Serve warm or at room temperature.

Note: To toast nuts, place in a single layer in a baking dish and toast at 350°F oven about 10 minutes or until golden.

Yield: 4 servings

Baked Goat Cheese Salad

Variation of a French classic

½ cup olive oil
4 sprigs plus 2 teaspoons chopped fresh thyme
8 rounds goat cheese, cut ¾-inch thick from Montrachet log
¾ cup fine white bread crumbs
¼ teaspoon salt
  pepper to taste
3 tablespoons balsamic vinegar
4 cups watercress (or endive, spinach, leaf lettuce or radicchio)

- Combine oil and sprigs of thyme. Pour over cheese rounds and marinate overnight.
- Preheat oven to 350°F.
- Combine bread crumbs, chopped thyme, salt and pepper in a bowl.
- Remove cheese from marinade, reserving marinade.
- Roll cheese rounds in bread crumb mixture. Place in baking dish and bake 15 minutes until crumbs are golden.
- Combine oil from marinade with vinegar and salt and pepper to taste. Toss oil and vinegar with salad greens.
- Serve four individual salads with two rounds of goat cheese on the side of each.

Yield: 4 servings

The U.S. now competes with France in producing a variety of goat's milk cheeses, or chèvres. Serve chèvre in the following ways:

- blended with a little cream and walnuts to serve with apples or pears
- a baked potato topping
- on toast with preserves
- atop your favorite pizza
- instead of cream cheese in dips and spreads

Cucumber and Feta Cheese Salad

A cool salad to complement grilled foods

1 medium cucumber, peeled, halved lengthwise and sliced ¼-inch thick
1 small Vidalia or other sweet onion, halved and sliced ¼-inch thick
6 Greek black olives, pitted
2 ounces (½ cup) feta cheese, crumbled
3 tablespoons olive oil
2 tablespoons white wine vinegar
½ teaspoon coarsely ground black pepper
  salt

- Combine cucumber, onion slices, olives and cheese in a bowl. Toss gently to mix.
- Stir together oil, vinegar, pepper and salt to taste in a cup. Pour dressing over salad and set aside 10 minutes for flavors to blend.

Yield: 2 servings

"To make a good salad is to be a brilliant diplomatist - the problem is entirely the same in both cases. To know exactly how much oil one must put with one's vinegar." Oscar Wilde, *Vera, or the Nihilists,* 1883

Roquefort is a blue cheese made from sheep's milk that must be aged for at least two months in the limestone caves of Cambalou in the south of France. Its sharp taste, combined with tart apples and walnuts and topped with a sweet dressing, makes a fabulous topping for fresh greens.

Green Salad
with Roquefort, Apples and Walnuts

Three distinct flavors combine to create a sensational autumn salad.

6 to 8	cups torn mixed salad greens (romaine, leaf lettuce, bibb, spinach, frisée)
1	large apple, peeled, cored and chopped
4	ounces Roquefort cheese, crumbled
½	cup walnuts, toasted
3	tablespoons bacon bits (optional)
	Celery Seed Dressing (recipe follows)

- Place lettuce, apple, cheese and walnuts in a large salad bowl.
- Pour on enough dressing to coat and toss lightly.
- Sprinkle with bacon bits and serve.

Celery Seed Dressing

2	cups vegetable oil
2	tablespoons salt
1	cup sugar
2	tablespoons celery seeds
1½	tablespoons minced onion
3 to 4	cloves garlic, minced (or more to taste)
⅔	cup white wine vinegar

- Whisk together all ingredients until sugar is dissolved.

Yield: 4 to 6 servings

Stuffed Avocados

Garnish with edible flowers such as Johnny jump-ups or nasturtiums for a stunning effect.

²⁄₃ cup crumbled feta cheese (about 4 ounces)
2   small ripe tomatoes, chopped
½   cup chopped red onion
2   tablespoons chopped fresh parsley
2   tablespoons olive oil
1   tablespoon balsamic vinegar or red wine vinegar
1   tablespoon chopped fresh oregano or 1 teaspoon dried
    lettuce leaves
2   large avocados, halved and pitted
    salt and pepper to taste

• Combine feta cheese, tomatoes, onion, parsley, olive oil, vinegar and oregano in a medium bowl. Season with salt and pepper.
• Arrange lettuce leaves on 4 plates. Place avocado halves on lettuce leaves and spoon cheese mixture into each avocado half.

Yield: 4 servings

To halve an avocado, use a sharp paring knife to cut it lengthwise all around. Gently twist the halves in opposite directions to separate. To remove the seed, insert the blade of a sharp, heavy knife into the seed with a quick, firm stroke, and use the knife to twist the seed and lift it from the fruit.

To minimize discoloration, lightly brush the avocado with lemon juice after slicing. Wrap tightly in plastic wrap and refrigerate until ready to use. Before use, scrape off any browned flesh.

Shoe Peg Corn Salad

Doubles easily for large crowds

2   (16-ounce) cans shoe peg corn, drained
1   (2-ounce) jar chopped pimientos, drained
½   cup chopped green bell pepper
½   cup chopped onion
2   stalks celery, chopped
½   cup sugar
½   cup vegetable oil
½   cup vinegar
1   teaspoon salt
½   teaspoon black pepper

• Mix together corn, pimientos, green pepper, onion and celery.
• Combine the remaining ingredients and pour over vegetables. Cover and chill overnight.
• Drain vegetables well before serving.

Yield: 6 to 8 servings

Southerners enjoy peanuts raw, roasted and boiled; hot and spicy or salted; ground into peanut butter or whole; as a garnish for vegetables, in dressings and stuffings or in candy and sweets. Also called ground-nuts and goober peas, we thank our African ancestors for introducing this nutritious bean to our diet.

Green Pea Salad

One of the tried and true covered dishes

1   (10-ounce) box frozen peas, thawed
1   head cauliflower, broken into pieces
½   cup diced celery
5   scallions, diced
½   pound bacon, fried and crumbled
½   (12-ounce) can salted peanuts
1   cup mayonnaise
    Dash of salt to taste

• Combine all ingredients in a large salad bowl and stir gently to coat.

Note: When making this salad ahead of time, add the peanuts just before serving to keep them crunchy.

Yield: 6 servings

Make-Ahead Grilled Salad

Fire up your grill...for vegetables!

4   yellow squash, sliced in half lengthwise
4   zucchini, sliced in half lengthwise
1   large onion, sliced in half through root end
2   tablespoons olive oil
1   cup bottled Italian salad dressing
1   teaspoon salt
½   teaspoon ground pepper

• Prepare a hot fire on the grill.
• Brush vegetables with olive oil.
• Grill 6 inches from heat, turning occasionally, until vegetables are slightly browned and tender. Remove from heat and let cool. Slice vegetables into bite-sized pieces when cooled.
• In a large bowl, combine the sliced vegetables, dressing, salt and pepper. Cover and marinate in refrigerator for 8 hours or overnight.
• Drain vegetables and arrange on serving platter or bowl.

Yield: 4 to 6 servings

Black Bean and Corn Salad

This multicolored side dish brings life to any menu.

½ **pound dried black beans**
   salt to taste
1 **(16-ounce) package frozen yellow corn, cooked and cooled**
1 **small red onion, diced**
2 **ribs celery, diced**
1 **small red bell pepper, seeded and diced**
1 **jalapeño pepper, seeded and diced**
1 **carrot, diced and blanched**
   Mustard Vinaigrette Dressing (recipe follows)

• Cook black beans until done. Do not overcook. Drain, rinse well and season.
• Combine all the vegetables with the dressing and marinate overnight.

Mustard Vinaigrette Dressing

⅓ **cup vinegar**
⅔ **cup olive oil**
1 **tablespoon dried basil**
1 **teaspoon dried thyme**
½ **cup Dijon mustard**
⅓ **cup sugar**
1 **teaspoon sesame oil**
2 **teaspoons coarsely ground pepper**

• Blend dressing ingredients in a food processor until smooth. Add more mustard to emulsify if necessary.

Yield: 8 to 10 servings

Black beans, also known as "turtle beans," are native to South America and are popular in soup, rice and salad dishes. When preparing the black beans, follow these guidelines to ensure that they are crisp, tender and full of their natural flavor:

• Drain off the soaking water and add fresh water to the pot before cooking. Do not add salt to the cooking water since the salt can toughen the beans.

• Always drain the beans when done to prevent further cooking in the hot liquid.

• Cooked beans can be stored in airtight containers in the refrigerator for up to 5 days.

Prepare pineapple for Summer Fruit Salad following these simple steps:

- Select a pineapple that is heavy for its size with deep green leaves at the crown.
- Cut off the base and leaves of the fruit so that it stands.
- Using a very sharp knife, cut away the skin in strips going from top to bottom; trim any eyes left after cutting away the skin.
- Slice the fruit in wedges, cut away the core, and cut the wedges into cubes for your salad.
- For an added twist, slice the core into strips and use as swizzle sticks for cocktails.

Summer Fruit Salad

Serve as salad or dessert. Either way, guests will rave.

1	fresh pineapple, peeled, cored and cubed
1	quart fresh strawberries, hulled
1	cup fresh blueberries
2	cups freshly squeezed orange juice
½	cup sugar
¼	cup cream sherry
½	teaspoon almond extract
½	teaspoon vanilla extract

- Combine pineapple, strawberries and blueberries in a large bowl.
- Combine remaining ingredients in a medium bowl, stirring until sugar dissolves.
- Pour orange juice/sherry mixture over fruit, tossing lightly.
- Cover and chill 2 to 3 hours.
- Serve salad with a slotted spoon.

Yield: 10 servings

To prevent the bananas from turning brown, dip slices in orange juice before combining them with the other fruit.

Fresh Fruit Salad

It's no longer necessary to bribe the children to eat nutritious fruit.

1½ to 2	pounds seedless grapes, halved
4	bananas, sliced
4	apples, diced (with or without peel)
1	egg, beaten
6	tablespoons apple cider vinegar
½	cup water
1	cup sugar
1	tablespoon all-purpose flour
	lettuce leaves

- Place fruit in a large mixing bowl.
- Place remaining ingredients in a double boiler. Cook until thick, stirring often.
- Pour dressing mixture over fruit. Chill for 1 hour.
- Serve on a bed of lettuce.

Yield: 6 to 8 servings

Frozen Fruit Salad

Keep in the freezer to refresh appetites on hot summer days.

2	cups sour cream
2	tablespoons lemon juice
½	cup sugar
⅛	teaspoon salt
1	(8-ounce) can crushed pineapple, drained
1	large banana, diced
3 to 4	teaspoons maraschino cherry juice, for color
½	cup chopped pecans
¼	cup maraschino cherries, drained and chopped

- Combine first seven ingredients until blended and a pretty pink color. Fold in nuts and cherries.
- Spoon into 12 paper muffin liners fitted into 3-inch muffin pan. Cover muffin pan with foil.
- Freeze.
- Can be removed and placed in a plastic storage bag after freezing. These will keep for 1 month in the freezer.
- Remove from freezer about 15 minutes before serving. Peel off paper liners and place on a bed of lettuce or other greens.

Yield: 12 servings

Individual salads in paper cups are a hit with children and adults. At your next backyard picnic, serve salads in decorative muffin liners topped with a dollop of vanilla yogurt and whole cherries. For more elegant brunches or luncheons, use shiny foil liners that you have decorated with glitter or beads, and top each salad with crystallized violets. (To crystallize violets, dip them in superfine sugar and dry for 1-2 days until brittle.)

Fresh Spinach and Strawberries

A sweet and tangy salad to dress your holiday table

1	pound fresh spinach, washed and dried
1	pint fresh strawberries
¾	cup sliced almonds, toasted
	Dressing (recipe follows)

- Toss spinach and strawberries.
- Pour dressing over salad, then top with toasted almonds.

Dressing

½	cup sugar
1	tablespoon poppy seeds
2	tablespoons sesame seeds
1½	teaspoons minced onion
¼	teaspoon paprika
½	cup red or white wine vinegar
¼	cup cider vinegar
½	cup salad oil

- Mix dressing ingredients and refrigerate.
- Dressing will keep for up to one month.

Yield: 6 to 8 servings

"Six of us have shared a holiday girls' dinner for several years. Though we cherish our friendship, our lives go in so many directions that it's difficult for us all to get together at other times. One friend is known for her strawberry and spinach salad. The flavors of the fresh green spinach leaves (renewing friendships), the sweetness of the strawberries she manages to find in December (celebrating our joys), and the tangy dressing (supporting our sorrows) somehow sum up the reasons why we continue our tradition each season."

The cool, sweet mango provides the necessary antithesis to the heat of the chilies. Since the mango's flesh clings tenaciously to the pit, you will need to use a sharp knife to cut the fruit away from the seed:

- Slice the fruit lengthwise on either side of the pit, cutting as close to the pit as possible.
- Slice the flesh of the 2 sections in a lattice pattern.
- For each section, cut down to the peel but do not pierce it.
- Using your thumbs, push the peel inside out.
- Cut away cubes with a small knife.

Turn on Jimmy Buffet and pass out the Margarita glasses - filled with slaw! Your guests will be amused and pleasantly surprised as they savor this unusual salad.

Mango Jalapeño Slaw

Fabulous with ribs and other grilled dishes

½   head green cabbage, shredded
    Salt and pepper to taste
2   jalapeño chiles, minced (wear rubber gloves)
3   tablespoons balsamic vinegar
¾   cup mayonnaise
1   ripe mango, peeled, seeded and cubed

- Combine green cabbage and jalapeños.
- Liberally salt and pepper mixture.
- Mix mayonnaise and vinegar and fold into cabbage mixture. Gently fold in mango.
- Refrigerate until served.

Note: Do not use light mayonnaise here; the result will be watery slaw.

Yield: 6 to 8 servings

Margarita Berry Slaw

Unexpected and enticing flavors for your backyard picnic

1½ pounds green cabbage, shredded
½   pound red cabbage, shredded
3   carrots, shredded
1   cup dried cranberries
2   medium Granny Smith apples, peeled, cored and cut into small cubes
    Margarita Dressing (recipe follows)

- Toss together cabbages, carrots, cranberries and apple cubes in a large mixing bowl.
- Pour Margarita Dressing over cabbage mixture and toss well. Cover and refrigerate a minimum of 6 hours or overnight.

Margarita Dressing

¾   cup frozen margarita mix, thawed
¼   cup apple cider vinegar
¼   cup vegetable oil
¾   teaspoon celery salt

- Combine dressing ingredients in a small bowl, stirring well.

Yield: 12 servings

Parslied Potato Salad

A prelude for picky appetites

8   medium potatoes
1½ cups mayonnaise
1   cup sour cream
1½ teaspoons horseradish
1   teaspoon celery seeds
½   teaspoon salt
1   cup chopped fresh parsley (do not omit or decrease)
2   medium sweet onions, finely minced

- Boil whole potatoes with jackets still on.
- After fully cooking and cooling, peel and cut into ⅛-inch slices.
- Mix mayonnaise, sour cream, horseradish, celery seeds and salt. Set aside.
- Mix parsley and onion. Set aside.
- In a large serving bowl, place a layer of potatoes; salt lightly. Cover with a layer of mayonnaise mixture. Then sprinkle with a layer of parsley and onion.
- Continue layering, ending with parsley and onion.
- DO NOT STIR.
- Cover and store in refrigerator for 8 hours.

Yield: 6 to 8 servings

Someone once said, "Happiness is like a potato salad - when shared with others, it's a picnic." Whether at a southern picnic, funeral, or family reunion, count on finding potato salad among the items on the buffet table. Second only to barbecue sauce in the debate for whose recipe is the best, potato salad has been a favorite side dish as long as any southerner can remember. Instead of entering this debate, we offer a new, colorful version to add to your entertaining files. But please, do keep grandmother's recipe on hand for those cherished family gatherings!

Mediterranean Rice Salad

Not for dieters only, this Riviera-inspired combination is great for lunch.

1   (6-ounce) package chicken flavored rice mix
2   green onions, sliced
½   green bell pepper, chopped
12 ripe black olives, sliced
⅓   cup mayonnaise
2   (6-ounce) jars marinated artichoke hearts, chopped, liquid reserved
¼   teaspoon curry powder

- Cook rice according to package directions and cool.
- Add green onions, green pepper and olives to the rice.
- In a small bowl, combine mayonnaise and artichoke liquid.
- Toss rice mixture with mayonnaise mixture.
- Fold in artichokes.
- Add curry powder and mix well.
- Chill well, preferably overnight, in an airtight container.

Yield: 6 to 8 servings

While you might look to Mediterranean rice salad for your chicken side dish, don't forget the sea. Serve with grilled fish and scallops, too.

Do you want people in your life to know, "There's someone who always goes the extra mile for me"? Use homemade mayonnaise here; they'll know.

Homemade Mayonnaise

2 egg yolks

1 whole egg

1 tablespoon Dijon mustard
   pinch of salt
   freshly ground pepper
   to taste

2 tablespoons fresh lemon juice

2 cups oil (corn, vegetable or olive)

- Combine all ingredients except oil in food processor. Process using steel blade for 1 minute.
- With the motor running, add oil through feed tube in steady stream.
- When finished, scrape sides of bowl and taste. Correct seasonings. (If you used vegetable oil, you may wish to add more lemon juice.)
- Store, covered, in refrigerator for up to 5 days.

Layered Basil Salad

A substantial salad of pasta, vegetables and ham

4   cups torn salad greens
4   medium carrots, julienned
1½ cups cooked macaroni shells
2   cups frozen peas, thawed
1   medium red onion, diced
¾   pound fully cooked ham, cubed
⅓   cup shredded Swiss cheese
⅓   cup shredded cheddar cheese
    Dressing (recipe follows)
2   hard-cooked eggs, cut into wedges (optional)

- In a 3½-quart glass bowl, layer greens, carrots, macaroni, peas, onion, ham and cheeses.
- Spread dressing over salad.
- Garnish with eggs, if desired.
- Cover and chill for several hours.

Dressing

1   cup mayonnaise
½   cup sour cream
2   teaspoons Dijon mustard
1½ teaspoons chopped fresh basil or ½ teaspoon dried basil
½   teaspoon salt
½   teaspoon pepper

- In a small bowl, combine dressing ingredients; mixing well.

Yield: 12 to 14 servings

Oriental Chicken Salad with Rice

Lovely to look at, better to taste (Wait a day if you can!)

1   (6-ounce) box seasoned long grain and wild rice
½   cup olive oil
¼   cup tarragon or red wine vinegar
2   tablespoons Dijon mustard
1   tablespoon grated fresh ginger
1   teaspoon pepper
1   pound cooked chicken or turkey, cut into cubes
1   (10-ounce) package frozen peas, thawed
½   cup chopped green onions
½   cup sliced almonds, toasted
¼   cup chopped red bell pepper

• Cook rice according to package directions.
• Whisk oil, vinegar, mustard, ginger and pepper in a large bowl.
• Stir in rice, chicken, peas, onions, almonds and red pepper.
• Serve warm or at room temperature.

Yield: 6 servings

> To prevent chicken or turkey cubes from being dry, allow meat to cool thoroughly in its broth before cutting.

Curried Chicken Salad

2   cups cubed, cooked chicken
1   cup raisins
1   cup chopped apple
1   tablespoon grated onion
½   cup mayonnaise
½   cup sour cream
½   teaspoon salt
½   teaspoon pepper
½   teaspoon curry powder

• Mix all ingredients well.
• Chill overnight before serving.

Yield: 4 to 6 servings

> Resist the urge to taste when you make Curried Chicken Salad. The flavors need to marry overnight.

Savory Rice Salad

Team up Chicken Enchiladas as compadre numero uno for Savory Rice Salad.

1½ cups brown rice
½   cup wild rice
4   cups water
5   chicken bouillon cubes
1   teaspoon Italian seasoning
½   teaspoon garlic powder
½   teaspoon thyme
½   cup diced onion
1   cup diced celery
1   (16-ounce) package frozen green peas, cooked per package instructions
½   cup sliced, blanched almonds
     mayonnaise to moisten salad

- Bring the brown rice, wild rice, water, bouillon cubes, Italian seasoning, garlic powder and thyme to boil in a large saucepan. Cover, reduce heat and simmer 40 minutes; check and cook 10 minutes longer if needed.
- Taste and add seasonings if needed.
- Combine rice mix with vegetables. Moisten with mayonnaise.
- Chill, but serve at room temperature.

Yield: 8 to 10 servings

Caviar Mayonnaise

1 cup mayonnaise
1 cup sour cream
1 tablespoon fresh lemon juice
2 teaspoons prepared mustard
1 ounce jar black caviar
- Mix together the first 4 ingredients. Fold in caviar. Makes 1¾ cups.

Tomato Aspic

An old-South favorite takes on a new dimension.

1   (3-ounce) package lemon-flavored gelatin
1   cup boiling water
1   envelope unflavored gelatin
1¾ cups vegetable juice cocktail, divided
½   cup white vinegar
1   tablespoon lemon juice
½   teaspoon hot sauce
1   cup chopped celery
½   cup chopped green bell pepper
½   cup pimiento-stuffed green olives, sliced
     lettuce leaves

(continued on next page)

Tomato Aspic *(continued)*

- Dissolve lemon gelatin in 1 cup boiling water.
- Sprinkle unflavored gelatin over 1 cup vegetable juice cocktail in a saucepan; let stand 1 minute.
- Cook over low heat, stirring until gelatin dissolves.
- Add remaining vegetable juice, lemon gelatin mixture, vinegar, lemon juice and hot sauce.
- Chill until it becomes the consistency of unbeaten egg white.
- Fold in celery, green pepper and olives.
- Pour into a lightly oiled 5-cup mold. Cover and chill.
- Unmold onto lettuce leaves.
- If desired, serve with Caviar Mayonnaise.

Yield: 8 servings

Creamy Cucumber Aspic
Use your decorative salad molds to showcase this refreshing aspic.

3 to 4	**medium cucumbers**
1	**(8-ounce) package cream cheese, softened**
1	**cup mayonnaise**
1/4	**cup minced onion**
1/4	**cup chopped fresh parsley,**
1	**envelope unflavored gelatin**
2	**tablespoons sugar**
3/4	**teaspoon salt**
2/3	**cup boiling water**
4	**tablespoons lemon juice**
	fresh parsley sprigs to garnish

- Halve and seed the cucumbers. Using a food processor, shred the cucumbers until you have 2 cups. Drain the shredded cucumbers thoroughly and squeeze them dry with paper towels.
- Mix the softened cream cheese with the mayonnaise, onion and parsley. Add the shredded cucumbers. Mix well.
- Mix the unflavored gelatin, sugar and salt together. Pour the boiling water over and stir until the sugar is dissolved. Add the lemon juice.
- Add the gelatin mixture to the cream cheese/cucumber mixture and stir well. Pour into one large mold or individual molds. Refrigerate.
- Unmold and garnish with fresh parsley sprigs.

Yield: 8 servings

> **"Couples who cook together stay together. (Maybe because they can't decide who'll get the Cuisinart.)"**
>
> *Erica Jong*

Greek Salad with Poached Salmon

Added salmon turns this crisp salad into a main course.

6	tablespoons water
1	tablespoon sauvignon blanc
1	carrot, cut into pieces
1	stalk celery, cut into pieces
¼	cup chopped onion
½	teaspoon thyme
½	teaspoon parsley
4	salmon fillets (skin off)
1	head romaine lettuce, washed and drained
1	cup cucumber, peeled and cut into ½-inch dice
1	cup green bell pepper, cut into ¾-inch dice
1	cup red bell pepper, cut into ¾-inch dice
1	cup crumbled feta cheese
6	pitted kalamata olives
2	ounces large croutons
2	tablespoons olive oil
2	teaspoons chopped fresh thyme

- Mix water, wine, carrot, celery, onion, thyme and parsley together in a skillet and bring to a simmer. Add the salmon fillets and poach for 5 to 6 minutes. Extra water may be added as needed.
- Tear lettuce into pieces and place on salad plate.
- Layer cucumber, peppers and cheese over lettuce.
- Brush salmon with olive oil and then sprinkle with thyme. Place warm salmon in center of salad.
- Garnish with croutons and olives.
- Serve with an herb-vinaigrette dressing.

Yield: 4 servings

Salad of Lettuce and Braised Quail

Dainty quail top off this impressive first course or luncheon entrée.

¼ **pound bacon**
2 **teaspoons sherry vinegar**
¼ **cup veal or chicken stock (use low-sodium if canned)**
½ **cup walnut oil**
   salt and freshly ground pepper
4 **quail**
2 **tablespoons vegetable oil**
   mixed lettuces (romaine, mâche, radicchio, arugula, etc)
2 **tablespoons pine nuts**
2 **tablespoons croutons (see Note)**
½ **avocado, thinly sliced**
4 **mushrooms, thinly sliced**

- Fry bacon in a heavy medium skillet until crisp. Remove using a slotted spoon and drain on paper towels. Crumble bacon and reserve drippings in skillet.
- Stir vinegar into skillet, scraping up any browned bits. Blend in stock. Whisk in walnut oil in a thin stream. Season with salt and pepper. Keep dressing warm over low heat.
- Pat quail dry. Sprinkle with salt and pepper. Heat vegetable oil in a heavy large skillet over medium-high heat. Add quail and cook until crisp, turning frequently, 5 to 6 minutes per side or until done. Quail may also be grilled, 6 minutes on each side.
- Mound lettuce on each plate. Top with quail. Sprinkle with crumbled bacon, pine nuts and croutons.
- Surround quail with avocado and mushrooms.
- Spoon dressing over salad and serve.

Note: Croutons may be prepared by cutting country bread into small pieces. Heat vegetable oil to 350°F. Drop bread pieces into hot oil and fry until golden brown, 20 to 30 seconds. Drain on paper towels and sprinkle with garlic salt. Commercial croutons are also suitable.

Yield: 4 servings

> "The annual ritual of the hunt is inaugurated each fall in the southern states, the young quail, rabbit, and deer reaching maturity and fattening on ripening berries, persimmons and nuts." (Bill Neal, *Bill Neal's Southern Cooking*)

Grilled Game Hen Salad

8   Cornish game hens, quartered
1½ cups freshly squeezed orange juice (about 3 oranges), divided
1   cup peanut oil, divided
3   tablespoons soy sauce, divided
3   cloves garlic, minced, divided
3   teaspoons minced fresh ginger, divided
¼   cup sherry vinegar
2   tablespoons Asian sesame oil
1½ teaspoons Oriental chili oil
    Salt and pepper to taste
4   ounces fresh shiitake mushrooms
1   head radicchio, torn into pieces
1   bunch mixed lettuces (enough for 12 servings)
3   oranges, peeled and cut into segments
4   green onions, chopped
    toasted almonds, chopped
    grated peel from 1 orange

- Arrange game hens in single layer in glass baking dish.
- Mix ½ cup orange juice, ¼ cup peanut oil, 2 teaspoons soy sauce, 1 minced garlic clove and 1 teaspoon minced ginger in medium bowl.
- Pour marinade over hens, cover, and refrigerate for at least 6 hours or overnight.
- Whisk remaining 1 cup orange juice, ¾ cup peanut oil, 2 tablespoons plus 1 teaspoon soy sauce, 2 minced garlic cloves and 2 teaspoons ginger in a medium bowl.
- Stir in vinegar, sesame oil and chili oil. Whisk to blend and season with salt and pepper.
- Bring hens to room temperature before grilling.
- Prepare grill for medium-high. Remove hens from marinade; reserve marinade.
- Grill hens until crisp and cooked through, turning occasionally, about 20 to 30 minutes. Transfer to platter.
- Brush mushrooms with reserved marinade. Grill mushrooms until light brown, about 1 minute per side.
- To prepare salad, arrange lettuces on platter. Place hens atop greens. Surround with mushrooms and orange segments.
- Sprinkle with green onions, almonds and orange peel.
- Drizzle enough dressing over salad to moisten. Pass remaining dressing separately.

Yield: 12 servings

Stir-fried Pork and Spinach Salad

A healthier way to enjoy stir-fried pork

2	teaspoons olive oil
1	clove garlic, crushed
1	pound boneless pork loin, cut into thin strips (2 x ¼-inch)
1	pound fresh spinach leaves, coarsely shredded
3	cups watercress sprigs
1	cup thinly sliced celery
1	cup seedless green grapes
½	cup thinly sliced green onions
1	(8-ounce) can sliced water chestnuts, drained
1	large Golden Delicious apple, cored and chopped
1	cup low-calorie Italian salad dressing
2	tablespoons dry white wine
2	tablespoons Dijon mustard
3	tablespoons light brown sugar
2	tablespoons toasted sesame seeds

- Heat olive oil and garlic in a nonstick skillet. Stir-fry pork strips until cooked through, about 4 minutes. Set aside; keep warm.
- In large serving bowl, toss spinach, watercress, celery, grapes, green onion, water chestnuts and apple; toss to mix.
- In small saucepan, combine salad dressing, white wine, mustard and brown sugar; heat just until brown sugar is dissolved, stirring constantly.
- Stir cooked pork into hot dressing to coat well.
- Remove pork from dressing. Pour half dressing over greens mixture in bowl; toss well.
- Place pork strips on top of salad.
- Sprinkle with sesame seeds. Pass remaining dressing.

Yield: 6 servings

Treat guests to an evening in the Far East by serving Carrot Ginger Soup and Stir-Fried Pork and Spinach Salad. Encourage them to leave their shoes at the door, and serve the meal on a low table for floor seating. Supply chopsticks (Keep forks ready.) and offer sake for refreshment. Background music, Chinese lanterns, lowered lights and candles perfect the evening's ambiance.

Grilled Shrimp with Corn and Black Bean Salad

A spicy homemade dressing enhances the grilled flavors.

5 tablespoons lime juice
¾ cup olive oil
1¼ cups chopped cilantro, divided
1½ tablespoons minced jalapeños
1 tablespoon ground cumin
   Salt and pepper
3 cups chopped, seeded tomatoes
1 (15-ounce) can black beans, rinsed and drained
1 cup chopped green onions
¾ cup chopped red onion
6 cups shredded iceberg lettuce (about 1 head)
2 ears corn, husked
24 large shrimp, peeled with tails intact (about 1½ pounds)
24 large tortilla chips

- For the dressing, place the lime juice in a medium bowl, Gradually whisk in the olive oil. Mix in 6 tablespoons cilantro, jalapeños and cumin. Season to taste with salt and pepper.
- Combine the tomatoes, beans, green onions, ¾ cup cilantro and red onion in a large bowl. (Can be prepared ahead.)
- Prepare the barbecue for medium-high heat.
- Mix lettuce into the salad. Pour ¼ cup dressing into a small bowl. Reserve the remainder for the salad.
- Brush the corn with the dressing from the small bowl. Grill corn until beginning to brown, about 5 minutes.
- Brush the shrimp with the dressing from the small bowl and grill, turning, about 5 minutes.
- Cut the kernels from the ears of corn and add to the salad.
- Toss the salad with enough dressing to coat.
- Season with salt and pepper.
- Top with shrimp.
- Garnish with tortilla chips and additional cilantro.

Yield: 4 servings

Freshly prepared tortilla chips add a marvelous touch to this unusual and elegant salad. To fry tortilla chips, heat oil in large pot to 350 degrees. (The oil must be this hot.) Tear 6-inch corn tortillas into 4 pieces and drop into oil. Fry until chips just begin to change color slightly, about 20 seconds. Drain on paper towels.

Penne Salad
with Tomatoes and Mozzarella

Feast often when local garden tomatoes are available.

5	large tomatoes, diced
½	cup chopped fresh basil
3	cloves garlic, minced
1	(4½-ounce) can chopped ripe olives
½	teaspoon salt
½	teaspoon ground black pepper
1	(16-ounce) package penne pasta, cooked al dente
⅓	cup olive oil
1	tablespoon sweet red pepper flakes
1	teaspoon chopped fresh mint
8	ounces mozzarella cheese, cubed
	fresh basil sprigs for garnish

- Combine diced tomatoes with next 5 ingredients in a large bowl; top with penne.
- Combine olive oil, red pepper flakes and mint in a 1-cup glass measuring cup; microwave at high for one minute.
- Pour over pasta; add cheese cubes and toss gently.
- Cover and chill.
- Garnish with fresh basil if desired.

Yield: 6 to 8 servings

"Salads have always been an important dish on the southern table. A century before 'green' salads became a regular element in the American diet, Mary Randolph, through *The Virginia Housewife,* gave detailed instructions on making a fresh garden salad with a dressing that included tarragon vinegar and hard-boiled eggs."
(Diana Rattray)

Greens vary in flavor from mild to peppery and spicy. When mixing greens, you want to mix stronger flavors with mild, balancing the greens so that none is overpowering. For example, arugula has tender dark green leaves with a nutty taste and is best when mixed with sweet mild lettuces such as Boston or bibb lettuce. The mild greens (e.g., bibb, Boston, iceberg, romaine) also mix well with a little watercress (spicy) or Belgian endive (bitter). Always select the freshest greens available, avoiding those with wilted, dry or yellowing leaves. The greens should smell fresh, and the stem should not be brown or slimy. Wash greens carefully in cold water and dry thoroughly before storing them in your crisper. If using plastic bags for storage, first wrap the greens loosely in paper towels to absorb excess moisture, then press air from bag before sealing.

Blender Caesar Salad Dressing

1   (2-ounce) can anchovies
    juice of ½ lemon
1   large clove garlic
1   teaspoon prepared mustard
1   tablespoon Worcestershire sauce
1   egg yolk
¼   cup vinegar
¼   cup Parmesan cheese
½   cup olive oil

- Combine all ingredients in a food processor or blender.
- Refrigerate up to three days.

Yield: 1 cup

Fresh Herb Vinaigrette

1   large shallot
1   large clove garlic
1   teaspoon fresh basil
1   teaspoon fresh thyme
1   teaspoon fresh parsley
1   teaspoon fresh tarragon
1   teaspoon fresh chives
1½ tablespoons white wine vinegar
¼   cup peanut oil
1   tablespoon virgin olive oil
    lemon juice to taste
    salt to taste

- Mince vegetables and herbs.
- Combine with vinegar in a small bowl. Whisk in oils.
- Season to taste with lemon juice and salt.
- Mix well to blend.

Yield: ½ cup

Spicy Catalina Dressing

1 cup vegetable oil
⅓ cup vinegar
½ cup chili sauce
1 teaspoon Worcestershire sauce
½ cup sugar
1 teaspoon salt
1 small onion, cut into wedges
1 clove garlic
blue cheese to taste

- Combine all ingredients except the blue cheese in a blender. Blend until smooth.
- Crumble in blue cheese to taste.
- Refrigerate.

Yield: 2½ cups

Southwestern Dressing

½ cup tahini
¾ cup water
2 tablespoons soy sauce
1 tablespoon plus ½ teaspoon freshly squeezed lemon juice
1 clove fresh garlic, mashed (or ⅛ teaspoon garlic powder)
¼ teaspoon cumin
5 dashes hot sauce, or more to taste
salt and pepper to taste

- Place tahini in bowl. Gradually add water, stirring until blended.
- Add remaining ingredients, mixing well.
- Chill.
- Always stir or shake before serving.

Yield: 1 cup

Use your imagination when selecting garnishes, keeping them simple and fresh. Fresh tomatoes (marinated in a vinaigrette dressing, if desired), cucumber slices, sliced red onion, radishes, sliced hard boiled eggs, cheeses, and strips of red, green or yellow peppers are always appreciated. To add sweetness, slice fresh oranges or pears, or top with seedless grapes. For crunchiness, sprinkle with toasted walnuts, almonds, pecans, pine nuts or sesame seeds. Surprise your table guests with toppings such as cooked baby beets (cut into rounds), dried berries, or black or white truffle slivers.

Salad suggestion: Boston lettuce, Belgian endive and radicchio with fresh orange slices and toasted sesame seeds. (Also makes a great dip for chicken strips.)

Balsamic Vinaigrette Dressing

²/₃ cup extra virgin olive oil
¹/₃ cup balsamic vinegar
2   teaspoons Dijon mustard
¹/₂ teaspoon salt
     freshly ground black pepper to taste

• Whisk together all ingredients to blend.

Yield: ²/₃ cup

Salad suggestion: Mesclun with sliced pears, toasted walnut halves and Parmesan curls.

Louise's French Dressing

1   teaspoon paprika
1   teaspoon ground black pepper
1   tablespoon salt
1   cup oil
¹/₂ cup plus 2 tablespoons vinegar
1   tablespoon dry mustard
1   (11-ounce) can tomato soup
1   small onion, grated
     Blue cheese to garnish (optional)

• Beat together all ingredients.
• Chill for 24 hours to blend flavors.

Yield: 2 cups

Salad suggestion: Lettuce wedge with a crumbled blue cheese garnish.

Poppy Seed Dressing

¹/₂ cup chopped onions
2¹/₂ tablespoons poppy seeds
¹/₂ cup sugar
1   tablespoon dry mustard
¹/₂ teaspoon Nature's seasoning mix
2   tablespoons plus 1 cup corn oil
³/₄ cup tarragon vinegar

• Combine onion, poppy seeds, sugar, mustard, Nature's seasoning and 2 tablespoons corn oil in a blender. Mix well.
• Add the remaining oil and the vinegar. Mix well.

Yield: 2 cups

Salad suggestion: Chinese cabbage and bean sprouts with sweet red pepper strips, golden raisins and toasted pecans.

Marinda Sapp

Summer Spread
oil on canvas, 1998

Fish and Shellfish

Edwina's Shrimp and Grits

8 cups water
1½ tablespoons salt
2 sticks butter, divided
¾ teaspoon ground cayenne pepper
1¾ cups quick grits
2 cups cremini (Italian) mushrooms, cleaned, dried and sliced
1 cup oyster mushrooms, cleaned, dried and sliced
1 cup portobello mushrooms, cleaned, dried and sliced
2 cups shiitake mushrooms, cleaned, dried and sliced
1½ pounds smoked bacon
12 Roma tomatoes or summer tomatoes
8 ounces sun-dried tomatoes packed in oil, drained and julienned
2 pounds fresh shrimp, peeled and deveined
1 (12-ounce) can beer
3 bay leaves
  crisp green onions to garnish

Edwina Shaw is a well-known local restaurateur and cooking instructor. This ingenious recipe which she shared with us has a casserole consistency and makes an exquisite dish for a brunch or casual dinner.

- Preheat oven to 400°F.
- In a 3-quart saucepan, bring 8 cups of water, salt, 1½ sticks of butter and cayenne pepper to a boil. Slowly stir in grits. Reduce heat to low and cook 10 minutes, stirring occasionally. Remove from heat and cover. Let stand covered for 10 minutes
- In a large skillet, melt ½ stick of butter over medium-high heat. When butter begins to sizzle, add 6 cups of mushrooms. Sauté rapidly, browning slightly. Quickly remove from pan, drain and cool.
- Cook bacon in preheated oven for 12 to 18 minutes, turning bacon once half way through. (Bacon should be crisp.) Drain on paper towels. After it cools, stack and chop coarsely. Cover and set aside. (If you are refrigerating the casserole, the bacon should be left at room temperature.)
- Dice tomatoes and add to sun-dried tomatoes. Toss and set aside for 30 minutes.
- Cook shrimp in boiling water, just until they turn pink.
- In another pot, bring 2 quarts of water to boil. Add beer, bay leaves and cooked shrimp. Cook for an additional 1 minute and drain.
- Place grits in the bottom of a greased 9x13-inch glass baking dish. Dish should be ½ full. Place shrimp on top of the grits and firmly press them down.
- Cover with drained mushrooms and then top with mixed tomatoes. At this point, the casserole may be refrigerated.
- After refrigeration, bring casserole to room temperature. Do this at least 3 hours before cooking.
- Before cooking, top with bacon.
- Bake at 325°F for 30 to 40 minutes. Remove from the oven and sprinkle with cold, crisp green onions and serve.

Yield: 12 to 14 servings

Wine Recommendations: Red Côtes du Rhone, Red Burgundy or Barrel-Fermented Chardonnay

A time-saving trick for preparing seafood dishes or appetizers for parties is to keep the fish, crabmeat or shellfish ready for use in your freezer. For shrimp, peel and devein, then pack the raw shrimp in ½ lb. and 1 lb. portions in plastic freezer cartons until approximately three-quarters full. Pour salted water, 1 t. per quart of water, to fill each container to the rim. Cover and freeze. Defrost in refrigerator before using. Once thawed, rinse in cool tap water. Use in dishes requiring fresh, uncooked shrimp or steam, chill and serve as an appetizer with cocktail sauce or dips.

Shrimp with Tabasco Butter

The butter should be prepared ahead of time and refrigerated.

Tabasco Butter (recipe follows)
1 **cup coarsely chopped red onion**
1 **red or green bell pepper, sliced**
1 **pound uncooked large shrimp, peeled and deveined**
 salt to taste
½ **cup dry vermouth**

- In a large skillet over medium heat, melt 2 tablespoons of prepared Tabasco butter. Add onion and bell pepper and sauté until almost tender, about 5 minutes. Push vegetables to the side of skillet.
- Melt another 2 tablespoons of the butter in the same skillet, add shrimp and sauté until just cooked through, about 3 minutes.
- Mix shrimp and vegetables and season with salt. Divide among plates.
- Add vermouth to skillet and boil 1 minute. Gradually add remaining prepared butter, whisking until just melted.
- Pour sauce over the shrimp.

Yield: 4 servings

Tabasco Butter

½ **cup butter, room temperature**
¼ **cup chopped fresh chives**
4 **teaspoons crab boil or seafood seasoning, such as Old Bay**
1½ **teaspoons Tabasco sauce**

- Mix butter, chives, crab boil and Tabasco sauce in a bowl. Refrigerate. Butter can be prepared 2 days ahead.

Yield: ⅔ cup

Wine Recommendations: California Sauvignon Blanc or Lightly Oaked California Chardonnay

The Big Easy Shrimp

Serve with crusty bread and mixed greens for a fabulous and spicy dinner.

½   cup olive oil
2   tablespoons powdered Cajun or Creole seasoning or seafood season-
    ing, such as Old Bay
2   tablespoons chopped fresh parsley
2   tablespoons freshly squeezed lemon juice
1½ tablespoons soy sauce
1   tablespoon honey
    pinch of cayenne pepper
1   pound uncooked large shrimp, peeled and deveined

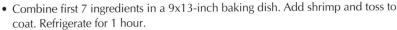

- Combine first 7 ingredients in a 9x13-inch baking dish. Add shrimp and toss to coat. Refrigerate for 1 hour.
- Preheat oven to 450°F.
- Bake until shrimp are done, stirring occasionally, about 10 minutes.

Yield: 4 to 6 servings

Nothing tops off seafood better than a squirt or two of fresh lemon or lime juice. To enhance the juice content within the citrus fruit, simply boil the entire lemon in water for 10 minutes. You can store the processed lemons in the refrigerator for use in recipes. Or try this fun serving idea; cut a tiny hole in the top and pass the lemon around the dinner table for your guests to season their own seafood platters!

Frogmore Stew

The coastline cook's equivalent to the mainland cook's barbecue

½   cup butter
4   teaspoons salt
1   bag Old Bay crab and seafood boil
2   pounds mild smoked sausage cut into 2-inch pieces
1   large onion, diced
5   ears fresh yellow or white corn, husked, cut in half
2   pounds medium red potatoes, quartered
3   pounds medium shrimp, shells on
    hot cooked rice

- Fill an 8 to 10-quart pot half full of water. Add butter, salt, crab boil, sausage and onion. Bring to a boil, uncovered. Let boil 10 minutes.
- Add corn and potatoes. Cook 5 minutes.
- Add shrimp, shells on, and cook 5 minutes more. Shrimp will turn pink and float to top when cooked.
- Turn heat off and let pot sit for 4 minutes.
- With slotted spoon, serve immediately in large bowls over prepared long-grain rice.

Yield: 5 to 6 servings

Wine Recommendations: Beaujolais, Côtes du Rhone or Rosé de Provence

It's just a name! No 4-legged, fly-catching creatures allowed in this stew pot! Tiny St. Helena Island lies just off the South Carolina coast. The post office there bears the name "Frogmore," the mailing address for the island's Gullah-speaking inhabitants. As the recipe connotes, this stew makes for sloppy eating, but when friends and relatives are gathered for a casual beach fest, who cares if you eat with your hands and drip food down your shirt?! Serve it at your gathering by first adorning your table top with the classifieds, then ladling the stew from a strainer directly onto the newspapers. Cleanup is a wrap!

Creole sauce may be made several days in advance and refrigerated. The uncooked shrimp should be added once the sauce has been brought back to a simmer, just before serving.

42nd Street Oyster Bar's Creole Sauce

Local seafood landmark, host to the lively discourse of North Carolina legislators

2   whole bay leaves
¾   teaspoon dried oregano
½   teaspoon white pepper
½   teaspoon cayenne pepper
½   teaspoon dried thyme
½   teaspoon paprika
¼   cup butter
1   cup peeled and chopped tomatoes
¾   cup chopped onions
¾   cup chopped green bell peppers
¾   cup chopped celery
1½ teaspoons minced garlic
1¼ cups chicken stock or broth
1   cup tomato sauce
1   teaspoon sugar
½   teaspoon Tabasco (optional)
2   pounds shrimp, peeled and deveined

- Combine first 6 ingredients in a small bowl. Set aside.
- Melt butter in a large skillet over medium heat. Add tomatoes, onions, peppers and celery. Then add garlic and mixed herbs. Stir thoroughly.
- Sauté until onions are transparent, about 5 minutes, stirring occasionally.
- Add chicken stock, tomato sauce, sugar and Tabasco. Bring to a boil. Add shrimp.
- Reduce heat to a simmer and cook for about 20 minutes or until vegetables are tender.
- Remove bay leaves before serving.
- Serve over rice.

Yield: 4 to 6 servings

Shrimp and Champagne Sauce

1	tablespoon olive oil
1	cup sliced mushrooms
1	pound medium shrimp, cleaned and deveined
1½	cups champagne
¼	teaspoon salt
2	tablespoons minced shallots or scallions
2	plum tomatoes, diced
¾	cup heavy cream
	salt and pepper to taste
1	(16-ounce) package angel hair pasta
3	tablespoons chopped fresh parsley

- Sauté mushrooms in hot olive oil over medium-high heat. Cook until juices evaporate. Remove mushrooms and set aside.
- In same pan, combine shrimp, champagne and salt. Heat to a simmer over high heat. When liquid boils and shrimp turn pink, remove from cooking liquid with slotted spoon. Set shrimp aside.
- Add chopped shallots and tomatoes to cooking liquid and boil over medium-high heat until reduced to approximately ½ cup, about 8 minutes.
- After liquid is reduced, add ¾ cup heavy cream and boil 1 to 2 minutes until slightly thickened.
- Add shrimp and mushrooms to sauce and heat through. Add salt and pepper to taste.
- Meanwhile, cook pasta according to package directions. Drain thoroughly and return to pot.
- Serve pasta and spoon shrimp sauce over the top. Garnish with chopped parsley.

Yield: 4 to 6 servings

Wine Recommendations: Champagne or Chablis

When serving shrimp dishes with a cream sauce, deveining the shrimp prior to preparing the dish is recommended. To clean and devein whole shrimp, first twist off the heads. Next, peel the shrimp by first peeling back the shell on the thick end and then pinching the end of the tail and pulling away the rest of the shell. Slide a sharpened paring knife along the back of the shrimp, exposing the vein. Pull out the vein with the tip of the knife or with your fingers. Rinse under cold running water. As a variation, you can slide the pointed end of a handheld can opener along the opening to help dislodge the vein. (adapted from *Fish & Shellfish,* by James Peterson)

Lock, Stock and Barrel Pasta

Much to do and worth the effort.

¼ teaspoon onion powder
¼ teaspoon cayenne pepper
¼ teaspoon dried oregano
½ teaspoon paprika
1 teaspoon salt, divided
½ teaspoon garlic powder
¼ teaspoon dried thyme
¼ teaspoon pepper
1 cup boneless, skinless chicken breast, chopped
2 tablespoons olive oil
4 ounces andouille sausage, chopped
½ pound peeled shrimp
¼ cup chopped green onions
1 tablespoon minced garlic
1½ cups heavy cream
¼ teaspoon Worcestershire sauce
¼ teaspoon hot pepper sauce
½ cup freshly grated Parmesan cheese, divided
8 ounces fettuccini

- Mix together first 8 ingredients and toss with chicken.
- Heat olive oil in skillet over medium-high heat. Add chicken and sauté 2 minutes. Add sausage and sauté 2 minutes. Add shrimp and sauté 2 minutes more.
- Stir in green onions, garlic and cream and cook 2 minutes.
- Stir in Worcestershire sauce, hot pepper sauce, ½ teaspoon salt and ¼ cup Parmesan cheese and simmer 2 minutes.
- Meanwhile, cook pasta according to package directions. Drain and toss with sauce.
- Sprinkle with remaining ¼ cup Parmesan cheese and serve.

Yield: 4 servings

Wine Recommendations: Beaujolais, Spanish Rioja or Italian Barbera

Scalloped Oysters

Perfect to accompany your Thanksgiving feast.

¼ cup butter, room temperature
3 tablespoons dry fresh bread crumbs
24 fresh oysters, shucked, liquor reserved
2 cups heavy cream
1 teaspoon Worcestershire sauce
½ teaspoon freshly ground white pepper
   salt to taste
½ cup grated Parmesan cheese or ¼ cup grated Romano cheese (optional)
½ cup soda cracker crumbs
   fresh chives for garnish

- Preheat oven to 400°F.
- Grease 13x9-inch casserole dish with butter. Sprinkle with bread crumbs.
- Mix oyster liquor, cream, Worcestershire sauce, pepper and salt. Add cheese at this time, if desired.
- Add oysters to dish and top with cream sauce.
- Sprinkle with cracker crumbs.
- Bake until cream bubbles and edges of oysters begin to curl, about 15 minutes.
- Top with fresh chives. Serve immediately.

Yield: 4 dinner servings or 8 side servings

Wine Recommendations: Champagne, Presecco or Muscadet

The south has long been enamored of the oyster. Indeed, these mollusks are as much a part of eastern North Carolina food history as butter beans, barbecue and speckled trout. In times past the oyster has been more than mere sustenance, evidenced by its use for making plaster, mortar, foundations for houses, roads, white wash, fertilizer, jewelry and ammunition!

The Rockford's Crab Cakes

A fabulous salad-and-sandwich restaurant for an appetizing workday lunch

5 pounds crabmeat, picked free of shell
1 green bell pepper, finely chopped
1 red onion, finely chopped
4 cups fresh bread crumbs
1 (8-ounce) package cream cheese
1 cup mayonnaise (optional)
2 eggs, whipped
2 teaspoons granulated garlic
   salt and pepper to taste
   vegetable oil

- By hand, mix all ingredients except oil in a large bowl.
- Form into patties.
- In a large skillet, heat vegetable oil. Fry cakes until browned, about 5 minutes per side. Drain on paper towels.

Yield: 10 servings

Wine Recommendations: Loire Valley Sauvignon Blanc (Sancerre, Pouilly Fumé) or New Zealand Sauvignon Blanc

The Rockford restaurant features this dish with an Aïoli sauce, or garlic mayonnaise. To prepare this flattering accompaniment, use the recipe offered with Portobello Mushrooms located in the Appetizers section.

Our southern forefathers thought nothing of consuming several dozen oysters as merely an appetizer to a follow-on meal! Today, our tastes are a bit more dainty, and twelve oysters a person are considered plenty.

Grilled Roast Oysters

Traditional and manageable oyster roast

- Prepare charcoal grill with enough briquettes to achieve a very hot fire.
- While grill is heating, pick through any quantity of whole oysters, discarding those which may have already opened.
- Scrub oysters thoroughly with a wire brush.
- Place on a prepared grill.
- Cover with damp cotton dish towels.
- Close grill lid and roast until oysters open, checking initially after 15-20 minutes.

Note: Serve with Shallot and White Wine Sauce (recipe follows), lemon, butter, cocktail sauce or oyster crackers and chilled dry white wine or icy cold beer.

Shallot and White Wine Sauce

4   tablespoons unsalted butter, or more as needed
¼   cup water
⅓   cup chopped shallots
¼   cup chopped red bell pepper
½   cup dry white wine

- Melt butter in the water in heavy skillet.
- Add shallots and bell pepper and simmer until water has boiled away, about 2 minutes.
- Add wine and simmer 5 minutes.
- Add more butter, if needed, to make the sauce smooth and creamy.
- Salt and pepper to taste.
- Serve over oysters.

Carolina Deviled Crab

Savor the delicate flavor of crab enhanced with subtle ingredients.

¾	**cup butter**
¾	**cup minced onion**
¼	**cup chopped fresh parsley**
2	**tablespoons minced green bell pepper**
1	**pound crabmeat, picked free of shell**
1½	**cups cracker crumbs**
2	**tablespoons freshly squeezed lemon juice**
1	**tablespoon Worcestershire sauce**
1	**teaspoon dry mustard**
½	**teaspoon salt**
	dash of cayenne pepper
2	**eggs, beaten**
½	**cup heavy cream**

- Preheat oven to 350°F.
- Place butter in a 9x9-inch casserole dish and place in the oven. When butter melts, place onion, parsley and green bell pepper into dish and return to oven for 3 to 5 minutes or until just browned.
- In a large bowl, add crabmeat, cracker crumbs, lemon juice, Worcestershire sauce, mustard, salt and cayenne pepper. Add cooked vegetables to this mixture.
- In a small bowl, beat eggs and cream until blended. Add this to crab mixture and mix well.
- Spoon into a 9x9-inch casserole dish.
- Bake 30 minutes.

Variation: For a gracious serving alternative, bake in individual decorative ovenproof ramekins or seashells. Sauté vegetable mixture in a saucepan until just browned. Prepare remaining ingredients according to recipe. Divide evenly into 4 ramekins or shells coated with no stick cooking spray. Place atop a broiler pan with 1 inch water in bottom compartment, not touching ramekins. Bake 20 minutes.

Yield: 4 servings

"'Get out your oldest pair of tennis shoes, socks and jeans, boys and girls!' My mother's words always brought squeals of delight as we prepared ourselves for the adventure of crabbing. Unlike many of our friends who vacationed at summer resorts, we always went to our family beach home where a small general store was the only shopping on the island. After stocking the necessary crabbing supplies; chicken necks, string and bottled soft drinks, we made our way to the marshes, ready to blacken our tennis shoes in the plough mud and haul in fresh crabs for dinner."

Cooked Atlantic blue crabs yield the bulk of the commercially prepared crabmeat. While there are three grades available, the best grade to use in recipes consists of large chunks of the body, known as lump, jumbo or backfin.

Crab and Asparagus Casserole

Beautiful brunch option or evening entrée with a fresh garden salad

2	pounds fresh asparagus
1	pound fresh lump crabmeat, picked free of shell
½	cup butter, divided
4	tablespoons all-purpose flour
1	teaspoon salt
¼	teaspoon pepper
1	teaspoon dry mustard
1	pint half-and-half
4	tablespoons lemon juice
¾	cup grated sharp cheddar cheese
1½	cups fresh bread crumbs

- Preheat oven to 350°F.
- Clean asparagus and snap off tough bottoms.
- In a large skillet, steam asparagus 5 minutes or until just tender.
- Drain asparagus and lay them in the bottom of a greased 9x13-inch casserole dish.
- Place crabmeat over asparagus.
- In a small pot, melt 4 tablespoons butter. Add flour, salt, pepper, mustard, half-and-half, lemon juice and cheese.
- Cook until thickened, over medium heat.
- Pour sauce over asparagus and crab.
- Melt remaining 4 tablespoons butter and mix with bread crumbs. Spread evenly over asparagus and crab meat.
- Bake for 30 minutes.

Yield: 4 servings

Crabmeat sold in cartons has been pasteurized to extend its shelflife. It need not be rinsed prior to use in recipes. Examine the crabmeat closely and remove any shell, but handle the meat minimally to keep the texture firm.

Simply Elegant Crab Casserole

Sun-dried tomatoes offer another touch of class.

6	tablespoons butter, divided
1	bunch scallions, minced
6	sun-dried tomatoes, packed in oil, drained and minced (optional)
2	teaspoons dried tarragon
3	teaspoons Dijon mustard, divided
1½	cups milk
½	cup heavy cream
1	large egg
1	pound lump crabmeat, picked free of shell
2	tablespoons cream sherry
	salt and pepper to taste
1½	cups fresh bread crumbs

(continued on next page)

Simply Elegant Crab Casserole *continued*

- Preheat oven to 375°F.
- Melt 2 tablespoons butter in medium-sized skillet over medium heat.
- Add scallions and sauté until transparent, about 4 minutes.
- Add tomatoes (optional). Add tarragon and sauté another minute.
- Add 2 teaspoons mustard, milk and cream. Whisk until blended.
- Bring to a boil and simmer, uncovered, for 5 minutes.
- In a small bowl, lightly beat egg and ½ cup milk mixture. Mix well and add back to remaining milk mixture.
- Add crabmeat, sherry, salt and pepper to taste. Cook over low heat for 2 to 4 minutes.
- Place crab mixture into a greased 9x9-inch casserole dish.
- Melt remaining 4 tablespoons butter and add 1 teaspoon mustard. Stir in fresh bread crumbs to coat, and top casserole.
- Bake uncovered for 30 minutes or until lightly browned.

Yield: 4 to 6 servings

Champagne Soft-Shell Crabs
Toast this classic Carolina treat!

1   **cup crushed almonds**
¼   **cup all-purpose flour**
      pinch of salt and pepper
½   **cup cornmeal**
1   **(12-ounce) can evaporated milk**
¼   **cup olive oil**
¼   **cup champagne**
1   **lemon wedge**
6   **soft-shell crabs**

- Combine almonds, flour, salt, pepper and cornmeal. Set aside.
- In another bowl, pour evaporated milk and dip soft-shell crabs in to coat, then dredge in flour mixture. Let sit 30 seconds to set.
- Heat olive oil in a large skillet over medium-high heat.
- Sauté crabs 4 minutes on each side. Remove to a platter.
- Drain oil from skillet and add champagne.
- Squeeze the juice from 1 wedge of lemon into the pan.
- Stir to combine and serve over crabs.

Yield: 4 servings

Wine Recommendations: Champagne or Chablis

Live soft-shell crabs may be purchased from the seafood market and remain refrigerated one week before perishing; however, cleaned soft-shells should be used within two days. For ease of preparation, ask the fishmonger to clean the crabs for you. The crabs may be eaten in their entirety once the gills are removed.

North Carolina has staked its claim among the top states in the nation for soft-shell crab production. In only a 24-hour cycle, the blue crab sheds its outer shell and is promptly harvested before its new outer shell hardens. Depending on warm water conditions in the bays and inlets of coastal Carolina, the soft-shell season runs from early May to September.

Soft-Shell Crabs with Lemon Garlic Sauce

North Carolina's well-kept secret seafood delicacy might be soft-shell crabs!

1	cup all-purpose flour
½	teaspoon cayenne pepper
¼	teaspoon ground black pepper
12	soft-shell crabs, cleaned
¾	cup butter
1	teaspoon minced garlic
4	tablespoons freshly squeezed lemon juice
2	tablespoons minced fresh parsley

- Stir together flour and peppers.
- Dredge crabs in flour mixture.
- Melt butter in a large skillet over medium-high heat.
- Sauté crabs in butter, about 5 minutes each side. Remove crabs to platter.
- Add garlic to skillet, stirring quickly. Add lemon juice and stir.
- Serve sauce over crabs and sprinkle with parsley.

Yield: 4 to 6 servings

Wine Recommendations: Unoaked Chardonnay or Unoaked California Sauvignon Blanc

The three types of scallops harvested along the Atlantic coast are sea, bay and calico scallops. The large white adductor muscle, shucked from the considerable shell, is what we know as the plump and meaty bivalve. The meat in a sea scallop is ¾-1½ inches. Usually shucked at sea, the scallops are often soaked in treated water for moisture retention. The term "dry packed" refers to scallops which have been stored only in their own juices. Although more expensive, dry packed sea scallops are preferred for their taste and cooking performance.

Savory Scallops

Rich, elegant starter for an intimate dinner

1½	tablespoons olive oil
12	ounces large sea scallops, dry packed
½	cup dry white wine
3	tablespoons thinly sliced oil packed sun-dried tomatoes, drained
¼	cup heavy cream
2	tablespoons butter, room temperature
2	teaspoons minced garlic
	Salt and pepper to taste

- Preheat large skillet. When pan is hot, add oil. This will prevent sticking.
- Add scallops and cook until brown and crusty on outside and cooked through, about 2 minutes on each side. DO NOT overcrowd; do in batches if necessary. Only turn once.
- Transfer scallops to plates, dividing equally.
- Add wine and tomatoes to skillet and stir 2 minutes, scraping up any browned bits.
- Add cream and boil until mixture is reduced to sauce consistency, about 2 minutes. Remove from heat. Add butter and garlic, whisking until melted.
- Season with salt and pepper to taste.
- Pour over scallops and serve.

Yield: 2 servings

Wine Recommendations: Barrel-Fermented Chardonnay or Alsace Riesling

Gruyère Scallop Bake

4	tablespoons butter, melted and divided
1	pound bay scallops
1	medium onion, finely chopped
½	pound mushrooms, sliced
1½	cups (6 ounces) shredded Gruyère cheese or Swiss cheese
½	cup mayonnaise
¼	cup white wine
1	(2-ounce) jar pimientos, chopped
	salt and pepper to taste
	chopped parsley to garnish

- In 2 tablespoons butter, sauté scallops for 2 to 3 minutes. Drain and set aside.
- In remaining 2 tablespoons of butter, sauté onion and mushrooms until tender. Add scallops, cheese, mayonnaise, wine and pimientos. Stir.
- Spoon mixture into lightly greased ramekins.
- Broil scallops in preheated broiler for 4 to 5 minutes, until lightly browned.
- Garnish with parsley.

Yield: 4 servings

Wine Recommendations: Unoaked Chardonnay or Dry Riesling

Bay scallops are generally sweeter than sea scallops and at ½ to ¾ inch, smaller in size. Harvested from October (peak) until March, shucked bay scallops should be slightly pink or pale orange and are usually more expensive. Take care not to mistake bay scallops with calico scallops, which do not have the sweet, delicate flavor. Calico scallops are smaller, about the size of mini-marshmallows, and are pale white and opaque around the edges.

Southwestern Scallops

Attractive and colorful combination of seafood and fresh produce

1½	teaspoons salt
1	tablespoon dried thyme, crumbled
1½	pounds sea scallops
2	tablespoons olive oil
4	scallions, thinly sliced
2	cups corn freshly cut from the cob
2	cups cherry tomatoes, halved
	salt and pepper to taste
4	slices bacon, cooked and crumbled

- Mix salt and thyme in a bowl; toss scallops in mixture.
- Heat oil in a large nonstick skillet over medium heat. Sear scallops 2 to 3 minutes, stirring often, until cooked through and golden. With a slotted spoon, remove scallops and place in a clean bowl.
- Sauté scallions in the same skillet about 1 minute, until browned. Add corn and tomatoes and cook about 3 minutes, until corn begins to brown.
- Return scallops to skillet and heat through. Season with salt and pepper.
- Sprinkle with bacon and serve.

Yield: 4 servings

Wine Recommendations: California Chardonnay or Barrel-Fermented Sauvignon Blanc

When purchasing sea scallops, choose similar-sized ones for even cooking. You should look for a cream-colored or slightly pink hue, avoiding the pure white or brownish varieties. You should also check the aroma of the scallops to eliminate a too-pungent batch.

The Bloomsbury Bistro exquisitely showcases the fish and shellfish in these recipes. To serve, the chef proprietor suggests a spiced basmati rice and English pea mixture for the center of each plate. Place the fish on top of the rice mixture and spoon the scallops with sauce around and over the fish.

Sautéed Carolina
Triggerfish

- 6 **(6-7 ounce) triggerfish fillets, black bass, snapper or grouper**
- ¼ **cup peanut oil**
- 2 **tablespoons butter**
  flour, salt and pepper
- **Rinse and towel dry the fillets.**
- **Generously salt and pepper each side of the fish and lightly dust with flour.**
- **Place a large sauté pan over very high heat. Once the pan is very hot, add the peanut oil and the butter. Allow the butter to melt and slightly brown.**
- **Shake off any excess flour from the fish and carefully place each fillet in the pan.**
- **Allow the fish to cook for about one minute or until nicely browned. Flip once and cook on other side.**

Curried Sweet Bay Scallops

Intriguing display of fish and shellfish combined

- ¼ **cup water**
- 3 **tablespoons sugar**
- 2 **tablespoons white wine vinegar**
- 3 **shallots, roughly chopped**
- 1 **clove garlic, roughly chopped**
- 2 **tablespoons hot Indian curry paste**
- 1 **cup freshly squeezed orange juice**
- ½ **cup dry white wine**
- 2 **cups heavy cream**
- 8 **ounces fresh bay scallops**
- 1 **tablespoon chopped fresh cilantro**
- 1 **tablespoon chopped fresh basil**
- 1 **tablespoon chopped fresh mint**
- 1 **red bell pepper, finely diced**
  salt and pepper to taste

- Place the water and sugar in a heavy-bottomed saucepot over high heat until the water is evaporated and the sugar begins to caramelize. When the sugar becomes light golden brown, quickly and carefully pour in the vinegar. Stir a few times to dissolve the caramel and cook until the vinegar is almost completely evaporated.
- Add the shallots, garlic, curry paste, wine and orange juice. Stir well. Continue cooking over high heat until liquid is reduced to half its original volume.
- Add the cream and bring to simmer. Allow the cream to gently boil until reduced to ¾ its original volume and becomes slightly thick. Remove from heat and liquefy the sauce in a blender. Pass through a fine meshed strainer into a clean pot.
- Add the scallops and bell pepper and return to a simmer. Remove from heat. Add the cilantro, basil and mint.
- Season with salt and pepper and keep warm until needed.

Yield: 2 main course or 6 side servings

Panfried Freshwater Bass

Store the prepared cornmeal mixture in the refrigerator for handy use.

1 (3-pound) largemouth bass, filleted and skin removed
½ cup all-purpose flour
½ cup yellow cornmeal
½ tablespoon salt
½ teaspoon white pepper or freshly cracked black pepper
⅛ teaspoon cayenne pepper
½ teaspoon garlic salt or celery salt
1 teaspoon onion powder
  dash of dry mustard
½ cup buttermilk or milk
2 tablespoons canola or corn oil
2 tablespoons unsalted butter

- Thoroughly rinse the bass fillets and dry on paper towels. Refrigerate until chilled.
- Mix together the flour, cornmeal and spices to make the coating.
- Heat the oil and butter in a large cast iron skillet or heavy frying pan.
- Brush the buttermilk on the fillets or dip in the milk and shake off the excess moisture. Dip fillets into the dry mixture to thoroughly coat.
- Carefully place the fillets in the pan and reduce heat to medium-low. Fry about 8 minutes, then turn and cook for 8 minutes more. The fillets will be done when the outside turns golden brown and the flesh turns white and flakes apart.
- Serve directly from the pan, piping hot.

Note: If the fillets are too large and thick to cook evenly, cut the fillets into strips before coating. Your frying time will be reduced and younger children will be more inclined to eat fish strips picked up with their fingers!

Yield: 4 servings

"My husband and sons enjoy the pleasure of a spring sunrise while drifting in the bass boat on Falls Lake, just 20 minutes north of downtown Raleigh. On lucky occasions this pre-dawn diligence results in fresh largemouth bass for breakfast or lunch." The delicate flavor of this white fish (low in fat and oil content) is best savored by gently panfrying and serving hot.

Campfire Trout in a Tent

Catch-of-the-day cooked outdoors or in

2 (12-ounce) whole rainbow or brown trout, cleaned
2 tablespoons prepared mustard
4 slices onion
4 sheets heavy duty foil

- Rinse and dry the trout.
- Spread the mustard inside the cavity of each fish. Fill each cavity with a slice of onion.
- Enclose the fish in the foil so that it is wrapped and folded in the shape of a tent.
- Steam the tented fish on a medium-hot grill for 45 minutes.

Note: If preparing indoors, tents may be placed on a baking sheet and baked in a 375°F oven for 45 minutes.

Yield: 4 to 6 servings

Leftover catfish cakes are delicious served on a Kaiser roll or atop mixed greens with a Dijon-vinaigrette dressing.

Catfish Cakes

Quite versatile if you have any leftovers

1½ pounds catfish fillets
1 large egg, beaten
2 tablespoons mayonnaise
1 tablespoon mustard
1 tablespoon butter, melted
1 teaspoon chopped fresh parsley
¼ teaspoon garlic salt
⅛ teaspoon red pepper flakes
¾ cup crushed corn flakes or bread crumbs
vegetable oil for frying

- Preheat oven to 400°F.
- In a medium casserole dish, bake fish, covered with foil, for 20 minutes.
- In a medium bowl, combine next 7 ingredients.
- Crumble cooked fish and stir into mixture.
- Refrigerate 1 hour. (necessary to prevent mixture from crumbling when shaping into patties)
- Shape into patties and roll in corn flakes or bread crumbs.
- Fry in hot oil 2 minutes each side. Drain.
- Serve hot.

Yield: 2 servings

Wine Recommendations: Dry Vouvray or Rosé de Provence

Fish steaks, such as halibut, are excellent to grill because the flesh is firm and holds together well. When grilling fish steaks and fillets, make sure they are at least ½ inch thick to achieve a crispy and flavorful surface and to avoid overcooking. This recipe was modified from its original version using Atlantic swordfish. In recent years, swordfish have experienced vast depletion by overfishing and longline fishing methods which snare immature female swordfish before breeding. Thus, no swordfish recipes are listed in this cookbook.

Grilled Halibut with Dill and Oregano

A tasty and healthy grilled fish dish

1 teaspoon chopped fresh dill
½ teaspoon dried oregano, or 2 tablespoons chopped fresh oregano
salt to taste
4 (6-ounce) halibut or wahoo steaks
¼ cup lemon juice
1 clove garlic, crushed
⅛ teaspoon paprika

- Prepare grill or broiler.
- In a small bowl, mix dill, oregano and salt.
- Dip fish in lemon juice, rub with garlic and sprinkle with herb mixture.
- Grill or broil 4 to 5 minutes per side or until fish flakes easily.
- Sprinkle steaks with paprika and serve.

Yield: 4 servings

King Mackerel with Avocado Salsa

Refreshing summer grill to enjoy with the neighbors

2	tomatoes, peeled, seeded, coarsely chopped
¼	red bell pepper, diced
¼	green bell pepper, diced
¼	yellow bell pepper, diced
¼	red onion, chopped
2	tablespoons olive oil
2	tablespoons freshly squeezed lime juice
1	tablespoon white wine vinegar
1	large clove garlic, minced
1	tablespoon chopped fresh basil
1	tablespoon chopped fresh dill
1	tablespoon fresh thyme
	dash of Tabasco
	salt and pepper to taste
1	avocado, peeled, seeded and chopped
4	(6-ounce) king mackerel or wahoo steaks or Spanish mackerel fillets

- Combine tomatoes, peppers, onion, olive oil, lime juice, vinegar, garlic, basil, dill, thyme and Tabasco. Season with salt and pepper. Gently fold avocado into salsa.
- Grill mackerel until cooked through, about 3 minutes each side.
- Transfer fish to plates and top with salsa.

Yield: 4 servings

Before placing fish on the grill, make sure the grill is perfectly clean, lightly oiled and very hot. The fish should be dry, then brushed with oil. Be careful when using a spatula to turn the fish. To prevent tearing, perhaps a better technique is to slide a long two-pronged fork under the fish—parallel with the grill rods—and then gently lift the fish in several places to detach it from the grill. It can then be flipped over by lifting with the fork and holding it with a spatula held over the top of the fish. (adapted from *Fish & Shellfish*, by James Peterson.)

Baked Rainbow Trout

Baking whole enhances the natural flavor of freshwater fish.

	no stick vegetable cooking spray
2	(12-ounce) whole rainbow or brown trout, gutted
2	tablespoons extra-virgin olive oil
¼	teaspoon lemon pepper seasoning

- Preheat oven to 375°F.
- Coat a 13x9-inch baking dish with cooking spray.
- Brush the two trout with olive oil and place in the dish side-by-side. Sprinkle with lemon pepper seasoning.
- Bake for 30 minutes or until fish flakes easily with a fork.

Yield: 4 servings

Once you've experienced salad made with fresh tuna, you'll never want to use canned varieties again! Simply add another steak or fillet to the grill when preparing your entrée. Refrigerate the leftover fish and concoct a veritable treat for your taste buds the next day!

Garlic Grilled Tuna

A tangy sauce adds zest to this "blackened" fish.

¼ cup lemon juice
1 clove garlic, minced
1 tablespoon olive oil
1 teaspoon dried mint or 2 teaspoons chopped fresh mint
2 teaspoons black peppercorns, crushed
4 (6-ounce) tuna steaks

- Combine lemon juice, garlic, olive oil and mint in a bowl. Mix well.
- Press peppercorns into both sides of tuna steaks.
- Grill 4 minutes per side, or until tuna is browned on the outside and slightly pink on the inside. Remove from heat.
- Serve tuna with garlic sauce.

Yield: 4 servings

Variation: For another simple marinade for grilled fish, coat four 8-ounce fillets with a mixture of ½ cup mayonnaise, ¼ cup soy sauce and 4 tablespoons prepared horseradish, reserving some sauce. Refrigerate until chilled. Grill as indicated in recipe above. Serve with a dollop of reserved sauce that has been amended with a sprinkling more soy sauce and horseradish.

Searing means to brown the surface of the food quickly on all sides, using high heat to seal in the juices. The process may take place in an oven or on top of the stove.

Seared Tuna with Red Wine Sauce

"Fish to taste right, must swim three times - in water, in butter and in wine."
—Polish proverb

2 tablespoons olive oil
4 (6-ounce) tuna fillets
salt and pepper to taste
½ cup red wine
¼ cup chicken stock
2 shallots, minced
2 tablespoons cream
6 tablespoons butter
1 tablespoon red wine vinegar

(continued on next page)

Seared Tuna with Red Wine Sauce *continued*

- Preheat oven to 350°F.
- Heat olive oil in oven proof sauté pan over medium heat.
- Salt and pepper tuna and add to pan. Sear 1 to 2 minutes on each side.
- Put pan into the oven for 7 to 10 minutes or until fish is done.
- Combine red wine, chicken stock and shallots. Boil in saucepan until reduced to 1 tablespoon. Add cream and bring to a boil. Add butter 1 tablespoon at a time until melted.
- Remove from heat and add vinegar. Serve over fillets.

Yield: 4 servings

Wine Recommendations: Chablis or California Sauvignon Blanc

Bloomsbury Bistro's Pan Seared Tuna with Spicy Citrus-Curry Vinaigrette

Creative Carolina cookery located in historic Five Points

2	shallots, finely minced
	juice of 1 lemon
	juice of 2 oranges
	juice of 1 lime
3	teaspoons balsamic vinegar
1	teaspoon sugar
1	tablespoon hot curry paste
1	teaspoon sambal oelek (available at an oriental market)
½	cup plus 2 tablespoons canola oil, divided
1	teaspoon chopped fresh mint
1	teaspoon chopped fresh basil
1	teaspoon chopped fresh cilantro
	salt and pepper to taste
4	(8-ounce) tuna steaks

- To make vinaigrette, combine shallots, juices, vinegar and sugar in metal bowl. Allow shallots to pickle in juice for 15 minutes.
- Whisk in curry paste, sambal oelek and ½ cup canola oil until mixed thoroughly.
- Stir in mint, basil, cilantro, salt and pepper. Set aside.
- Place a large, heavy sauté pan over very high heat. While the pan is heating, towel dry any moisture off the tuna. Sprinkle generously with salt and pepper.
- Add 2 tablespoons oil to pan. Allow to heat until the first signs of smoke appear. Very carefully, place tuna steaks into pan. Cook one minute each side for a medium rare steak.
- Remove from pan, spoon vinaigrette over the tuna and serve.

Yield: 4 servings

Wine Recommendations: Australian Chardonnay or California Viognier

Certain seafood experts, such as James Peterson, insist that "tuna cooked all the way through is never as satisfying as tuna cooked like a rare steak, with a dark streak of red down the middle. Just one bite always convinces even the most squeamish."

(from *Fish & Shellfish*, by James Peterson.)

Although the name is
Hawaiian, mahi mahi do
thrive in Atlantic waters
and are plentiful in late
spring through summer.
Also known as dolphin,
this catch is not the
mammal we recognize as
Flipper!

Citrus Baked Mahi Mahi

The pronounced flavor of dolphin can stand up to strong citrus ingredients.

1½ **pounds mahi mahi**
¼   **cup orange juice**
2   **tablespoons lemon juice**
     salt and pepper to taste
¾   **teaspoon cornstarch**
1½ **tablespoons water**
1   **tablespoon orange marmalade**
1   **tablespoon grated lemon zest**

- Preheat oven to 400°F.
- Place fish into greased 9x13-inch baking dish. Drizzle with orange and lemon juices. Season with salt and pepper. Set aside for 15 to 20 minutes, turning once to marinate.
- Bake fish 11 to 15 minutes or until fish flakes. Place fish on platter and cover to keep warm.
- Pour fish juice from baking dish into a saucepan. In a small bowl, dissolve cornstarch in water and add to fish juice. Add marmalade and lemon zest. Stir over medium heat 4 to 5 minutes or until sauce thickens.
- Serve over fish.

Yield: 4 servings

Grouper with Ginger Sauce

For an oriental flair, serve with a rice, chopped pecan and raisin mixture.

1   **tablespoon olive oil**
    salt and pepper to taste
    cayenne pepper to taste
2   **(6-ounce) grouper fillets**
2   **tablespoons butter**
2   **teaspoons julienne of peeled fresh ginger, chopped**
½   **teaspoon minced garlic**
½   **cup white wine**
½   **cup fish stock or clam juice**
½   **cup heavy cream**
1   **tablespoon freshly squeezed lemon juice**

- Preheat oven to 350°F.
- Heat olive oil in skillet over medium-high heat.
- Salt, pepper and add a slight sprinkling of cayenne pepper to the fish.
- Place fish in skillet and sauté 2 minutes on each side to sear.
- Place in oven and cook for 7 to 10 minutes until fish is cooked through.
- To prepare sauce, melt butter in a small skillet over medium heat. Add ginger and garlic. Sauté about 2 minutes.
- Add wine and cook until liquid evaporates, about 3 minutes.
- Add fish stock or clam juice and cream to pan and boil until reduced to ½ cup, about 6 minutes.
- Add lemon juice and season with salt and pepper.
- Serve over fish fillets.

Yield: 2 servings

Numerous varieties of grouper, a subspecies of the sea bass family, swim in southern Gulf and Atlantic waters. Several grouper types are bottom fished from Gulf Stream waters off the North Carolina coast, red grouper comprising the bulk of the commercial catch. Groupers yield firm, white meat that is medium to low in oil content. They are excellent prepared any way but whole (skin intact) or raw.

"When my children were toddlers and eating finger food, I wanted to give them food more similar to our adult fare. Instead of offering them frozen processed fish sticks, try this easy recipe derived from a parenting book, *What To Expect The First Year:*"

Fishy Fingers

1-2 oz. fresh fish fillets, such as orange roughy, sole, flounder or haddock

1-2 slices fresh whole wheat bread, may be slightly stale

1 T. grated Parmesan cheese

dash garlic powder

1 t. mayonnaise

- Preheat the oven to 350°F.
- In a mini food processor, mix the bread, Parmesan cheese and garlic powder and set aside.
- Slice the fish fillets into ½ inch strips.
- Spread the mayonnaise to coat each strip. Roll the fish strips in the bread crumbs.
- Coat the bottom of a shallow baking pan with no stick cooking spray.
- Lay the strips on the pan and bake for 5 minutes. Turn the strips once and continue baking for an additional 5 minutes. Serve the homemade fish sticks atop a clean high chair!

Lemon Grouper

A relaxing meal to prepare after a day at the beach

1	tablespoon olive oil
4	(6-ounce) skinless grouper fillets (½-inch thick)
½	cup chicken stock
3	teaspoons capers, drained
1	lemon, divided
1	tablespoon unsalted butter
1	teaspoon chopped fresh parsley

- Heat oil in a medium nonstick skillet over medium heat. Sauté grouper 4 minutes per side or until the fish flakes easily.
- Place grouper onto a platter. Cover to keep warm.
- Add chicken stock, capers and ½ the lemon cut into ¼-inch slices and halved, into skillet and stir. Simmer for 2 minutes. Remove from heat.
- Add butter and stir until melted.
- Serve sauce over grouper. Garnish with parsley and extra lemon slices.

Note: If grouper is not available, choose another mild white fish such as triggerfish, black bass or red snapper.

Yield: 4 servings

Wine Recommendations: Pinot Grigio or Macon

Pecan Encrusted Salmon

A convenient way to prepare fish after a busy day at work.

4	salmon fillets
	salt and pepper to taste
2	tablespoons Dijon mustard
2	tablespoons butter
1½	tablespoons honey
¼	cup bread crumbs
2	teaspoons chopped fresh parsley
¼	cup finely chopped pecans

- Preheat oven to 450°F.
- Sprinkle salmon with salt and pepper. Set aside.
- Combine mustard, butter and honey. Brush fish on both sides with this mixture.
- Combine bread crumbs, parsley and pecans. Dip fish in this to coat.
- Place in greased 9x9-inch casserole dish and spoon extra crumb mixture on top.
- Bake for 15 to 20 minutes or until salmon flakes.

Yield: 4 servings

Wine Recommendations: California Chardonnay or Beaujolais

Salmon with Herb Sauce

An elegant entrée for dinner guests

½   cup dry white wine
1   cup heavy cream
4   tablespoons unsalted butter, room temperature, divided
4   (6-ounce) skinless salmon fillets
½   cup dry vermouth
1   large shallot, minced
2   tablespoons minced fresh herbs (tarragon, basil, dill and chives)
      juice of one lemon
      salt and pepper to taste

- Preheat oven to 400°F.
- Boil wine in small saucepan until reduced to 1 tablespoon, about 5 minutes.
- Add cream and boil until reduced to ½ cup, about 10 minutes. Set aside.
- Use ½ tablespoon butter to grease large ovenproof skillet. Place fillets in skillet. Pour vermouth over fish and top with the shallot. Bring to a simmer. Cover skillet with foil and place into the oven.
- Bake salmon until just cooked, about 10 minutes.
- Sear cooked salmon one minute on each side on stovetop in the same skillet. This helps to caramelize the shallots.
- Place salmon onto a platter. Cover with foil to keep warm.
- Mix liquid in skillet into the sauce that was set aside. Cook over medium heat until reduced to sauce consistency, stirring occasionally, about 5 minutes. Remove from heat.
- Whisk in remaining 3½ tablespoons butter and minced herbs. Season with lemon juice, salt and pepper.
- Spoon sauce over salmon.

Yield: 4 servings

Wine Recommendation: White Burgundy

Atlantic salmon has a medium to high fat content, affording much flexibility in preparation. When cooked, the appearance will be pale pink to red.

Pine Nut and Basil Crusted Salmon with Caramelized Onion Mashed Potatoes

An often-requested dish from Lofton's in the North Raleigh Hilton

¾ **cup finely chopped pine nuts**
¼ **cup chopped fresh basil**
1 **tablespoon all-purpose flour**
   pinch of seasoned salt
1½ **pounds deboned salmon, cut into 4 servings**
¼ **cup olive oil**
   Caramelized Onion Mashed Potatoes (see below)
   Wine Cream Sauce (see below)
   chopped fresh basil to garnish

- Preheat oven to 375°F.
- Combine pine nuts, chopped basil, flour and a pinch of seasoned salt. Mix well.
- Brush the top side of salmon with olive oil and then dip the oiled side into the pine nut mixture to coat.
- Heat olive oil in a nonstick sauté pan over medium heat.
- When heated, place salmon, nut-side down and cook until golden brown.
- Cook only on one side, then place onto a baking sheet nut-side up.
- Place into oven and bake for 8 to 10 minutes until done. Keep warm.
- Place a mound of mashed potatoes in center of plate.
- Place salmon on top and drizzle sauce around the plate. Garnish with basil.

Potatoes

3 **russet potatoes, peeled and quartered**
½ **cup unsalted butter**
¼ **cup milk**
   salt and pepper to taste
¼ **cup butter**
1 **Walla Walla onion**
¼ **cup Chardonnay wine**

- Boil potatoes until soft. Drain and mash with ½ cup unsalted butter, milk, salt and pepper to taste. Keep warm.
- Melt ¼ cup butter in skillet over medium heat. Add onions and stir until they caramelize. Turn down heat; add Chardonnay and cook until softened and golden brown, about 20 minutes.
- Stir in mashed potatoes and taste for seasoning. Keep warm.

(continued on next page)

Pine Nut and Basil Crusted Salmon *continued*

Wine Cream Sauce

1	shallot, finely minced
1	cup Chardonnay wine
1	ounce heavy cream
½	cup unsalted butter, cubed
1	teaspoon lemon juice
¼	cup finely julienned fresh basil

- In a small saucepan combine shallot, Chardonnay and cream. Over medium heat, reduce to ¼ cup of liquid.
- Reduce heat and whisk in butter cubes, a few at a time. Add lemon juice and julienned basil. Keep warm.

Yield: 4 servings

Wine Recommendation: Barrel-Fermented Chardonnay

Roasted Salmon with Spring Asparagus

A wonderful springtime dish!

1	pound medium asparagus
2	tablespoons extra-virgin olive oil, divided
	salt and pepper to taste
1½	pounds salmon fillets, 1-inch thick
1	tablespoon freshly squeezed lemon juice
½	teaspoon dried thyme
2	teaspoons finely chopped fresh cilantro
	lemon wedges to garnish

- Preheat oven to 450°F.
- Clean asparagus and snap off bottoms. Place in roasting pan. Sprinkle evenly with 1 tablespoon oil, salt and pepper. Toss to coat.
- Place fish in separate roasting pan. Coat with remaining 1 tablespoon oil and rub with lemon juice. Sprinkle with thyme, salt, pepper and cilantro.
- Place both pans in the oven. Roast uncovered for about 12 minutes. Turn asparagus once while roasting. When done, asparagus should be crisp and fish should flake.
- Garnish with lemon wedges.

Yield: 4 servings

Wine Recommendations: Sancerre or White Bordeaux

With fishing innovations borrowed from the Norwegians, most Atlantic salmon is farmed in tremendous cages in the open sea. This method enables the salmon found in our seafood markets to be quite fresh, of excellent quality and easily affordable.

Grilled Salmon with Strawberry Salsa

If you can't beat it, join the summer heat with this tangy grilled meal.

½ cup unsalted butter
1 clove garlic, minced
1 tablespoon honey
2 tablespoons soy sauce
1 tablespoon freshly squeezed lemon juice
6 salmon fillets, (or fish of choice) skinless
  Strawberry Salsa (see sidebar)

- To prepare sauce, in a small saucepan melt butter. Stir in garlic, honey, soy sauce and lemon juice and cook 3 minutes.
- Brush fish on both sides with sauce before grilling. Grill 6 to 7 minutes per side or until fish flakes easily. Brush again with sauce.
- Place fish on a platter and top with salsa.

Yield: 6 servings

Wine Recommendations: *Côtes du Rhone or Bandol Rosé*

Strawberry Salsa

1 seedless cucumber, finely chopped
1 yellow bell pepper, finely chopped
1 green onion, thinly sliced
2 tablespoons chopped cilantro
4 tablespoons rice wine vinegar
2 cups fresh strawberries, hulled and diced small

- Make salsa at least one hour ahead of serving.
- Mix cucumbers, yellow pepper, green onion, cilantro and vinegar. Cover and chill. Just before serving, add strawberries.

Pasta with Smoked Salmon and Vodka Cream

This seafood dish needs only a green salad and crusty bread to complete an elegant meal.

4 tablespoons butter, divided
2 shallots, minced
1 clove garlic, minced
1 cup vodka
1 cup heavy cream
8 ounces smoked salmon, chopped
  salt and pepper to taste
½ (16-ounce) package fettuccini
  freshly grated Parmesan cheese

"My brother-in-law from the northwestern part of the country sends us smoked salmon each year for Christmas. This delicacy is a perfect appetizer served with thin crackers or for lunch flaked above a mixed green salad."

(continued on next page)

Pasta with Smoked Salmon and Vodka Cream *continued*

- In a medium saucepan, melt 2 tablespoons butter and sauté shallots until translucent. Add garlic and sauté 2 minutes.
- Add vodka and simmer until liquid is reduced by half. Add cream and simmer until thickened.
- Stir in salmon and cook just until heated through. Season with salt and pepper to taste.
- Meanwhile, cook fettuccini until al dente. Drain pasta; transfer to a warm serving plate and toss with remaining 2 tablespoons butter. Toss again with sauce.
- Serve with plenty of freshly grated Parmesan cheese.

Yield: 4 servings

Wine Recommendations: Barrel-Fermented Chardonnay or Champagne

Sensational Salmon

Unusual seasonings combine for an intriguing flavor.

2	**cups tamari**
2	**tablespoons cornstarch**
2	**tablespoons Asian sesame oil**
2	**tablespoons peeled and minced fresh ginger**
2	**tablespoons dry sherry or rice wine**
1	**tablespoon honey**
1	**teaspoon Tabasco**
1	**teaspoon ground black pepper**
2	**cloves garlic, chopped**
½	**teaspoon turmeric**
2	**bunches green onions**
⅔	**cup water**
8	**(8-ounce) salmon fillets (1-inch thick)**

- Preheat oven to 400°F.
- Purée first 10 ingredients in a blender until almost smooth. (This can be prepared 1 day ahead. Cover and refrigerate.)
- Lightly grease 2 (9x9-inch) baking dishes. Divide fish between the two dishes. Add 1 bunch whole green onions to each dish.
- Pour half of sauce over each dish, dividing evenly between the two.
- Bake until just cooked, about 15 to 20 minutes, basting often with remaining sauce.
- Add ⅓ cup water to dish if sauce begins to burn.

Note: Substitute low-sodium soy sauce for tamari, if needed.

Yield: 6 to 8 servings

A Catchy Way to Display Seafood Sauces. . .

The next time you stroll along the shoreline, gather up the oyster and clam shells that you find. Scrub them thoroughly with a toothbrush. At mealtime, fill the shells with various sauces to complement your menu. Arrange the decorative shells alongside the seafood on a large platter or on individual plates.

Traditional Tartar Sauce

1	cup mayonnaise
2	tablespoons freshly squeezed lemon juice
1	teaspoon Worcestershire sauce
	dash of Tabasco sauce
¼	cup finely sliced dill pickles
¼	cup chopped fresh Italian parsley
2	tablespoons finely minced shallots
2	tablespoons small capers, drained
	salt and pepper to taste

- Mix together mayonnaise, lemon juice, Worcestershire sauce and dash of Tabasco.
- Gently fold in pickles, parsley, shallots and capers.
- Season with salt and pepper.
- Cover and refrigerate 1 hour before serving.

Yield: 1½ cups

Basil-Lemon Tartar Sauce

½	cup packed fresh basil leaves
½	cup mayonnaise
1	tablespoon sour cream
1	teaspoon freshly squeezed lemon juice
½	teaspoon minced garlic
⅛	teaspoon salt
	dash of cayenne pepper
	dash of hot pepper sauce

- Rinse basil leaves in hot water and pat dry in paper towels.
- Place all ingredients in food processor and process until well blended.
- Refrigerate until ready to serve.

Yield: 1 cup

Cocktail Sauce

⅔	cups chili sauce
¼	teaspoon Tabasco sauce
¼	cup lemon juice
2 to 3	tablespoons prepared horseradish
2	teaspoon Worcestershire sauce

- Mix all ingredients well and chill for 2 hours before serving.

Yield: 1 cup

Nora Shepard

Places I Have Been
oil on canvas, 1997

Poultry and Meats

Chicken

Turkey

Game

Beef

Veal

Pork

Lamb

Citrus Grilled Chicken with Avocado Lime Sauce

The bright flavors of lemon and lime make this chicken and avocado combination something special.

6	tablespoons freshly squeezed lime juice
2	teaspoons finely grated lime zest
²⁄₃	cup freshly squeezed lemon juice
2	tablespoons vegetable oil
2	teaspoons minced garlic, divided
1	bunch fresh cilantro, stemmed and chopped
	salt to taste
6	boneless, skinless chicken breast halves
2	large ripe avocados, peeled and seeded
2	green onions, finely chopped
	hot sauce to taste
	purchased salsa
	sour cream

- Combine juices, zest, oil, 1 teaspoon garlic, cilantro and salt in a large mixing bowl. Reserve ¼ cup citrus mixture for garnish.
- Add chicken to remaining citrus mixture in bowl and marinate for 1 hour.
- To make the sauce, mash avocados in a medium bowl. Add reserved citrus mixture, green onions, 1 teaspoon garlic and several dashes of hot sauce to taste. Stir well.
- Remove chicken from marinade and grill chicken over medium heat, turning once, until done.
- To serve, place chicken on plates and top with avocado sauce. Garnish with avocado slices, purchased salsa and sour cream.

Yield: 6 servings

Wine Recommendations: Australian Chardonnay or California Viognier

Reserve extra Avocado Lime Sauce for the following uses:

- **dip for tortilla chips**
- **light salad dressing over shredded lettuce greens**
- **filler for warmed flour tortillas with black beans and yellow corn**
- **topping for grilled white fish or fish steaks, such as tuna**

Leftover sauce may be kept, refrigerated, for 2-3 days.

Kitchen shears are indis-
pensable, making it a snap
to cut boneless chicken
into chunks. Remember to
wash thoroughly all
utensils and dishes used in
chicken preparation to
prevent bacteria from
spreading to other foods.

Crunchy Cashew Chicken

Vary ingredient amounts according to your taste and enjoy over warm rice.

4	boneless, skinless chicken breast halves, cut into chunks
¼	cup red wine vinegar
¼	cup soy sauce
2	tablespoons sugar
1	(1-inch) piece fresh ginger, chopped
2	tablespoons cornstarch
4	tablespoons vegetable or sesame oil
1 to 3	cloves garlic, chopped
2 to 4	green onions, chopped
1	(8-ounce) can sliced water chestnuts, drained
1	cup cashews
½	cup low-sodium chicken broth
¼	teaspoon crushed red pepper flakes

- In a small bowl, combine vinegar, soy sauce, sugar and ginger.
- Toss chicken with cornstarch until coated. Heat 2 tablespoons oil in heavy skillet and sauté chicken until done. Remove chicken from skillet.
- Add 2 tablespoons oil, garlic, onions, water chestnuts and cashews to skillet and broth. Stir in vinegar mixture and simmer over low heat.
- Add chicken pieces to skillet and red pepper flakes to taste. Simmer for 5 minutes.

Yield: 4 to 6 servings

Southern Fried Chicken

Traditional southern standard that dresses up for Sunday afternoon dinner or travels casually in a picnic basket.

1   fresh 3 to 3½ pound chicken, cut into pieces
1   cup buttermilk
1   cup all-purpose flour
1½ teaspoons salt
1   teaspoon coarsely ground fresh pepper
1   cup peanut oil
1   cup shortening

- Place chicken in a large mixing bowl and coat with the buttermilk. Let the chicken soak in the buttermilk for at least two hours.
- Put the flour, salt and pepper in a large paper bag and drop in the chicken pieces, one at a time, tossing each piece to coat.
- Heat the peanut oil and shortening in a large, cast iron skillet to medium high heat.
- Add the chicken to the skillet, reduce heat to medium, and cover. Fry for 15 minutes. Turn chicken and fry another 10 to 15 minutes uncovered.
- Drain on paper towels before serving.

Yield: 4 to 6 servings

Wine Recommendations: Spanish Rioja or Beaujolais

Sherried Sesame Chicken

The sweetness of sherry and the crunch of sesame combine for a distinctive flavor.

6   boneless, skinless chicken breast halves
1   tablespoon minced onion
¼   cup soy sauce
3   tablespoons sherry
1   tablespoon sugar
3   tablespoons vegetable oil
¼   teaspoon ground ginger
    dash of cayenne pepper
1½ teaspoons sesame seeds

- Arrange chicken in a lightly greased 2-quart baking dish.
- Combine remaining sauce ingredients (except sesame seeds) in a small bowl.
- Pour sauce over chicken.
- Cover and bake at 350°F for 30 minutes.
- Turn chicken and sprinkle with sesame seeds.
- Bake uncovered for 10 minutes more or until done.

Yield: 6 servings

"I grew up in a neighborhood with 22 kids, only three girls. The three of us lived side by side, were born in the same year, and were best friends. It was a given that one of our mothers would be frying chicken for Sunday dinner, and that the girl of that home had from Sunday School until about 1:00 p.m. to get the other two invited over. After church, we met in the holly hedge between the houses. Once we determined our direction, we held hands and skipped toward the food chanting, 'Chicken and biscuits and tea, whoopee! Chicken and biscuits and tea, whoopee!'"

Africans who brought the sesame seed to America referred to it as benne seed. You may still find southern recipes that call for benne seed, perhaps the most well-known being the Benne Seed Wafer, a thin cookie long enjoyed at tea time.

Accompany Chicken
Enchiladas with the
following light, Mexican
style salad.

Combine in a serving bowl:

1 medium jicama, peeled
   and cut into thin strips

1 red onion, thinly sliced

2 seedless oranges, peeled
   and sectioned

2 avocados, peeled and
   sliced

Dress with:

4 tablespoons fresh
   lime juice

¼ cup white vinegar

2 tablespoons honey
   pepper to taste

Whisk ingredients and toss
with salad.

Set a seasonal mood by
decorating your buffet
table with brilliantly
colored fall squash, Indian
corn and branches of fall
berries, such as pyracantha
and nandina. Serve this dish
in a large tureen surrounded
by miniature pumpkins
hollowed and filled with
chopped candied ginger,
toasted coconut, chopped
scallions, raisins, chopped
cashews and dried
cranberries.

Creamy Chicken Enchiladas

Use leftover chicken to create a Mexican theme dinner.

4   tablespoons butter
1   medium onion, thinly sliced
1½ cups shredded cooked chicken
½   cup canned green chiles, diced
2   (3-ounce) packages cream cheese, diced
    salt to taste
¼   cup corn oil
8   (6-inch) corn tortillas
⅔   cup heavy cream
2   cups grated Monterey Jack cheese
    prepared salsa

- Melt butter in large skillet over low heat.
- Sauté onion until limp but not brown, about 10 minutes.
- Remove from heat and add chicken, chiles and cream cheese. Season with salt.
- Heat oil in small skillet over medium heat.
- Add tortillas, one at a time, and fry until just beginning to blister, about 1 minute.
- Drain on paper towels.
- Spoon ½ cup chicken filling down center of each tortilla and roll.
- Place enchiladas seam side down in a 4-quart baking dish.
- Pour cream over enchiladas. Sprinkle with cheese.
- Bake at 350°F until cream thickens and cheese bubbles, about 20 minutes.
- Serve hot with salsa.

Yield: 4 servings

Autumn Chicken Curry

Cool autumn evenings are perfect for entertaining guests with chicken curry.

16 boneless, skinless chicken breast halves cut into chunks
1   cup all-purpose flour
1   tablespoon butter
1   tablespoon vegetable oil
2   onions, diced
2   cloves garlic, chopped
2   teaspoons curry powder
3   (14-ounce) cans chicken stock
2   pints heavy cream
2   apples, finely diced
2   bananas, finely diced

(continued on next page)

Autumn Chicken Curry *continued*

- Dredge chicken breast chunks in flour.
- In a large saucepan over medium-high heat, sauté chicken in butter and oil until brown. Set chicken aside.
- In same saucepan, sauté onion and garlic until golden brown.
- Sprinkle curry in while cooking.
- Add chicken stock, cream, apples and bananas.
- Reduce heat and let simmer for 1 hour until thickened and reduced.
- Add chicken chunks and simmer for 30 minutes.

Yield: 10 servings

Wine Recommendations: California Viognier or Alaska Gerwurztraminer

Creamed Chicken in Puff Pastry

Pastry shells full of hot, creamy chicken

1	tablespoon chopped onion
3	tablespoons margarine
1	(3-ounce) package cream cheese
2	cups cooked, cubed chicken
¼	teaspoon salt
⅛	teaspoon pepper
2	tablespoons milk
1	tablespoon chopped pimientos
1	package puffed pastry shells, baked according to package directions

- Sauté onion in margarine until translucent.
- Blend cream cheese with onion until smooth.
- Add chicken, salt, pepper, milk, and pimientos to cream cheese mixture, mixing well.
- Fill baked pastry shells with chicken mixture.
- Bake at 250°F for 15 minutes or until chicken mixture is hot.

Yield: 6 servings

Wine Recommendations: Chardonnay or Beaujolais

Create your own shells with prepackaged puff pastry sheets and large cookie cutters. Simply thaw the pastry sheets and cut with cookie cutters in your favorite shapes. Using a sharp knife, cut almost through the pastry cutouts to form a shell to hold the chicken. Bake the pastry as directed and lift out the center while still hot. Use the center as a lid for the shell after it has been filled with chicken.

The warm, moist climate along the Mediterranean is perfect for growing the wild shrubs that produce capers. The buds of the caper plant are picked by hand before they open and then sun dried. Capers are commonly packed pickled in a vinegar brine and can be stored in the refrigerator up to 9 months in a tightly sealed container.

Lemon Chicken with Capers and Black Olives

A fresh taste reminiscent of warm summer skies and deep blue seas.

4	boneless, skinless chicken breast halves
2	tablespoons all-purpose flour
1	tablespoon olive oil
1	(15-ounce) can chicken broth
4	tablespoons capers
2	tablespoons sliced black olives
2	tablespoons lemon juice
1	tablespoon cornstarch
⅓	cup water
	wild rice, cooked according to package directions

- Dredge chicken in flour.
- Sauté chicken in olive oil in medium saucepan until cooked through.
- Remove chicken and add chicken broth to saucepan.
- Bring broth to boil, reduce heat and simmer.
- Mix cornstarch with warm water until blended; stir into broth.
- Add capers, black olives and lemon juice to broth mixture.
- Serve chicken with sauce over wild rice.

Yield: 4 servings

Wine Recommendations: Pinot Grigio or an Unoaked Chardonnay

"My son just doesn't like anything...but he loves Winnie-the-Pooh and honey! That's how I came up with this recipe and its name. He likes it with Rabbit's carrots and long grain wild rice that cooks in 5 minutes."

Honey Bear Chicken

Chicken inspired by bears' temptation.

4	boneless, skinless chicken breast halves
2	tablespoons lemon juice
1	tablespoon honey
2	tablespoons purchased barbecue sauce

- Mix lemon juice, honey and barbecue sauce. Marinate chicken in mixture in the refrigerator overnight or at room temperature for one hour.
- Grill chicken over medium heat, turning once, until done.

Yield: 4 servings

Spicy Caribbean Chicken

A taste of the islands for your table

8	boneless, skinless chicken breast halves
1	cup purchased Jamaican jerk marinade
½	cup freshly squeezed lime juice
1	cup mango juice
2	tablespoons white wine vinegar
¼	cup country-style mustard
3	tablespoons chopped onion
2	teaspoons dried rosemary
2	teaspoons dried basil
1	tablespoon peeled, chopped fresh ginger
1	teaspoon salt
1	teaspoon freshly ground pepper
1	bunch fresh mint, chopped
1	mango, peeled, seeded and diced

- In a large bowl combine all ingredients except chicken. Pour marinade over chicken in a large resealable plastic bag.
- Marinate 2 hours at room temperature or up to 8 hours in the refrigerator.
- Grill chicken over medium heat, basting frequently with marinade, for 30 minutes or until done.
- Pour remaining marinade into a saucepan and boil for 3 minutes. Serve marinade with chicken.

Yield: 8 servings

Wine Recommendations: California Chardonnay or Rosé de Provence

Caribbean Night

Bring the islands to life at your dinner party with features from a Caribbean menu and a few creative decorations. Black beans and rice and a cool marinated salad are apropos. Top your table with linens in bright pink, hot yellow and the azure blue of the Caribbean Sea. String twinkling lights around your dining area. As your centerpiece, fill a large glass bowl with whole fresh mangoes, papayas, passion fruits, star fruits and kiwis. After dinner pass around knives and encourage guests to pick and peel their own dessert, served with yogurt dipping sauce.

Yogurt Dipping Sauce:

1 cup plain or vanilla
   yogurt

1 tablespoon orange juice

1 tablespoon brown sugar
   dash of cinnamon

The bright red and black toppings of bell peppers and olives make Checkered Chicken attractive and full of flavor. Bring out your checkers and checkerboards for a fun, old-fashioned night of games and refreshments. To keep leftover olives, refrigerate in an airtight glass jar for 1-2 months. Float a thin layer of vegetable oil on the surface of the brine to keep olives from turning soft.

What's In a Name?

Southerners do love nicknames. In fact, our state has two nicknames, the Old North State and the Tarheel State. We became the Old North State in 1710 when the land called Carolina was divided into two sections, North Carolina and South Carolina. Since North Carolina was both the northern and older settlement, we were thereafter called the Old North State. This nickname has endured, and both our official state song and state toast refer to our land as the Old North State.

Checkered Chicken

Your favorite opponent will give you points both for presentation and for taste.

4	bone-in chicken breasts
1	cup all-purpose flour
¼	cup olive oil
4	cloves garlic, minced
1	red bell pepper, seeded and diced
½	cup large black olive halves
1	cup chicken broth
½	cup lemon juice

- Dredge chicken breasts in flour.
- Brown chicken breasts in olive oil in large skillet over medium heat until nearly done. Remove chicken from skillet and place in a 4-quart baking dish.
- Sauté garlic, bell pepper and black olives in the skillet for 10 minutes.
- Add chicken broth and lemon juice to skillet and simmer over low heat for 10 minutes, stirring frequently.
- Pour sauce over chicken and bake for 20 minutes at 350°F or until chicken is tender.

Yield: 4 servings

Old North State Barbecued Chicken Breasts

Our own vinegar-based barbecue sauce makes this a Carolina classic.

4	boneless, skinless chicken breast halves
1½	cups vinegar
1	tablespoon chili powder
1	teaspoon salt
1	teaspoon pepper
1	teaspoon celery seed
1	tablespoon creamy peanut butter
	juice of one lemon

- Place chicken breasts in a 2-quart casserole dish.
- Combine remaining ingredients in saucepan over medium heat until peanut butter melts.
- Pour over chicken.
- Bake at 350°F for one hour, or until the chicken is tender.

Yield: 4 servings

Crab Stuffed Chicken Roll-ups

In a hurry? Use your microwave to save time with this dish.

3	tablespoons butter
½	cup plus 2 tablespoons chopped green onion
½	cup chopped celery
½	cup seasoned stuffing mix
1	(5-ounce) can crabmeat, drained and picked over for shells
3	tablespoons white wine
6	boneless, skinless chicken breast halves
	salt and pepper
	paprika

Sauce

⅓	cup grated Swiss cheese
⅓	cup white wine
3	tablespoons butter
3	tablespoons all-purpose flour
1	pint half-and-half

- Melt butter in heavy skillet and sauté onion and celery until tender, about 5 minutes.
- Stir in stuffing mix, crabmeat and wine. Remove from heat.
- Pound chicken breasts between two layers of waxed paper until thin. Lightly salt and pepper chicken.
- Place stuffing mixture down the center of each breast, roll up and secure with toothpicks. Sprinkle with paprika. Place chicken roll-ups in a 2-quart baking dish lightly sprayed with oil.
- Bake at 375°F for 45 minutes.
- To prepare sauce, melt butter in saucepan, stirring in flour until well mixed.
- Gradually add cream and stir constantly until smooth.
- Add wine and cheese and continue stirring until cheese is melted.
- To serve, remove toothpicks from chicken, pour sauce over chicken, and garnish with green onions.

Yield: 6 servings

Timesaving Method

- **Place butter in large microwaveable bowl and cook at half power for 40 seconds.**
- **Add onion and celery and cook 2 minutes on high power, uncovered, stirring once.**
- **Add stuffing, crabmeat and wine, mixing well.**
- **Pound chicken and roll with stuffing as directed in recipe. Place in microwaveable baking dish and cover with waxed paper.**
- **Cook for 10 minutes on high power, turning dish once.**

Slow Cooked Greek Chicken

Start this in the morning and come home to the aromas of Greece.

¼	**cup dry sherry**
	juice of one lemon
3	**cloves garlic, minced**
1	**onion, chopped**
1	**(16-ounce) can cut tomatoes with basil**
2	**cinnamon sticks**
1	**bay leaf**
⅛	**teaspoon pepper**
4	**boneless, skinless chicken breast halves**
1	**teaspoon olive oil**
1	**tablespoon all-purpose flour**
2	**tablespoons water**
8	**ounces broad noodles, cooked al dente**
¼	**cup crumbled feta cheese**

- Combine sherry, lemon juice, garlic, onion, tomatoes, cinnamon sticks, bay leaf and pepper in an electric slow cooker.
- Brown chicken on both sides in oil in skillet over medium-high heat.
- Transfer chicken to cooker.
- Cover and cook on low for 8 to 10 hours.
- Before serving, place cooked noodles on a serving plate and top with chicken breasts.
- Pour sauce from cooker into a large saucepan.
- Mix together one tablespoon flour and two tablespoons warm water and add to sauce.
- Stir sauce over medium heat until sauce is thickened.
- Pour sauce over chicken and noodles and sprinkle with feta cheese.

Yield: 4 servings

Wine Recommendations: Pinot Grigio or an Unoaked Chardonnay

Roasted Pesto Chicken

A roasted chicken infused with the taste of pesto makes summertime supper a special occasion.

1   **(6-pound) whole roasting chicken**
1   **(7-ounce) container pesto sauce**
3   **tablespoons dry white wine**
¾   **cup low-salt canned chicken stock**
2   **tablespoons all-purpose flour**
3   **tablespoons heavy cream**

- Gently separate chicken skin from the breast and thigh to form pockets.
- Reserve one tablespoon of pesto for sauce.
- Spread remaining pesto under skin, in the cavity and on the outer skin of the chicken.
- Place the chicken in a large roasting pan and roast at 450°F for 15 minutes.
- Reduce heat to 375°F and roast until juices run clear, basting occasionally, for about 1 hour 15 minutes.
- Transfer chicken to serving platter.
- Pour pan juices into a measuring cup and pour off the fat from the top.
- In a small saucepan, bring wine and scrapings from roasting pan to a boil.
- Add wine mixture to pan juices.
- Add enough chicken stock to equal one cup and pour back into saucepan.
- Combine 2 tablespoons chicken stock and flour in a small bowl, whisking until smooth.
- Add to saucepan.
- Bring to boil, whisking constantly.
- Boil until thickened, stirring often, about 5 minutes.
- Mix in cream, reserved pesto, salt and pepper to taste.
- Serve chicken with sauce.

Yield: 4 to 6 servings

Wine Recommendations: Côtes du Rhone or Dolcetto

Leftover Roasted Pesto Chicken transforms into a decidedly different chicken salad. Chop leftover chicken to desired consistency. For 2 cups chicken, mix together ¼ cup sour cream, ¼ cup mayonnaise, freshly ground pepper and a spritz of fresh lemon juice. Toss lightly with chopped chicken. Add one or more of the following to complete your Roasted Pesto Chicken Salad:

- **cherry tomato halves**
- **chopped sun-dried tomatoes**
- **chopped walnuts**
- **chopped black olives**
- **chopped scallions**

This recipe is made simple by using canned artichoke hearts. If you prefer fresh artichokes, substitute with baby artichokes which are usually available in the spring, or fresh artichoke hearts. To prepare fresh artichokes, cover them with water, add lemon slices and salt, and boil until tender, about 25-45 minutes.

Artichoke Baked Chicken

Delicious over rice or noodles

¼ cup butter
6 boneless, skinless chicken breast halves
1 (14-ounce) can artichoke hearts, drained and halved
1 clove garlic, minced
¾ cup chopped onion
3 tablespoons all-purpose flour
¼ teaspoon salt
1¼ cups dry white wine
1 cup chicken broth
1 (3-ounce) package cream cheese
½ cup toasted almond slices

- Melt butter in large skillet. Sauté chicken until brown, about 5 minutes on each side. Remove chicken to a 2-quart baking dish and top with artichoke hearts.
- Sauté garlic and onion in same skillet over medium heat until tender.
- Stir in flour and salt. Cook for one minute, stirring constantly.
- Stir in wine and broth, cooking and stirring until thickened. Add cream cheese and cook until melted.
- Spoon cream cheese mixture over chicken and bake at 350°F for 45 minutes. Garnish with toasted almonds

Yield: 6 servings

Creamy Chicken Pasta with Jalapeños

A spicy twist to ordinary pasta

1 pound boneless, skinless chicken breasts
5 tablespoons olive oil, divided
4 cloves garlic, minced
2 jalapeños, chopped
1 large onion, chopped
¾ cup chicken broth
1 (16-ounce) package sour cream
   salt and pepper to taste
¼ cup fresh cilantro
1 (16-ounce) package rotini, cooked al dente
   Parmesan cheese

(continued on next page)

Creamy Chicken Pasta with Jalapeños *continued*

- Thinly slice chicken breasts across the breast.
- Heat 3 tablespoons olive oil in a large skillet over medium-high heat and sauté chicken until chicken changes color. Remove from heat.
- Add 2 tablespoons of oil to the same skillet and sauté the next 3 ingredients for 2 to 3 minutes or until the onions are slightly transparent.
- Return the chicken to skillet.
- Add broth and sour cream to pan; reduce until sauce coats spoon, about 5 minutes.
- Add salt and pepper to taste.
- Remove from heat and add cilantro.
- Serve over pasta with Parmesan cheese.

Yield: 4 to 6 servings

Pasta with Chicken, Sun-dried Tomatoes and Gorgonzola

Substitute a creamy blue cheese if Gorgonzola is not available.

½	**cup chopped, drained, oil-packed sun-dried tomatoes (2 tablespoons oil reserved)**
2	**boneless, skinless chicken breast halves**
1	**pound gnocchi pasta or medium shell pasta**
4	**cloves garlic, minced**
½	**cup chopped fresh basil**
½	**cup canned low-salt chicken broth**
½	**cup crumbled Gorgonzola cheese (about 2 ounces)**
¼	**cup chopped prosciutto**
¼	**cup pine nuts, toasted**

- Heat 1 tablespoon oil reserved from tomatoes in heavy large skillet over medium-high heat.
- Add chicken to skillet, and sauté until cooked through, about 3 minutes per side.
- Transfer chicken to plate and cool; do not clean skillet.
- Cut chicken into ½-inch pieces.
- Cook pasta in large pot of boiling water until tender but still firm to bite. Drain pasta; transfer to large bowl.
- Meanwhile, heat remaining 1 tablespoon tomato oil in same skillet over medium-high heat.
- Add garlic; sauté until tender, about 1 minute. Add sun-dried tomatoes, chicken, basil, broth, cheese and prosciutto to skillet and bring to the boil.
- Add sauce to pasta and toss with salt and pepper. Top with toasted pine nuts and serve.

Yield: 4 servings

Prosciutto, an Italian-style ham which is seasoned, salt-cured and air-dried, adds marvelous flavor to this pasta dish. In Parma, Italy, a strain of pigs is bred specifically for prosciutto, and these pigs are fed the whey left over from making Parmesan, giving the ham a very delicate flavor. In San Daniele, which is located in northern Italy, the pigs are fed acorns, and the prosciutto is very tender and sweet. Enjoy prosciutto in cooked dishes, or slice thinly and serve with melon or figs as an appetizer.

Old-Fashioned Roasted Turkey

The aroma of roasting turkey and homemade dressing always brings holiday memories to mind.

"My grandfather lit a fire
for every Thanksgiving
lunch, even if it was 85
degrees outside. We ate
country ham and fried
chicken until it grew
trendy to roast turkeys.
The turkey gravy was
made with hard-boiled
eggs. The stuffing was
prepared from cornbread
crumbs and old biscuits,
shaped into patties and
then baked."
(Ben Barker, *Bon Appétit*,
November 1992)

1	14 to 16-pound turkey
½	cup butter, melted
1	tablespoon salt
½	teaspoon pepper
2	teaspoons seasoned salt
1	teaspoon poultry seasoning
1	teaspoon garlic powder
½	teaspoon ground ginger
1	teaspoon paprika
¼	teaspoon cayenne pepper
¼	teaspoon dried basil

- Clean and dry turkey, reserving giblets if desired.
- Brush turkey with melted butter.
- Mix dry seasonings and rub thoroughly into cavity and on outside of turkey. Truss and tie up securely.
- Place breast side up in roasting bag in large roasting pan. Add one cup water, seal bag and place meat thermometer into thigh meat.
- Bake at 350°F for approximately 3 hours or until thermometer registers 180°F.

Yield: 6 servings

Turkey Stuffing with Swiss Chard and Sausage

Use sourdough bread for an even more unusual stuffing.

5	tablespoons butter or margarine
1	pound mild Italian sausage, crumbled with casing removed
1¼	cups chopped celery
1	large onion, chopped
¼	pound mushrooms, sliced
1½	pounds Swiss chard or spinach (ends trimmed), rinsed well and finely chopped
½	cup raisins
1¼	cups grated Parmesan cheese
1¼	teaspoons dried rosemary
1¼	teaspoons dried oregano
½	pound French bread, cut into ¼-inch cubes
1	cup dry white wine
	turkey

(continued on next page)

Turkey Stuffing with Swiss Chard and Sausage *continued*

- In a large skillet or Dutch oven, melt butter on medium heat.
- Add sausage and cook, stirring often, until browned, about 10 minutes. With slotted spoon, remove sausage to a large bowl.
- Add celery and onion to the skillet and cook until limp, about 5 minutes. Remove with a slotted spoon and add to sausage.
- Add mushrooms to skillet and stir often until liquid has evaporated and mushrooms are lightly browned, about 5 minutes. Remove with slotted spoon and add to sausage.
- Add chard or spinach to skillet and stir until wilted and juices are evaporated.
- Stir chard into sausage mixture with raisins, Parmesan cheese, rosemary and oregano.
- Soak bread in wine and work it with your hands until it is mashed.
- Combine sausage and bread mixture, mixing well.
- Fill turkey with stuffing.
- Place excess stuffing about 1 inch deep in a medium buttered baking dish. Bake at 350°F, uncovered, until top is lightly browned, about 25 minutes.

Yield: 8 to 10 servings

Roasted Turkey Breast for Sandwiches
As welcomed in your picnic basket as on your buffet table

1	turkey breast, up to 8 pounds
½	cup butter
½	cup sherry

- Turn breast cavity side up and place butter and sherry in cavity.
- Wrap in foil and seal.
- Bake on rack in roasting pan at 325°F for one hour 15 minutes or until tender.

Yield: 12 or more servings

A boring turkey sandwich? Hardly! Try some of these sandwich combinations to dress up this popular bird:

- whole wheat rolls with brown mustard and smoked Gouda cheese
- Kaiser rolls with cream cheese and cranberry relish
- rye bread with sauerkraut and Thousand Island dressing
- pumpernickel bread with chutney
- white bread, toasted, with American or Provolone cheese (for the kids)
- toasted whole wheat bread with lettuce, bacon and sliced tomatoes
- pita pockets filled with sprouts, chopped cucumber, chopped tomato and buttermilk dressing
- toasted sesame seed bread with honey mustard, thinly sliced Granny Smith apples and Havarti cheese

Fresh basil gives turkey scaloppine a pizazz that dried basil just can't match. Eliminate waste by freezing fresh herbs for other uses. First, strip the leaves from the stems and fill muffin cups halfway with the leaves. Then, fill the muffin cups with water and freeze until solid. Transfer the frozen herb cubes to plastic bags, seal tightly and keep in your freezer for up to 6 months. When ready to use, place cubes in strainer and run under cold water. Use immediately.

Summer Turkey Scaloppine

Perfect to serve at the end of the summer, when gardens brim with tomatoes and basil is knee high

Summer Tomatoes

6 cups cherry tomato halves
1 cup chopped red onion
10 large basil leaves, cut into strips
½ cup olive oil
   salt and freshly ground pepper to taste

Turkey Cutlets

2 pounds turkey cutlets, thinly sliced
1 cup all-purpose flour
2 eggs
2 cups soft bread crumbs
   salt and pepper to taste
3 tablespoons olive oil
3 tablespoons butter

- To prepare summer tomatoes, combine tomato ingredients and let stand at room temperature for at least two hours before serving.
- To prepare turkey, dredge cutlets in flour, then dip in eggs and coat with bread crumbs. Sprinkle slices with salt and pepper.
- Melt butter and olive oil in heavy skillet and cook turkey slices until browned, about 3 minutes on both sides.
- To serve, top each cutlet with summer tomatoes.

Yield: 6 to 8 servings

Wine Recommendations: Barbera or Beaujolais

Rock Cornish Game Hens with Grapes

Begin a new tradition for Thanksgiving dinner.

Game Hens

2   **Rock Cornish game hens**
    salt and pepper to taste
6   **slices bacon**
2   **slices bread, trimmed and cut into triangles**
2   **tablespoons butter**

Sauce

½   **cup cognac**
½   **cup heavy cream**
2   **scallions, finely chopped**
1   **tablespoon butter**
1   **(8-ounce) can light, seedless grapes, drained**
½   **cup port**
1   **teaspoon lemon juice**
    cayenne pepper to taste

- To prepare hens, sprinkle with salt and pepper and place in buttered roasting pan. Arrange 3 half-slices of bacon on each hen.
- Bake at 350°F for 50 minutes, basting occasionally.
- Sauté bread triangles in butter, turning once until both sides are golden. Drain on paper towels.
- Remove hens from oven, cut in half lengthwise and arrange each half on a bread triangle. Keep warm.
- To prepare sauce, put roasting pan over direct heat. Add cognac and cook until reduced by half.
- Add cream and boil until sauce is reduced to a creamy consistency.
- In a small saucepan, sauté scallions in butter for 2 minutes. Add grapes and port.
- Heat through and ignite wine, stirring until flame burns out.
- Strain the cream gravy from the roasting pan into the wine and grape sauce. Add lemon juice and a dash of cayenne pepper.
- To serve, pour sauce over hens and garnish with watercress, if desired.

Yield: 4 servings

Wine Recommendations Red Burgundy or an Oregon Pinot Noir

Game hens are quite appetizing and, because of their small size, make elegant single servings that require less cooking time than a whole chicken.

Wild Rice Pilaf

- Cover ½ cup long-grain brown rice with cold water and let stand for 1 hour, changing water several times. Rinse.
- Meanwhile, rinse ½ cup wild rice and add to pan of boiling, salted water and simmer, uncovered, until tender, about 35-40 minutes.
- Soften a small chopped onion in oil in a medium to large sauté pan. Add brown rice; stir over moderate heat until grains begin to burst.
- Stir in 1 cup heated chicken stock, add salt, cover and reduce heat. Simmer for 15 minutes.
- Combine 2 rices and any chopped cooked vegetables or seasonings desired.
- Serve as bed for Roast Duck Breasts.

Roast Duck Breasts

This unusual treatment of duck breasts is simple but elegant.

1	boneless duck breast (2 halves)
2	cloves garlic
1	sprig fresh rosemary
1	tablespoon raspberry vinegar
1	tablespoon balsamic vinegar
2	tablespoons red wine
1	tablespoon soy sauce
½	teaspoon dried, crushed rosemary
	salt and freshly ground pepper to taste
	Wild Rice Pilaf

- Rub breast with 1 halved garlic clove and fresh rosemary. Score skin but do not cut through flesh.
- Place duck in heavy-bottomed skillet, skin-side down, and cook over medium heat to render fat, about 5 minutes.
- Combine raspberry vinegar, balsamic vinegar, wine, soy sauce, 1 minced garlic clove and dried rosemary in shallow, ovenproof glass pan. Add duck and set aside 30 minutes to marinate. Season with salt and pepper.
- Place pan with duck and marinade in oven and cook at 400°F until duck breast is browned outside and rare inside, about 15 minutes.
- Remove duck from pan and thinly slice (remove and discard skin). Pour pan liquids into a small pan and cook over high heat until reduced by one-fourth and slightly thickened, about 5 minutes. Pour pan liquids over duck and wild rice pilaf and serve immediately.

Note: 2 tablespoons balsamic vinegar plus 1 teaspoon sugar may be substituted for 1 tablespoon raspberry vinegar and 1 tablespoon balsamic vinegar.

Yield: 2 servings

Wine Recommendations: Bandol Rouge or Châteauneuf-du-Pape

Duck with Tangerine and Port Sauce

The centerpiece for a special occasion

2   **ducks**
    salt and pepper
2   **tangerines, peeled and sectioned**
½   **cup chopped onion**
½   **cup chopped celery**
4   **bay leaves**
½   **cup minced onions**
1   **cup port wine**
    salt and pepper

- Rinse ducks and pat dry. Salt and pepper ducks all over and inside.
- Stuff ducks with chopped onion, celery, bay leaves and one tangerine.
- Gently separate skin from breasts and thighs and insert sections from second tangerine.
- Roast ducks in a deep roasting pan for 25 minutes at 500°F. Reduce heat to 350°F and roast for 35 minutes. Increase heat to 475°F and roast until dark and crispy, about 20 minutes.
- Remove ducks from roasting pan and pour off the fat. Sauté minced onions in remaining juices and stir in port, cooking until reduced to ¾ cup. Add salt and pepper to taste.
- Serve on platter garnished with caramelized tangerine slices.

Yield: 6 servings

Wine Recommendations: California Pinot Noir or Barrel-Fermented Chardonnay

Embellish your serving platter with caramelized tangerine slices. To prepare, stir 1¼ cup sugar and ¾ cup water in a heavy pan, and bring to a boil. Lower heat and swirl pan so syrup colors evenly. DO NOT STIR. Add 2 tangerines, sliced, and cook briefly until caramelized. Remove slices and garnish with parsley.

Bourbon Shallot Sauce

½ **cup unsalted butter, divided**

3 **shallots, diced**

½ **cup bourbon whiskey**

½ **cup chicken broth**

½ **cup heavy cream**

- Melt 1 tablespoon of the butter in a skillet and sauté the shallots until translucent.
- Add the bourbon and cook until reduced slightly.
- Add the chicken broth and cream and simmer until reduced by one third.
- Remove from heat and whisk in remaining butter.

Stuffed Quail with Bourbon Shallot Sauce

Quail are dressed with flavors of the south in this special occasion entrée.

7 **slices bacon, divided**
2 **shallots, diced**
½ **cup wild rice**
1 **cup chicken broth, divided**
   salt and pepper to taste
3 **tablespoons butter, divided**
4 **ounces wild mushrooms (oyster, shiitake, chanterelle or morel)**
½ **cup broken pecan halves**
2 **tablespoons bourbon whiskey**
½ **boneless chicken breast, fully cooked and chopped**
¼ **cup heavy cream**
1 **egg**
6 **boneless quail**
   Bourbon Shallot Sauce (see sidebar)

- Dice 1 slice bacon. In a large skillet, sauté until crisp.
- Add 1 shallot, wild rice, ¾ cup chicken broth, salt and pepper. Reduce heat, cover and simmer until rice is done, about 40 minutes, adding more chicken broth if needed. Remove from heat.
- In another skillet, melt 1 tablespoon butter and sauté mushrooms and remaining shallot until shallot is translucent. Add pecans and 1 tablespoon bourbon. Cook for 3 minutes. Remove from heat.
- Place chicken breast in food processor or blender and chop fine.
- With motor running, add cream, egg and remaining tablespoon bourbon, blending until smooth.
- Transfer to a bowl and fold in rice mixture and mushroom and pecan mixture. Let stuffing cool.
- Form the stuffing into six 2-inch balls.
- Place one quail, skin side up, over each ball of stuffing. Form the quail around the stuffing and place the legs in an upward position.
- Wrap a bacon slice around each quail and secure with a toothpick.
- Place stuffed quail in a baking dish and brush with 2 tablespoons melted butter.
- Bake for 20 to 25 minutes until quail are a rich brown color.
- Serve with Bourbon Shallot Sauce.

Yield: 4 to 6 servings

Grilled Beef Tenderloin with Dijon Bourbon Marinade

The flavor of bourbon complements any cut of beef.

1   **4 to 5-pound beef tenderloin, trimmed**
1   **cup bourbon whiskey**
1   **cup soy sauce**
1   **cup Dijon mustard**
1   **cup brown sugar**
2   **large onions, finely chopped**
2   **teaspoons salt**
¼   **cup Worcestershire sauce**
     pepper to taste

- Mix ingredients together except tenderloin. Pour over tenderloin.
- Marinate beef 6 hours or overnight.
- Grill to your taste.

Note: This marinade is also excellent with pork tenderloin.

Yield: 8 to 10 servings

Champagne Steak

Serve bubbly alongside — dinner guests will want to toast the chef.

4   **New York strip steaks (6-ounce), bone and fat removed**
1   **teaspoon cracked black pepper**
3   **tablespoons unsalted butter**
½   **cup red wine**
4   **tablespoons champagne mustard**
1½   **cups heavy cream**

- Season steaks with cracked pepper.
- Melt butter in large heavy skillet. Sauté steaks about 4 minutes per side over medium heat.
- Remove steaks to platter and keep warm in 180°F oven.
- Add red wine to skillet and turn heat to high. Add mustard and stir for about 1 minute. Add cream.
- Reduce heat and simmer 4 minutes. Sauce should be thick enough to coat back of spoon.
- Remove steaks from oven. Pour sauce over and serve.

Yield: 4 servings

If rain, sleet, snow or hail prevent you from grilling, roast the beef tenderloin in your oven:

- **Place prepared meat in a roasting pan, or use a large shallow pan with a wire rack in the bottom (a cake rack will do). This prevents the beef from stewing in its juices and allows the heat to penetrate evenly from all sides. If using beef with a layer of fat, always place fat side up so the juices will baste the meat as it cooks.**
- **Do not add water and do not cover pan.**
- **Insert meat thermometer into center of thickest part of cut or use instant reading thermometer near the end of the roasting time (see below).**
- **Roast at 425°F for 15 minutes. Reduce heat to 350°F and roast an additional 20-45 minutes to achieve desired doneness as indicated by meat thermometer:**
  Rare — 125°F to 130°F
  Medium — 135°F to 140°F
- **Remove roast from oven and allow to rest 10-15 minutes before carving. The beef will continue to cook internally during this time, and the juices will settle.**

"The southerner is indeed hospitable to this day, loving nothing more than to entertain family and friends with as much as he can afford." (Encyclopedia of Southern Culture)

"Growing up, we enjoyed wonderful meals and late-night family talks in the kitchen at a long table with benches on either side. With six children to feed, my mother spent much time in the kitchen. To this day, her birthday dinners for us are still very special and always include the birthday person's favorite dishes. This tenderloin is requested often, along with scalloped potatoes, steamed asparagus with dill and a layered salad. Our traditional Christmas brunch always includes another family favorite, cheese grits. If I ever had to leave the South, grits would be the first thing in my suitcase so that I'd never have to do without this 'southern caviar'!"

Elegant Beef Tenderloin

1	(5-pound) beef tenderloin, trimmed
1¼	teaspoon garlic salt
1	cup red wine
¼	cup soy sauce
¾	cup butter
1	teaspoon lemon-pepper seasoning
	grapes (optional)
	celery leaves (optional)
	lemon zest (optional)

- Preheat oven to 425°F.
- Place meat in a lightly greased shallow roasting pan.
- Sprinkle with garlic salt.
- Bake for 10 minutes.
- Combine wine, soy sauce, butter and lemon-pepper seasoning in a small saucepan.
- Cook until mixture is thoroughly heated.
- Pour over tenderloin.
- Bake an additional 30 to 40 minutes or until a thermometer registers 140°F (rare), basting occasionally with pan drippings. Bake until thermometer registers 150°F for medium rare or 160°F for medium.
- If desired, garnish beef with grapes, celery leaves and lemon zest.

Variation: Elegant Beef Tenderloin served cold and sliced makes an ideal centerpiece for your cocktail buffet. An assortment of rolls and pretty dishes filled with interesting mustards (label them) and Dijon mayonnaise completes the ensemble.

Yield: 10 servings

Wine Recommendations: *Washington Merlot or Young Bordeaux (Cru Bourgeoise)*

Filet Mignon with Balsamic Mushrooms

Serve a superb steak without firing up the grill.

2	filet mignon, 1½-inch thick
	cracked black pepper
2¼	teaspoons chopped fresh rosemary, divided
3½	tablespoons olive oil, divided
2¼	teaspoons fresh minced garlic
5	ounces whole oyster mushrooms
5	ounces shiitake mushrooms
2½	tablespoons balsamic vinegar, divided
¼	cup canned beef broth

- Press peppercorns and ¾ teaspoon rosemary into steaks.
- Heat 2 tablespoons olive oil in a heavy medium skillet over medium-high heat.
- Add garlic and remaining rosemary and sauté for 30 seconds.
- Add all mushrooms and sauté until beginning to soften, about 2 minutes.
- Add ½ tablespoon vinegar and stir to coat.
- Season with salt and pepper
- Heat 1½ tablespoons olive oil in heavy large skillet over high heat.
- Sprinkle steaks with salt. Add to skillet and cook 2 minutes on each side to brown.
- Reduce heat to medium-high and cook 2 more minutes on each side for rare.
- Add remaining 2 tablespoons vinegar and broth to steak skillet. Boil until syrupy, scraping bits, about 1 minute.
- Pour over steaks. Top with mushrooms.

Yield: 2 servings

Wine Recommendations: Châteauneuf-du-Pape or Gigondas

Cook a filet mignon on the stove?! Believe it or not, you will discover that grilling isn't the only acceptable option for cooking fine cuts of beef. Much of the flavor of this delectable sauce comes from the pan drippings, flavor otherwise lost on a grill.

Mango Salsa

2 cups diced tomatoes

1 fresh mango, peeled and diced

1 green bell pepper, seeded and diced

6 green onions with tops, diced

1 large fresh jalapeño, seeded and diced

¼ cup lime juice

½ cup fresh cilantro, chopped

¼ cup pecan pieces, toasted

• **Combine all ingredients and toss gently.**

Grilled Rib-Eyes with Mango Salsa

Add a bite to your beef.

4　beef rib-eye or chuck top blade steaks, cut ¾-inch thick
¼　cup Worcestershire sauce
¼　cup soy sauce
¼　cup lime juice
2　tablespoons vegetable oil
2　cloves garlic, crushed
1　tablespoon chili powder
1　tablespoon brown sugar
　　Mango Salsa (see sidebar)

• Mix Worcestershire, soy sauce, lime juice, oil, garlic, chili powder and brown sugar for marinade.
• Marinate steaks 30 to 45 minutes.
• Grill steaks 4 to 6 inches from medium coals for 8 to 10 minutes, turning once.
• Cut steaks in ¼ inch slices if desired.
• Serve steaks with mango salsa.

Yield: 4 servings

Wine Recommendations: California Cabernet or a Big California Red Zinfandel

Capital City Flank Steak

Thoughtful preparation makes a less tender cut of beef juicy and delicious.

1　1½-pound flank steak
⅓　cup vegetable oil
1　tablespoon red wine vinegar
2　cloves garlic, minced
　　salt and freshly ground pepper

• Trim excess fat from steak.
• Score steak on both sides in 1½-inch squares.
• Set steak in a deep bowl or zip-top plastic bag.
• Combine oil, vinegar, and garlic.
• Pour over meat, and marinate 3 hours in refrigerator turning once.
• Remove from marinade and place on a lightly greased rack in broiler pan.
• Broil 4 inches from heat 4 to 5 minutes.
• Sprinkle with salt and pepper to taste and turn.
• Broil an additional 4 to 5 minutes.
• Sprinkle with salt and pepper to taste.
• To serve, slice across grain into thin slices.

Yield: 4 to 6 servings

As the capital city of North Carolina, Raleigh is also home to the governor and his family. The governor's residence is the executive mansion, a Queen Anne style architectural treasure that was completed in 1891. The mansion sits on a city block near the heart of downtown Raleigh surrounded by a brick and iron fence. The brick sidewalk encircling the property bears the signatures of some of the state prisoners who made the bricks and scratched their names into the hardening clay.

Calf's Liver
with Bacon, Sage and Vermouth

An epicure's delight that will redefine your taste for liver.

4	bacon slices, chopped
3	tablespoons butter
1	pound calf's liver
½	medium red onion, thinly sliced
1	tablespoon all-purpose flour
¼	cup dry vermouth
½	cup beef stock
½	cup chicken stock
1	tablespoon chopped fresh or 1 teaspoon dried, rubbed sage
	salt and pepper to taste
	chopped fresh parsley

- Cook bacon in heavy large skillet over medium heat until crisp, about 6 minutes.
- Using a slotted spoon, transfer bacon to paper towels and drain. Drain drippings from skillet.
- Melt butter in same skillet over high heat. Add liver and sauté just until firm to the touch, about 3 to 4 minutes on each side.
- Transfer liver to platter. Tent with foil.
- Discard all but 1 tablespoon drippings from the skillet.
- Add onion to skillet and sauté over medium-high heat until golden, about 4 minutes. Add flour. Stir for 1 minute.
- Add vermouth. Bring to boil, scraping up any browned bits. Whisk in both stocks, sage and bacon.
- Boil until reduced to sauce consistency, stirring frequently, about 4 minutes.
- Season with salt and pepper.
- Spoon sauce over liver.
- Sprinkle with parsley and serve.

Yield: 2 servings

Wine Recommendations: Cru Beaujolais or California Zinfandel

"Considering my early dislike for liver, I am astonished that I now prepare it for my family - and they actually like it! As a child, I hid under my bed whenever I smelled Mom's favorite recipe, liver smothered in onions and gravy, cooking in the cast iron skillet. Mom eventually found my hiding place, forcing me to the table for 'at least 3 bites' before I was excused."

Picante Pot Roast

Lone Star Dry Rub

¾ cup paprika

¼ cup ground black
   pepper

¼ cup chili powder

¼ cup salt

¼ cup sugar

2 tablespoons garlic
   powder

2 tablespoons onion
   powder

1 tablespoon ground
   cayenne

- **Mix thoroughly in a bowl. Store leftover rub in a jar in the refrigerator.**

1	**3-pound boneless shoulder chuck roast**
3 to 4	**cloves garlic, slivered**
1 to 2	**pickled jalapeños, slivered**
	Lone Star Dry Rub
2	**tablespoons bacon drippings or corn oil**
¼	**cup all-purpose flour**
2	**(10-ounce) cans Ro-Tel Tomatoes and Green Chiles**
½ to 1	**cup unsalted beef stock**
6	**small carrots, cut in halves**
1½	**medium onions, sliced into rings**

- Insert the garlic and jalapeño slivers into openings in the meat's surface.
- Rub the meat well with the dry rub and let sit for 30 minutes to come close to room temperature.
- Preheat oven to 300°F.
- Heat the bacon drippings in a heavy lidded skillet or Dutch oven.
- Dredge the meat in the flour and brown it in the drippings. Turn off heat.
- Pour in tomatoes and ½ cup of stock and add the carrots and onions to the pan.
- Cover the pan tightly and bake the roast for 4 hours.
- Check the meat after 3 hours and add more stock if it is getting dry.
- If it seems soupy, uncover for the last 30 minutes of baking.
- The meat should be falling apart tender.

Yield: 4 to 6 servings

Barbecue Beef Brisket

Beef brisket is comfort for the appetite and the soul.

1	4 to 6 pound beef brisket
2 to 4	ounces liquid smoke
	celery salt
	garlic salt
	onion salt
2 to 4	tablespoons Worcestershire sauce
	favorite barbecue sauce

- Using a very sharp knife, remove all the fat from brisket.
- Place in large ziplock bag and sprinkle liberally with liquid smoke.
- Seal and place in refrigerator for 12 hours or overnight.
- Place in a large baking pan.
- Sprinkle liberally with Worcestershire sauce, celery, onion and garlic salt.
- Cover with foil and bake at 275°F for 4 to 5 hours. Smaller brisket 4 hours, larger brisket 5 hours.
- Remove from pan, draining juices and let cool.
- Slice against the grain.
- Place back in baking pan and cover with your favorite barbecue sauce.
- Bake uncovered at 350°F for 1 hour.

Note: As an alternative, chop or shred the meat and serve on Kaiser buns.

Yield: 6 to 12 servings

"I always prepare this for those who are ill, have had a baby, have moved to a new home, etc., and it is always well-received. I even use it as a round-robin gift exchange for our Sunday school Christmas party."

Sesame Beef

3	pounds lean beef (flank steak or London broil)
1	cup sugar
1	cup soy sauce
4 to 5	cloves garlic, pressed
3	bunches green onions, diced
1½	teaspoons sesame seeds, toasted and crushed
3 to 4	tablespoons olive oil

- Slice beef as thinly as possible. Toss with sugar and let stand for half an hour at room temperature.
- Meanwhile, combine soy sauce, garlic, onions, sesame seeds and olive oil in a bowl. Pour marinade over meat and sugar mixture and refrigerate approximately 3 hours.
- Stir-fry beef and marinade over high heat until meat is cooked through.
- Serve over rice or Asian noodles.

Note: Partially frozen meat is easier to slice thinly.

Yield: 6 servings

Leave it to the Russians to understand beef that really beats the cold weather blues.

Russian Beef Stroganoff

A panacea for chilly, drizzly weather

1   1½-pound piece beef filet
   salt and pepper
1   tablespoon vegetable oil
3   tablespoons unsalted butter, divided
1   cup chopped onion
4   large cloves garlic, minced
½   pound portobello mushrooms, trimmed and sliced thin
½   pound shiitake or white mushrooms, trimmed and sliced thin
½   cup dry white wine
½   cup beef broth
2   cups sour cream
2   tablespoons Dijon mustard
   egg noodles

- Cut filet crosswise into 1-inch slices and cut slices into ⅓-inch strips.
- Season beef with salt and pepper.
- In a 12-inch heavy skillet, heat oil and 1 tablespoon butter over high heat and sear beef, in batches, 30 seconds to 1 minute on each side or until browned but still rare.
- Transfer beef with tongs to a plate.
- Add remaining 2 tablespoons butter to a skillet and cook onion and garlic, stirring until softened.
- Add mushrooms and salt and pepper to taste.
- Cook over high heat, stirring until liquid evaporates.
- Add wine and boil, stirring, for 3 minutes.
- Add beef with any juices that have accumulated on plate, broth, sour cream, mustard and salt and pepper to taste.
- Cook, stirring until heated through. Do not boil.
- Serve over cooked noodles.

Yield: 6 servings

Italian Meatloaf

¾ **pound ground sirloin**
½ **pound ground veal**
½ **medium onion, chopped**
2 **cloves garlic, minced**
1 **tablespoon dried Italian herb blend**
¼ **cup fresh parsley, chopped**
1¼ **cup fresh bread crumbs**
1 **large egg**
½ **cup tomato juice**
1 **teaspoon freshly ground pepper**
4 **ounces thinly sliced prosciutto**
6 **ounces sliced provolone**

- In food processor or by hand mix ground meats, onion, garlic, Italian herb blend, parsley and bread crumbs.
- Add egg and tomato juice to bind together. Add pepper.
- On a large sheet of wax paper, pat mixture out to ½-inch thick rectangle about 9 x 13 inches.
- Preheat oven to 350°F.
- Cover ground meat mixture with prosciutto slices.
- Use ½ of cheese and cover prosciutto.
- Starting at long side of rectangle, roll up, jelly-roll style.
- Pat ends to create a good shape.
- Ease onto baking sheet.
- Bake 50 minutes.
- Place remaining provolone slices on top of meatloaf.
- Bake about 10 minutes more, until cheese is lightly browned.
- Serve hot or cold.

Note: Substitute ground sirloin for the ground veal, if desired.

Yield: 6 servings

Wine Recommendations: Chianti Classico or California Cabernet

"Worth the extra trouble! My dad has enjoyed making this meatloaf for as long as I can remember. Now, I enjoy serving it to my family, and my four-year-old has fun helping me...That's what the south is all about—continuing traditions that bind families for generations."

Quick Tomato Beef Bake

A quick and simple meatloaf that is cooked in the microwave

1   (8-ounce) can tomato sauce
¼   cup brown sugar
1   teaspoon prepared mustard
2   eggs, lightly beaten
1   medium onion, minced
¼   cup saltine cracker crumbs
2   pounds lean ground beef
1½   teaspoons salt
¼   teaspoon pepper

- In small bowl, combine tomato sauce, brown sugar and mustard. Set aside.
- In large mixing bowl, combine eggs, onion, cracker crumbs, ground beef, salt and pepper.
- Add ½ cup of tomato sauce mixture and stir.
- Place meat mixture in 2-quart ovenproof round casserole that has been coated with a no stick cooking spray.
- Pour remaining tomato sauce over meat.
- Cook in microwave, uncovered, on high (maximum power) 12 to 14 minutes.
- Let stand 5 minutes before serving.

Yield: 6 servings

Roast Beef Sandwiches with Roquefort and Caramelized Shallots

3   tablespoons butter
¾   pound shallots, thinly sliced
4   Kaiser rolls, split
1   pound thinly sliced medium rare roast beef
6   ounces chilled Roquefort cheese, crumbled

- Melt butter and cook shallots about 15 minutes on medium heat until golden.
- Preheat oven to 375°F.
- Assemble sandwiches with cheese first, then roast beef, then shallots.
- Place sandwiches on a baking sheet and cover with foil.
- Bake 10 minutes or until cheese has melted and sandwiches are hot.

Yield: 4 servings

Wine Recommendations: Cru Beaujolais or Red Zinfandel

Beef and Black Bean Burritos

Authentic Mexican taste north of the border

4 to 6	(10-inch) flour tortillas
½	pound lean ground beef
1	cup chopped white onion
1	(15-ounce) can black beans, drained
1	(10-ounce) can diced tomatoes with green chili peppers
2	teaspoons cumin
	chopped green onions

- Wrap tortillas in foil. Heat in oven according to package directions to soften.
- While heating tortillas, cook ground beef and onion until meat is brown and onion is tender. Drain.
- Stir in black beans, undrained tomatoes with chili peppers and cumin.
- Simmer uncovered for 5 minutes or to desired consistency.
- Reserve ¼ cup filling.
- Spoon about ¼ remaining filling into each tortilla, just below center.
- Fold bottom edge of tortilla up and over filling.
- Fold opposite sides of tortilla in, just until they meet.
- Roll up and over from the bottom.
- Top with some of the reserved filling.
- Sprinkle with green onions.

Yield: 4 to 6 servings, depending on how much filling used in each burrito

Wine Recommendation: California Red Zinfandel

"A stickler for nutrition, my mother never served a meal without meat, vegetables and bread...except on Sloppy Joe Nights. And were we excited! While our friends were happy with the canned version on their plates, Mom always cooked hers from scratch, making certain to include nutritious ingredients. I guess this made her feel better about skipping the vegetables. After being spoiled with such great-tasting food, it sure was hard to adjust to cans and fast food when we went to college!"

Sloppy Janes

1¾ pounds ground round
1 cup chopped onion
¾ cup chopped celery
1 large clove garlic, minced
2 (14½-ounce) cans whole tomatoes, undrained and chopped
1 (13¾-ounce) can beef broth
1 (6-ounce) can tomato paste
½ teaspoon pepper
½ teaspoon dried thyme
¼ teaspoon salt
1 large bay leaf
¼ cup chopped fresh parsley
⅓ cup finely chopped green bell pepper
2 tablespoons brown sugar
2 tablespoons cider vinegar
3 teaspoons Worcestershire sauce
8 buns

- Combine ground round, chopped onion, celery and garlic in a large Dutch oven. Cook over medium-high heat until meat is browned, stirring until it crumbles.
- Drain and pat dry with paper towels.
- Wipe drippings from Dutch oven with paper towel.
- Return meat mixture to Dutch oven. Add tomatoes, beef broth, tomato paste, pepper, thyme, salt and bay leaf, stirring well.
- Bring mixture to a boil. Reduce heat and simmer, uncovered, 35 minutes, stirring occasionally.
- Add parsley; cook 5 minutes.
- Remove and discard bay leaf.
- Combine meat sauce with green pepper, brown sugar, cider vinegar and Worcestershire sauce in a saucepan.
- Bring to a boil; reduce heat and simmer, uncovered, 20 minutes or until almost all liquid is absorbed, stirring occasionally.
- Spoon meat mixture evenly onto bottom halves of buns. Top with remaining halves of buns.

Yield: 8 servings

Burgers Stuffed with Feta and Mushrooms

1   pound lean ground beef
2   tablespoons Worcestershire sauce
2   teaspoons garlic salt
1   tablespoon butter
8   ounces mushrooms, sliced
4   tablespoons crumbled feta cheese
4   sandwich buns

- Mix Worcestershire sauce and garlic salt thoroughly into ground beef. Form into 4 patties.
- In medium skillet over medium-high heat, melt butter. Add mushrooms and sauté until tender and lightly browned.
- Split patties in half horizontally. Place 1 tablespoon feta and 1 tablespoon mushrooms in the center of each patty. Replace top on each burger and seal edges well.
- Grill burgers 4 to 6 minutes per side or until desired doneness.
- Serve on rolls with any additional sautéed mushrooms and usual hamburger condiments.

Yield: 4 servings

Governor Robert W. Scott, former governor of North Carolina, is often remembered for his annual Possum Dinner, an annual affair for close friends. One year, "a guest of Mrs. Scott's who was in the Mansion the same evening was somewhat squeamish. The first course was soup served in the impressive Mansion china. The soup was creamy in color and in its midst floated two portions of meat. The guest left the soup in order to avoid eating possum but enjoyed the rest of the dinner which consisted of superbly roasted spare ribs, greens, field peas, candied sweet potatoes, hot rolls and a delicious persimmon pudding for dessert. Afterward she was shocked to discover that the possum was not in the soup but was the spare ribs!" *(The Governor,* Nancy Roberts, 1972)

Veal Chops with Wild Mushrooms

Rich and luscious, these veal chops will please the most discerning palate.

vegetable cooking spray
4 **(6-ounce) lean veal chops (¾-inch thick)**
½ **cup thinly sliced fresh shiitake mushrooms**
½ **cup thinly sliced fresh oyster mushrooms**
1 **cup canned chicken broth**
½ **cup evaporated skim milk**
¼ **cup (1 ounce) shredded Swiss cheese**
1 **teaspoon minced fresh thyme**

- Coat a large nonstick skillet with cooking spray; place over medium heat until hot.
- Add veal chops. Cook 2 to 3 minutes on each side or until browned.
- Remove chops from skillet. Drain and pat dry with paper towels. Set chops aside.
- Wipe drippings from skillet with a paper towel. Coat skillet with cooking spray. Place over medium-high heat until hot. Add mushrooms; sauté until tender.
- Remove mushrooms from skillet. Set aside.
- Return chops to skillet. Pour broth over chops. Bring to a boil. Cover, reduce heat and simmer 20 to 25 minutes or until chops are tender.
- Remove chops from skillet. Set aside and keep warm
- Add milk to liquid in skillet. Bring to a boil. Cook, stirring constantly, 1 minute or until thickened.
- Stir in mushrooms, cheese and thyme. Cook, stirring constantly, until cheese melts.
- Spoon sauce evenly over chops.
- Serve immediately.

Yield: 4 servings

Wine Recommendations: Red Burgundy or Oregon Pinot Noir

Margaux's Wild Mushroom Braised Osso Buco

Richard Hege, Margaux's Restaurant

6   (12-ounce) veal shanks (1½-inch thick)
    salt and pepper to taste
5   tablespoons olive oil, divided
2   cups white wine
1   quart chicken stock
1   quart veal stock
8   ounces portobello mushrooms, stemmed and sliced
8   ounces oyster mushrooms, stemmed
8   ounces shiitake mushrooms, stemmed
10 shallots, sliced
3   cloves garlic, minced
½   ounce fresh thyme, minced
¼   ounce fresh oregano, minced
¼   ounce fresh rosemary, minced

- Preheat oven to 350°F.
- Heat a large cast iron skillet over medium-high heat. Season veal shanks with salt and pepper.
- Place 2 tablespoons oil in skillet. Sear veal, two pieces at a time, until golden brown on both sides. Remove from pan. Repeat with remaining four pieces veal.
- Drain excess oil from pan and deglaze with white wine. Reduce by half.
- Combine chicken and veal stock and bring to a boil. Add wine from skillet to stocks.
- Place a cast iron skillet back on the stove and bring to medium heat.
- Put 3 tablespoons oil in pan and allow to warm. Add garlic and allow to slightly color. Add shallots and let cook for another 30 seconds. Add mushrooms and cook for 3 to 5 minutes until tender. Remove pan from heat.
- Choose a roasting pan with a heavy bottom that is large enough to accommodate all veal shanks in a single layer.
- Place veal shanks in roasting pan and add cooked mushrooms, stock and fresh herbs.
- Cover with foil or a tight fitting lid and place in oven.
- Cook for 2 hours or until meat is tender and begins to fall off the bone.
- Serve over risotto with asparagus, broth and fresh Parmesan cheese for garnish.

Yield: 6 servings

Risotto

2   cups arborio rice
9   cups chicken stock
1   onion, minced
1   carrot, minced
2   stalks celery, minced
1   cup white wine
½   cup grated Parmesan cheese
6   tablespoons olive oil

- Do not rinse the rice before cooking. Select a very heavy pot that heats evenly for cooking the rice.
- In another pot, bring the chicken stock to a boil, reduce the heat, and keep at a simmer.
- Heat olive oil in the heavy pot. Add onion, carrot, celery, and wine and sauté over low heat until soft and wine is reduced by half.
- Add the rice and cook, stirring, another 3 minutes.
- Slowly add 1 cup of the stock to the rice. Stir, and allow it to simmer. When the stock has been absorbed, add another cup of stock, stir and simmer. Repeat until all stock has been added and absorbed.
- Garnish with Parmesan cheese.

Ragoût of Veal

A sumptuous meal for two

½	pound lean, boneless veal
1	tablespoon all-purpose flour
½	teaspoon freshly ground pepper
	no stick olive oil cooking spray
1	teaspoon olive oil, divided
1	cup beef broth
¼	cup plus 2 tablespoons dry vermouth
¾	cup sliced leeks
¾	cup peeled, seeded and chopped tomato
1½	teaspoons chopped garlic
¼	teaspoon dried rosemary
3	bay leaves
1½	cups sliced fresh mushrooms
3	tablespoons chopped fresh parsley
3	tablespoons coarsely chopped pitted ripe olives
⅛	teaspoon salt

- Trim fat from veal; cut veal into 1-inch cubes.
- Combine flour and pepper in a shallow dish; dredge veal in flour mixture.
- Coat a medium nonstick skillet with cooking spray; add ½ teaspoon olive oil.
- Place over medium-high heat until hot. Add veal; cook until browned on all sides, stirring frequently.
- Drain and pat dry with paper towels. Wipe drippings from skillet with a paper towel.
- Add beef broth and vermouth to skillet; bring to a boil.
- Add veal, leeks, tomato, garlic, rosemary and bay leaves.
- Cover, reduce heat, and simmer 1 hour.
- Coat a small nonstick skillet with cooking spray; add remaining ½ teaspoon oil.
- Place over medium heat until hot.
- Add mushrooms; sauté 4 minutes or until tender.
- Add parsley, olives and salt; stir well.
- Add mushroom mixture to veal. Cook, covered, 15 minutes or until veal is tender.
- Remove and discard bay leaves.

Yield: 2 servings

Wine Recommendations: Red Côtes du Rhone, Red Corgieres or Spanish Rioja

To update an old saying, "The way to a person's heart is through her stomach." With so many men now enjoying kitchen duty, we can remove the gender identification from that statement to make it impartial. Ragoût of Veal is a memorable meal that anyone who enjoys being in the kitchen will be proud to create for his or her soul mate. Add fresh herbed rolls, a simple salad, and raspberries splashed with Grand Marnier for an unforgettable dinner. Don't forget the candles!

Veal with Capers

¼ cup all-purpose flour
1½ pounds veal scallops
    salt and pepper to taste
2 cups sliced mushrooms
4 teaspoons minced garlic
4 teaspoons minced shallots
¼ cup capers, drained
4 teaspoons Dijon mustard
½ lemon
½ cup cognac
1 cup Madeira wine
½ cup heavy cream
4 teaspoons chopped scallions

- Dredge veal in flour, being sure to shake off excess flour.
- Melt butter in large skillet over medium-high heat. Sauté veal until lightly browned. Add salt and pepper.
- Add mushrooms, garlic, shallots, capers and mustard to skillet. Add juice of ½ lemon.
- Pour cognac around the edge of the pan. Deglaze with Madeira.
- Remove veal to serving platter and keep warm.
- Add cream to skillet and reduce sauce.
- Just before removing sauce, add scallions.
- Pour sauce over veal and serve.

Yield: 4 servings

Capers are pungent little flower buds found on bushes native to the Mediterranean and parts of Asia. The buds are hand-picked and sun-dried then packed in vinegar or brine. If possible, select capers packed in brine and rinse before using to remove excess salt. Most capers are imported from Italy, Morocco and Greece; however, the petite nonpareil variety from the south of France are considered the finest.

Sherried Pork Roast

½ cup soy sauce
½ cup dry sherry
2 cloves garlic, minced
1 tablespoon dry mustard
1 teaspoon ground ginger
1 teaspoon dried thyme
1 4 to 5-pound pork loin roast boned, rolled and tied

- Combine soy sauce, sherry, garlic, mustard, ginger and thyme.
- Place roast in large clear plastic bag.
- Pour in marinade and seal bag tightly.
- Marinate 2 to 3 hours at room temperature or overnight in refrigerator.
- Remove meat from marinade.
- Place on rack in roasting pan.
- Roast uncovered at 325°F for 3 hours.
- Baste occasionally with marinade during last hour of roasting time.

Yield: 6 to 8 servings

While grilling the pork, add sweet potatoes to the grill for an incomparable accompaniment. Wash the potatoes and slice cross-wise into ½-inch thick rounds. Brush with melted butter and lay on the grill, broiling about 10 minutes on each side until brown and tender. Brush with melted butter when turning.

Pork Medallions with Dijon Cream Sauce

vegetable cooking spray
1½ pounds boneless pork chops (½-inch thick)
¾ cup milk
1½ tablespoons all-purpose flour, divided
3   tablespoons Dijon mustard
2   tablespoons dry white wine
¼ cup sour cream
⅛ teaspoon pepper
    fresh rosemary sprigs (optional)

- Coat grill rack with cooking spray and place on grill over medium-hot coals (350° to 400°F).
- Place chops on rack.
- Grill, covered, 10 to 15 minutes or until juices run clear, turning occasionally.
- Remove and keep warm
- Combine milk and 1 tablespoon flour in a saucepan, stirring until smooth.
- Cook over medium heat, stirring constantly, until thickened.
- Stir in mustard and wine; remove from heat.
- Combine remaining 1½ teaspoons flour and sour cream; add to milk mixture, stirring well.
- Stir in pepper.
- Serve sauce with chops.
- Garnish with rosemary, if desired.

Yield: 6 servings

Wine Recommendations: Unoaked Maconais White or Red Burgundy

Clove-Studded Ham
with Orange Rum Glaze

1   **precooked smoked ham with bone in (about 16 pounds)**
     whole cloves, enough to cover surface of ham
¼   **cup Dijon mustard**
1   **cup dark brown sugar**
2   **cups canned pineapple chunks, with syrup**
1   **cup bitter orange marmalade**
1   **cup dark rum**
3   **bunches red seedless grapes, cut into small bunches**

- Preheat oven to 350°F.
- Peel skin from ham and trim fat to leave a ¼ inch layer all around.
- With a sharp knife, score the fat in a diamond pattern.
- Place ham in a large shallow baking pan lined with foil.
- Insert cloves at points of diamonds.
- Spread mustard over ham with rubber spatula.
- Sprinkle sugar evenly over the top.
- Bake for 30 minutes.
- While ham is baking, heat pineapple chunks with syrup and marmalade together in a saucepan.
- Remove from heat and add rum.
- Remove ham from oven, pour sauce over ham, return to oven and bake for 1½ hours, basting frequently.
- Remove ham from oven and place on serving platter.
- Decorate top of ham with pineapple chunks from pan, held on by toothpicks.
- Arrange grapes around ham.
- Slice ham very thin and serve on biscuits or bread with a selection of your favorite mustards and chutney.

Yield: 25 to 30 servings

The juices from the ham mixed with the pineapple and seasonings make a great sauce. First remove the pineapple chunks with a slotted spoon and skim the fat off the juices. Add the defatted juices to the pineapple, heat, and serve alongside the ham in a bowl or gravy boat.

Peppered Pork Roast with Cherry Salsa

1   (3-pound) pork loin roast
1 to 2 tablespoons cracked black pepper
2   teaspoons garlic salt
        Cherry Salsa (recipe follows)

- Rub pepper and garlic salt onto all surfaces of pork roast.
- Place pork in a shallow pan and roast in a 350°F oven for one hour, or until thermometer registers 155 to 160°F.
- Let roast stand for 10 minutes before slicing.
- Serve with Cherry Salsa.

Cherry Salsa

⅓ cup chopped onion
⅓ cup chopped green bell pepper
⅓ cup chopped green chiles
⅓ cup dried cherries, chopped
⅓ cup red cherry jam
1½ tablespoons vinegar
1½ tablespoons chopped fresh cilantro

- Combine onion, green pepper, green chilies, dried cherries, jam, vinegar and cilantro.
- Mix well.
- Cover and chill several hours or overnight.

Yield: 6 servings

Wine Recommendations: Red Côtes du Rhone or California Syrah

"When he was about four years old, my husband started asking for 'Sunday gravy.' His mother fixed chicken gravy, pot roast gravy and country fried steak gravy trying to figure out what he meant by Sunday gravy, but to no avail. Finally, during a visit to Grandmother's house for Sunday dinner, he excitedly thanked her for fixing his favorite Sunday gravy. She had prepared a pork roast for dinner."

Grilled Pork Tenderloin with Honey-Beer Marinade

1	1½ to 2-pound boneless pork tenderloin
1	cup beer
½	cup honey
½	cup Dijon mustard
¼	cup vegetable oil
1	small onion, finely chopped
2	teaspoons rosemary leaves, crushed
3	cloves garlic, minced
1	teaspoon salt
½	teaspoon ground black pepper

- Place pork roast in 3-quart bowl or plastic container.
- Combine remaining ingredients and pour over pork.
- Cover and marinate at least one hour or overnight in refrigerator.
- Remove pork from marinade.
- Place on grill over coals or indirect flame.
- Grill or bake at 350°F, 30 to 45 minutes or until thermometer reaches 160°F, basting occasionally.
- Simmer leftover marinade 5-10 minutes and serve with roast.

Yield: 8 to 10 servings

Wine Recommendations: Barrel-Fermented Chardonnay or Young, Red Zinfandel

Since cutting a tenderloin to check doneness allows the escape of too many good juices, we suggest using a meat thermometer. Insert the thermometer in the thickest section of the tenderloin and make sure the internal temperature has reached 150°F to 160°F. This temperature range ensures that the meat is safe to eat but not dry and overcooked.

Marinade variation:

⅓ cup soy sauce

¾ teaspoon ginger

5 cloves garlic

3 tablespoons brown sugar

4 tablespoons honey

2 teaspoons dark sesame oil

- Marinate pork in soy sauce, ginger and garlic overnight.
- Combine remaining ingredients and cook over low heat until sugar dissolves.
- Baste tenderloin with honey sauce; serve remaining sauce on the side.

Honey-Lime Tenderloin Sandwich

So elegant, we hesitate to call it a sandwich.

2   **pounds pork tenderloin**
½   **cup freshly squeezed lime juice**
¼   **cup honey**
¼   **cup water**
2   **cloves garlic, minced**
8   **hard rolls, split**

- Combine lime juice, honey, water and garlic.
- Place pork tenderloins in plastic bag or utility dish.
- Add marinade, turning pork to coat.
- Seal bag securely or cover dish and marinate in refrigerator 6 hours or overnight, turning pork once.
- Drain, reserving marinade.
- Place pork on a rack in open roasting pan.
- Roast at 375°F for 35 to 40 minutes.
- Place reserved marinade in a small saucepan, cover and cook 5 minutes; keep warm.
- Carve pork into thin slices, place in a shallow serving dish.
- Pour warm marinade over pork.
- Serve sliced pork in rolls.

Yield: 8 servings

Wine Recommendations: California Tank-Fermented Sauvignon Blanc or Australian Chardonnay

Skillet-Barbecued Pork Chops

Looking for a new family favorite? Here it is!

	vegetable cooking spray
4	(4-ounce) lean boneless center-cut loin pork chops (¾-inch thick)
¼	cup minced onion
4	teaspoons minced garlic
1	cup water
½	cup tomato paste
¼	cup brown sugar
3	tablespoons soy sauce
4	teaspoons lemon juice
	dash of salt

- Coat a nonstick skillet with cooking spray; place over medium-high heat until hot.
- Add pork chops and cook 2 minutes on each side or until browned.
- Remove chops from skillet.
- Drain and pat dry with paper towels.
- Wipe drippings from skillet with a paper towel.
- Coat skillet with cooking spray; place over medium-high heat until hot.
- Add onion and garlic; sauté 1 minute.
- Add water and tomato paste, brown sugar, soy sauce, lemon juice and salt to skillet; stir well.
- Return chops to skillet; bring to a boil.
- Reduce heat and simmer, uncovered, 20 minutes or until tender.

Yield: 4 servings

Barbecued Spareribs with Caramelized Onions

3 cups sliced onions
3 cups ketchup
3 cups water
¼ cup salt
⅓ cup Worcestershire sauce
1½ cups cider vinegar
1½ cups brown mustard
2 tablespoons paprika
6 pounds spareribs

- Preheat oven to 350°F.
- Mix together all ingredients except spareribs.
- Cut and braise the ribs to seal juices.
- Pour sauce over ribs and cook 3 to 4 hours, stirring every hour.
- To grill, prepare the ribs as above and cook for 2 hours. Remove onions and set aside.
- Grill ribs over medium coals until well done.
- Serve with the warmed caramelized onions.

Yield: 6 to 8 servings

Fiesta Pork Tenderloin

Pork tenderloins are usually packaged in pairs. When putting tenderloins in baking dish, place fat and skinny sides opposite each other for more even cooking.

1½ pounds pork tenderloin
½ cup butter
½ cup soy sauce
⅛ teaspoon ground cumin
⅛ teaspoon ground ginger
⅛ teaspoon ground coriander
¼ teaspoon hot sauce
1 tablespoon lemon juice
2 cloves garlic, minced

- Place tenderloin in a 13 x 9-inch baking dish.
- Combine remaining ingredients in a saucepan and bring to a boil.
- Pour marinade over pork tenderloin and marinate overnight.
- Bake at 325°F for 45 to 60 minutes, covered with foil.
- Can also be grilled over low to medium heat for 12 to 16 minutes per side.

Yield: 4 servings

Wine Recommendations: California Viognier or Australian Chardonnay

Slow Cooker Pig Pickin' Barbecue

An everyday version of the Carolina Pig Pickin' featured in our entertaining section

1⅓ cups apple cider vinegar
⅔ cup ketchup
½ teaspoon Worcestershire sauce
½ teaspoon cayenne pepper (or more to taste)
½ ounce crushed red pepper flakes
1 ounce honey
⅓ teaspoon salt
⅓ teaspoon ground black pepper
    juice from 1 lemon wedge
    pinch of ground coriander
1 3 to 5 pound pork roast

- Place all ingredients except pork roast in a large stockpot and heat until well combined.
- Remove from heat and let stand 2 to 3 hours at room temperature.
- Cook pork roast in slow cooker on high for 6 hours.
- Add barbecue sauce. Cook 30 minutes more on low.
- Slice pork across the grain and serve immediately.

Yield: 6 to 8 servings

Local journalist Dennis Rogers refers to his favorite food as "Holy Grub." He writes in his column, "The secret of barbecue is in the sauce. You would no more ask a barbecue man for his sauce than you would for the use of his dog, his motorcycle, or his wife..."
(The News & Observer, April, 1996)

Caribbean Pork Chops

4 pork loin chops, 1 inch thick
1 cup unsweetened pineapple juice
⅔ cup dry sherry
2 tablespoons brown sugar
½ teaspoon dried rosemary leaves, crushed
1 clove garlic, minced
    no stick cooking spray

- Combine all ingredients except pork chops. Mix well.
- Place chops in a shallow dish. Pour marinade over chops.
- Cover and refrigerate overnight, turning meat occasionally.
- Remove pork chops from marinade.
- Place on rack of broiling pan that has been coated with a non-stick spray.
- Broil or grill 6 to 9 minutes on each side, turning and basting once with marinade.

Yield: 4 servings

Wine Recommendations: California Chardonnay or Beaujolais

The marriage of fruit and meat in recipes is a centuries-old tradition, especially in Oriental, African and Middle Eastern cultures. This marinade combines an outstanding mingling of flavors.

Grilled Leg of Lamb with Rosemary and Red Wine

Your guests will feel like royalty when served grilled lamb.

This scrumptious dish deserves a lovely presentation. Slice lamb on the diagonal. For each serving, garnish with a sprig of rosemary and a spoonful of chutney and mustard on either side. Voilà!

1	leg of lamb
1	cup freshly squeezed lemon juice
1	cup dry red wine
6	tablespoons chopped fresh or 1 tablespoon dried rosemary
2	tablespoons finely chopped garlic
2	tablespoons hot red pepper flakes
3	teaspoons salt
1½	teaspoons freshly ground black pepper
1½	cups olive oil

- Ask your butcher to butterfly leg of lamb into 2 parcels.
- Mix the marinade ingredients in a food processor.
- Place lamb in glass baking dish and pour marinade over lamb.
- Marinate overnight, turning in the morning.
- Grill lamb over hot coals or gas grill about 10 minutes per side.

Yield: 8 to 10 servings

Wine Recommendations: Bandol Rouge or Cline Mourvedre

Minted Lamb Chops
with Jalapeño Chutney

8   lamb loin chops
1   cup loosely packed fresh mint leaves
1   cup loosely packed fresh cilantro
12 large garlic cloves, peeled
3   tablespoons ground cumin
1   tablespoon freshly ground black pepper
2   teaspoons salt
1   teaspoon cayenne pepper
½   cup olive oil
    Jalapeño Chutney (see sidebar)

- In food processor combine 1 cup mint, 1 cup cilantro, 12 cloves of garlic, cumin, coriander, pepper, 2 teaspoons salt and 1 teaspoon cayenne pepper.
- Process, stopping occasionally to scrape sides of bowl, until well blended.
- With processor running, slowly pour olive oil through feed tube.
- Continue processing until mixture is smooth.
- Place lamb in glass pan and spread evenly with marinade mixture.
- Cover with plastic wrap and chill overnight.
- Preheat grill to medium-high.
- Grill 12 to 15 minutes per side or until done to your taste.
- Serve with Jalapeño Chutney.

Yield: 8 servings

Wine Recommendations: Bandol Rouge, California Syrah or Australian Shiraz.

Jalapeño Chutney

5 cups loosely packed
   fresh mint leaves
1 cup loosely packed fresh
   cilantro
1 small onion, quartered
2 medium cloves garlic,
   peeled and quartered
1 medium jalapeño
   pepper, seeded and
   quartered or to taste
2 tablespoons fresh lemon
   juice
½ teaspoon salt
½ teaspoon dried dill weed
½ teaspoon paprika
½ teaspoon cayenne
   pepper

- In food processor combine 2 cups mint, 1 cup cilantro, onion, 2 cloves garlic, jalapeño, lemon juice, salt, dill, paprika and cayenne pepper.
- Process until well blended.
- Place in tightly covered jar and store in refrigerator up to 1 month.
- Serve leftover chutney as a dip with pita wedges.

Mediterranean Shish Kebabs

1	pound lamb, cut in cubes; use sirloin or leg
2	teaspoons red wine vinegar
½	teaspoon ground cumin
½	teaspoon ground coriander
¼	teaspoon ground cinnamon
2	garlic cloves, chopped
	salt and pepper to taste
2	teaspoons olive oil
8 to 12	mushrooms
1	red bell pepper, cut into 1 to 1½-inch pieces
1	green bell pepper, cut into 1 to 1½-inch pieces
5	cherry tomatoes
1	medium onion, sliced into wedges

- Put lamb in glass casserole just large enough to hold in 1 layer.
- In small bowl combine wine vinegar, cumin, coriander, cinnamon, mustard, garlic, salt and pepper and olive oil.
- Pour over lamb cubes and stir well.
- Cover and marinate in refrigerator for several hours.
- Return to room temperature before cooking.
- Thread lamb cubes on skewers alternating with vegetables.
- Put on hot grill or under broiler about 2 to 3 inches from heat.
- Cook about 5 to 6 minutes, turning occasionally and brushing with marinade until browned and desired doneness is reached.

Yield: 6 to 8 servings

Wine Recommendations: Languedoc Red, Gigondas or California Rhone blend.

Zesty Venison Chili

Outstanding taste and healthier than traditional chili recipes

4	large onions, thinly sliced or finely chopped
2	cloves garlic, finely chopped
2	tablespoons vegetable oil or olive oil
2	pounds ground venison
2	tablespoons chili powder
1	teaspoon ground coriander
½	teaspoon ground cumin
	dash of hot sauce
1	cup beer
½	cup tomato paste
1½	teaspoons salt

- Sauté onions and garlic in oil until they are limp and golden.
- Add ground venison, stirring until browned.
- Add the rest of the ingredients and blend.
- Reduce heat and simmer for 45 minutes to 1 hour.
- Taste for seasonings and correct.
- Add more beer if mixture gets too dry.
- Cook until well thickened and rich in flavor.

Yield: 6 servings

Wine Recommendations: Chianti Classico, Big Spanish Rioja or Châteauneuf-du-Pape.

For nine years, two Raleigh couples have hosted incredible, wild game feasts at Robertson's Mill Pond. Hunters, local and from out of state, contribute more than 200 pounds of dove, pheasant, duck, swan, quail, goose, boar, bear and venison. It is an extraordinary tasting experience.

Grilled Rosemary-Crusted Pizzas with Sausage, Bell Peppers, Onions and Cheese

Entertain your guests by letting them top and grill their own pizzas.

Dough

1   **cup warm water (105 to 115°F)**
1   **tablespoon sugar**
1   **envelope dry yeast**
3   **tablespoons olive oil**
3   **cups (or more) all-purpose flour**
1½ **teaspoons salt**
1   **tablespoon chopped fresh rosemary**

Toppings

¾   **cup olive oil**
6   **tablespoons balsamic vinegar**
3   **tablespoons chopped fresh rosemary**
1   **pound hot Italian sausages**
2   **yellow or red bell peppers, cored, quartered lengthwise**
1   **large red onion, peeled, cut through root end into ½-inch thick wedges**
    salt and pepper to taste

Final Ingredients

2   **cups grated mozzarella cheese**
½   **cup freshly grated Parmesan cheese**
2   **cups crumbled chilled soft fresh goat cheese, such as Montrachet**
4   **plum tomatoes, halved, seeded and chopped**
¾   **cup chopped green onion tops**

- To prepare dough, combine water and sugar in food processor equipped with a metal blade.
- Sprinkle yeast over and let stand until foamy, about 10 minutes.
- Add oil, then 3 cups flour and salt. Process until dough comes together, about 1 minute.
- Turn dough out onto floured work surface. Sprinkle with rosemary.
- Knead until dough is smooth and elastic, adding more flour as needed, by the tablespoons if dough is sticky, about 5 minutes.
- Lightly oil large bowl. Add dough; turn to coat with oil.
- Cover bowl with plastic, then towel.
- Let stand in warm draft-free area until dough doubles, about 1 hour.
- Punch dough, knead dough in bowl until smooth, about 2 minutes.

(continued on next page)

Grilled Rosemary-Crusted Pizzas *continued*

- To prepare toppings, whisk together oil, balsamic vinegar and rosemary in a medium bowl. Stir in sausages.
- Let vinaigrette stand 15 minutes at room temperature or refrigerate 2 hours.
- Prepare barbecue to medium heat.
- Arrange sausages, peppers and onion on baking sheet. Sprinkle with salt and pepper.
- Grill sausages until cooked through, about 12 minutes, and peppers and onion until slightly charred and crisp-tender, about 8 minutes, turning and basting occasionally.
- Transfer sausages and vegetables to cutting board. Cut sausages into 1 to 2-inch pieces and peppers into thin strips.
- For final preparation, add coals to barbecue if necessary.
- Divide dough into 4 equal pieces. Stretch out each piece on a floured surface to a 9-inch round.
- Place 2 dough rounds on grill.
- Grill over medium heat until top of dough puffs and underside is crisp, about 3 minutes. Turn rounds over.
- Grill 1 minute. Transfer to baking sheet with well-grilled side up.
- Repeat with remaining 2 dough rounds.
- Sprinkle each with ¼ of sausage, peppers and onions, then with ¼ of goat cheese, tomatoes and green onions.
- Drizzle each with 1½ tablespoons vinaigrette.
- Using a large spatula, return 2 pizzas to grill. Close grill or cover pizzas loosely with foil.
- Grill until cheeses melt and dough is cooked through and browned, using tongs to rotate pizzas for even cooking about 5 minutes.
- Transfer to plates and repeat grilling for remaining 2 pizzas.

Yield: 4 pizzas

Wine Recommendations: Red Zinfandel or Italian Barbera

Poultry and Meats

Linda Turner

Provence Luncheon
oil on canvas, 1998

From the private collection of
M. Eleanor Fisher, Raleigh, NC.

Side Dishes and Pasta

Vidalia Onion Casserole

Sweet southern onions dress up in a classic casserole

2	pounds Vidalia onions, coarsely chopped
¼	cup butter
3	eggs
1	cup sour cream
3	tablespoons all-purpose flour
	salt and pepper to taste
2	dashes hot sauce
¾	cup grated Parmesan cheese

- Sauté onion in butter over medium-high heat, 10 to 15 minutes or until tender.
- Preheat oven to 350°F.
- Beat eggs in a medium sized bowl and add sour cream, flour, salt, pepper and hot sauce, stirring to mix well. Add onions and combine thoroughly.
- Turn onion mixture into a greased 2-quart casserole. Top with Parmesan cheese and bake for 20 minutes, or until golden brown.

Yield: 6 servings

"Southerners seem to like onions as much anybody, and a lot better than most," according to John Edgerton in *Southern Food.* And, one could easily argue that the favorite onion of southerners is the Vidalia, named after the Georgia town where these sweet, yellow onions are the major agricultural product. Since the Vidalia onion derives its distinctive taste from the soil in which it is grown, a true Vidalia cannot be duplicated. Vidalias are in season in the summer. Substitute Maui or Walla Walla onions at other times.

Grated Sweet Potato Custard

2½	cups milk
5	medium sweet potatoes
1½	cups sugar
2	teaspoons cinnamon
3	eggs
½	cup butter, divided

- Put milk in 2½-quart casserole dish.
- Grate sweet potatoes in food processor, adding to casserole dish until milk just covers the sweet potatoes.
- Preheat oven to 300°F.
- In a separate bowl, beat eggs well, adding sugar gradually while beating. Stir cinnamon into sugar-egg mixture. Add egg mixture to sweet potatoes and milk and stir to mix well.
- Dot casserole generously with butter and bake for 2 hours or until firmly set.

Yield: 10 servings

"My grandmother called this recipe 'likker pudding' for the pot likker (liquid resulting from cooking vegetables or meats) which is left in the bottom of the casserole. This was always our Thanksgiving sweet potato dish."
To avoid fights over the pot likker, bake and serve in ramekins so that everyone gets a taste.

Noted Tarheel newscaster Charles Kuralt was asked by *Bon Appétit* magazine to describe a typical Christmas dinner from his North Carolina childhood. He replied, "Everything we ate came from what was raised on my grandparents' farm. The main course was roast pork-usually over-cooked-served with sweet potatoes and homemade preserves. My favorite memory is of the Christmas Day I snuck into the kitchen and ate a whole jar of spiced apples."

Lowfat Sweet Potato Soufflé

Rest assured, they won't know it's lowfat unless you confess.

	no stick cooking spray
3	cups fresh cooked sweet potatoes
1/3	cup sugar
1	teaspoon vanilla extract
2	tablespoons all-purpose flour
4	egg whites

Topping

3	tablespoons all-purpose flour
1/2	cup brown sugar
2	tablespoons margarine
1/2	cup chopped pecans

- Preheat oven to 350°F.
- Spray 1½-quart casserole dish with nonstick cooking spray.
- In mixing bowl or food processor, smooth together sweet potato, sugar, vanilla and 2 tablespoons flour.
- Beat egg whites on high speed until soft peaks form. Fold egg whites into sweet potato mixture and spoon into prepared casserole dish.
- Combine 3 tablespoons flour and brown sugar and cut in margarine with a pastry blender until mixture is crumbly. Stir in pecans and sprinkle over sweet potato mixture.
- Bake for 30 minutes or until topping is golden brown.

Yield: 8 servings

Good Luck Black-Eyed Peas

A spicy version of a southern favorite, and you don't have to soak the peas!

1   tablespoon olive oil
¼   cup finely chopped onion
2   ounces country ham, chopped
1   tablespoon minced garlic
1½ cups dried black-eyed peas
¼   teaspoon chili powder
¼   teaspoon ground cumin
⅛   teaspoon cayenne pepper
⅛   teaspoon crushed red pepper flakes
⅛   teaspoon ground coriander
4   cups chicken stock
1   teaspoon salt
    freshly ground black pepper to taste

- Heat oil in 2-quart heavy saucepan over high heat. Add onions and sauté 1 minute.
- Add ham, garlic, peas, chili powder, cumin, cayenne pepper, red pepper flakes and coriander and sauté 1 additional minute.
- Add chicken stock and bring to a boil. Reduce heat to medium, cover and cook for 15 minutes. Uncover and stir. Recover, reduce heat and simmer 15 minutes more.
- Add salt and pepper. Stir, cover and simmer another 10 minutes or until peas are tender.

Note: For an even spicier version, use 2 ounces tasso instead of country ham.

Yield: 3 cups

Collard Greens

2 bunches collard greens
6 pieces market style bacon
1 large onion

- Fry bacon in a large skillet until crisp. Remove bacon and reserve for another use.
- Sauté onion in bacon fat until translucent. Add freshly washed collards with water clinging to the leaves and cover.
- Simmer over medium heat for about 1 hour, stirring often until done.
- Chop collards and season with salt and pepper.

Sautéed Squash Medley

As squash grows in over-abundance in the garden, it's time for inventive Squash Medley.

3   **tablespoons olive oil**
1   **pound zucchini, thinly sliced**
1   **pound yellow crookneck squash, thinly sliced**
1   **medium yellow onion, thinly sliced**
1   **clove garlic, minced**
½   **cup chopped scallions**
1   **teaspoon freshly ground pepper**
¼   **cup V-8 Juice**
1   **teaspoon sugar**

- Sauté squashes, onion and garlic in oil over medium-low heat, about 5 minutes.
- Add scallions, pepper, juice and sugar and mix well. Cover and simmer over low heat, stirring occasionally, until just tender, approximately 5 more minutes. Serve immediately.

Yield: 6 servings

New Squash Fritters

Patties of zucchini flavored with spicy seasonings

Your antique salt bowl and silver salt spoon are just the right size for the cocktail sauce or spicy mustard that will add zing to squash fritters.

4   **medium zucchini squash**
1   **cup plain dry bread crumbs**
1   **egg, beaten**
2   **tablespoons butter, melted**
1   **tablespoon Old Bay seasoning**
4   **tablespoons all-purpose flour**
1   **small onion, finely chopped**
    vegetable oil for frying (½ inch in cast iron skillet)

- Wash and grate unpeeled squash to measure 2½ cups.
- Combine grated squash with all remaining ingredients except oil, mixing until well blended. Shape into patties about 2 inches in diameter.
- Heat about ½ inch of oil in heavy cast iron skillet over medium-high heat until drops of water sizzle when dropped into the oil.
- Fry patties in oil until golden brown on each side, turning only once, about 3 minutes on each side. Serve hot.

Yield: 6 servings

Asparagus and Prosciutto Bundles

Welcome spring with a fancy preparation of asparagus.

30	spears fresh pencil-thin asparagus
6	slices prosciutto ham
½	cup grated Parmesan cheese
¾	teaspoon freshly ground pepper
2	cloves garlic, minced
¼	cup butter, melted

- Preheat oven to 350°F.
- Grease 13x9x2-inch baking dish and set aside.
- Blanch asparagus 4 minutes until crisp-tender, then immediately submerge in ice water. Pat asparagus dry.
- Wrap 5 asparagus spears in each slice of prosciutto. Place bundles, seam side down, in prepared baking dish. Sprinkle Parmesan cheese across center of each bundle and season generously with pepper.
- Combine garlic with melted butter and drizzle over bundles. Bake 10 to 15 minutes or until cheese is melted and light brown and asparagus is heated through. The prepared bundles may be kept in the refrigerator for up to 2 hours prior to baking.

Yield: 6 servings

Baked Squash with Parmesan, Onion and Bacon

1	bacon slice, chopped
1	small onion, thinly sliced
2	pounds butternut squash, seeded and thinly sliced
	salt and pepper to taste
3	tablespoons freshly grated Parmesan cheese

- Preheat oven to 350°F.
- Mix bacon and onion in 13x9x2-inch baking dish. Arrange squash slices on top of onion mixture. Season with salt and pepper to taste. Cover dish with foil and bake until squash is almost tender, about 30 minutes.
- Increase oven temperature to 400°F. Uncover squash and continue baking until tender, about 10 minutes.
- Sprinkle with Parmesan cheese and bake until cheese melts, about 10 minutes more.

Yield: 4 servings

"My mother had a wide-mouthed Ball jar designated 'the asparagus jar.' Her storage method keeps asparagus fresh for up to two weeks."

To keep asparagus fresh, store it in the refrigerator standing up in a large jar partially filled with water. Place a damp paper towel over the top of the stalks, cover with a plastic bag and secure the bag with a rubber band.

Once the early southern settlers established swine herds, pork was consumed at every meal, either in the form of meat, lard, chitterlings, knuckles, livers or sausages. According to the *Smithsonian Folklife Cookbook,* "Many foods were either cooked in lard or flavored with it. Corn bread became crackling bread when cracklings were added for flavor. Pork grease added zest to vegetables, which many Southerners considered inedible if they did not contain enough grease to 'wink back' at the dinner guest."

"The tastes of my childhood are sweetened with memories of the honey my grandfather used to harvest from the bee hives on his farm. When he tended the hives, he stoked his pipe with tobacco and puffed himself into a cloud of blue smoke. The bees never touched him. He told me the smoke made them sleepy. My cousins and I would watch from our safe post inside the house until he pulled one of the honeycomb compartments from the hive. Then we dashed to the back porch to watch Granddaddy extract the honey. He put the comb in a contraption that looked like a giant washtub with a wringer in the center. He let us take turns cranking the wringer until the honey was squeezed out of the comb. As a treat we were given a little piece of the comb, dripping with honey and warm from the humid summer weather."

Honey-Ginger Green Beans

Add to your "Honey Do" List: "Honey, do make these Ginger Green Beans."

4	tablespoons olive oil
1	pound fresh green beans, trimmed, cut into 2-inch lengths
6	ounces fresh mushrooms, quartered
¼	cup soy sauce
1	tablespoon minced garlic
1	tablespoon honey
2	teaspoons peeled, minced fresh ginger
3	tablespoons chopped walnuts

- Heat oil in heavy, large skillet over high heat until hot but not smoking. Reduce to medium heat, add green beans and mushrooms and sauté until beans are crisp tender, about 5 minutes.
- Add soy sauce, garlic, honey and ginger. Bring to a boil over medium heat and cook until sauce thickens slightly and coats vegetables, about 2 minutes.
- Transfer to serving dish, sprinkle with chopped walnuts and serve hot.

Yield: 4 servings

Marinated Asparagus

Luncheons are prime occasions for chilled asparagus in a delicious marinade.

1	pound fresh asparagus spears
1	green onion, finely chopped
3	tablespoons olive oil
3	tablespoons balsamic vinegar
1	tablespoon Italian seasoning
2	tablespoons diced pimento
¼	teaspoon salt
¼	teaspoon white pepper

- Snap off tough ends of asparagus. Remove scales from stalks with a knife or vegetable peeler, if desired. Blanch asparagus 4 minutes until crisp-tender, then immediately submerge in ice water. Pat asparagus dry and place in shallow baking dish.
- Combine all remaining ingredients in a small bowl, stirring well. Pour over asparagus, cover and chill overnight. Drain any excess marinade before serving. Allow to sit at room temperature for 15 minutes before serving.

Yield: 4 servings

Bombay Green Beans

A spicy side dish for plain fish, grilled or broiled

2 inches peeled fresh ginger, chopped coarsely
10 whole garlic cloves, peeled
½ cup chopped onion
1¼ cups water, divided
4 tablespoons vegetable oil
3 teaspoons whole cumin seeds
2 teaspoons ground coriander seeds
2 medium tomatoes, peeled, seeded and finely chopped
1½ pounds green beans, trimmed and cut into 2-inch lengths
1 teaspoon salt
½ teaspoon cayenne pepper
1-2 teaspoons freshly ground pepper
3 tablespoons lemon juice

- Process ginger, garlic, onion and ¼ cup water in a food processor until a smooth paste is formed.
- Heat the oil in a large heavy skillet over medium heat until hot, but not smoking. Add cumin seeds and stir for 30 seconds. Add the ginger-garlic mixture; stir and cook for 2 minutes. Stir in the coriander.
- Add the tomatoes and cook for 2 minutes, mashing the tomatoes with the back of a slotted spoon.
- Add the beans, salt and remaining 1 cup of water. Bring to a boil, cover, reduce heat to low and simmer for 10 minutes or until beans are tender.
- Remove cover, stir in lemon juice and freshly ground pepper. Increase heat and boil away the remaining liquid, stirring the beans frequently. Serve immediately.

Yield: 6 servings

One positive note on the progression of southern cooking is that we no longer have to simmer our green beans until they are limp, dull and lifeless. Bombay Green Beans are redolent with spices and brightened with red tomatoes.

Menus can become predictable. Cookouts feature a monotonous parade of hot dogs, hamburgers, potato chips and ketchup-laden baked beans. Adding something new to the spread, without changing the comfort of familiar favorites, can turn you from host to hero. Serve bratwurst on dark bread, grilled portobello mushrooms on kaiser rolls, sweet potato chips, and Baked Butter Beans to your cookout crowd and revel in the compliments.

Flavored butters add the crowning touch to simply prepared vegetables. Add them to vegetables before presentation or make the most of those neat butter molds you found at the flea market. Guests will admire your excellent find and be as generous or as stingy as they choose with butter.

Maitre D'Hotel Butter

½ cup butter, softened

2 teaspoons fresh lemon juice

2 teaspoons chopped fresh parsley

½ teaspoon chopped fresh thyme

¼ teaspoon salt

⅛ teaspoon pepper

- **Combine all ingredients in food processor. Process until fluffy. Chill. Serve with green beans, peas or carrots.**

Baked Butter Beans

An unbeatable alternative to traditional baked beans

3 cups fresh butter beans or 2 (10-ounce) packages frozen baby limas
½ pound bacon, diced
1 cup finely chopped onion
½ cup finely chopped red bell pepper
1½ cups shredded Monterey Jack cheese
¼ teaspoon white pepper
1 teaspoon Worcestershire sauce

- Cook beans in 1½ cups boiling salted water until tender (30 minutes for fresh, 15 minutes for frozen). Drain beans and set aside in mixing bowl.
- Fry diced bacon over medium-high heat until done, but not too crisp. Remove with slotted spoon and drain bacon on a paper towel. Reserve 3 tablespoons of bacon drippings in skillet.
- Preheat oven to 350°F.
- In reserved drippings, sauté onion and bell pepper until tender. Pour into mixing bowl with beans. Add bacon, cheese, white pepper and Worcestershire sauce and toss lightly so as not to mash beans, but so that ingredients are mixed well.
- Spoon into greased 2-quart casserole dish and bake 25 minutes or until lightly browned.

Yield: 8 servings

Broccoli with Balsamic Butter

This butter dresses a bounty of vegetables.

1 large head broccoli, trimmed of leaves and tough end of stems
2 tablespoons balsamic vinegar
2 tablespoons dry red wine
6 tablespoons butter

- Separate broccoli into spears and steam 5 minutes or until just tender.
- Combine vinegar and wine and cook over medium-high heat until reduced by half. Reduce heat and add butter, one tablespoon at a time, whisking until sauce is creamy.
- Pour sauce over broccoli, toss to coat and serve immediately.

Yield: 6 servings

Drunken Beans

Beer and jalapeños add a punch to baked beans.

¾	**pound bacon slices, chopped**
3	**large onions, chopped**
6	**(15-ounce) cans pinto beans, drained**
3	**(12-ounce) bottles dark beer**
3	**cups beef stock**
3	**large tomatoes, peeled, seeded and chopped**
1½	**cups fresh chopped cilantro**
3	**jalapeño peppers, seeded and finely chopped**
1	**tablespoon sugar**
	salt and pepper to taste

- Cook bacon in large pot over medium-high heat until crisp, reserving bacon drippings in pot. Transfer cooked bacon to bowl using a slotted spoon.
- Add onions to bacon drippings and sauté 15 minutes or until tender.
- Add bacon, beans, beer, stock, tomatoes, cilantro, jalapeño pepper and sugar to onions in pot and bring to a boil over medium-high heat. Season with salt and pepper to taste.
- Reduce heat and simmer uncovered until slightly thickened, about 1½ hours.

Yield: 12 cups

The ubiquitous covered dish supper serves a variety of functions... church social, supper club, block party, informal office party, family reunion and board get-together. Relish the opportunity to bring only one dish yet to taste dozens of others.

Garlic Broccoli

Subtle Asian influences complement pork tenderloin or fish.

1½	**pounds fresh broccoli spears**
1½	**teaspoons dark sesame oil**
1½	**teaspoons vegetable oil**
1	**teaspoon dried crushed red pepper**
2	**cloves garlic, minced**
¼	**cup soy sauce**
1	**tablespoon sugar**
1	**tablespoon lemon juice**
1	**tablespoon water**

- Steam broccoli 5 minutes or until just tender. Remove from heat but keep warm.
- Heat sesame and vegetable oils in small pan until hot but not smoking. Remove from heat. Add red pepper to heated oils and let stand 10 minutes.
- Add remaining ingredients to oil, stirring to dissolve sugar. Toss broccoli spears gently with oil mixture. Reheat briefly in a 350°F oven if necessary. Serve hot.

Yield: 6 servings

Cabbage and apples are plentiful in September, October and November. Select them from a farmers market and not only get locally grown, quality products at a good (even negotiable) price, but take a moment and get to know the growers. Visit the State Farmers Market, 201 Agricultural Street, Raleigh, featuring produce, crafts, jams, cut flowers, garden center, fish market and two restaurants. Hours: Monday-Friday, 5 a.m.-6 p.m.; Sunday, 1 p.m.-6 p.m. 733-7417.

Red Cabbage with Apples

A cool weather accompaniment for marinated veal medallions or venison steaks

½ cup water
½ cup red wine
1 head red cabbage, shredded
1 small bay leaf
1 medium onion, peeled and studded with 4 whole cloves
3 tart apples, peeled, cored and shredded
3 tablespoons butter
1 tablespoon all-purpose flour
¼ cup packed brown sugar
⅓ cup apple cider vinegar
½ teaspoon salt
¼ teaspoon freshly ground black pepper
½ teaspoon ground allspice

- Bring water and wine to a boil in a large, heavy stockpot. Add cabbage, bay leaf and onion. Cover and cook over medium heat 10 minutes.
- Stir in apples and continue cooking, covered, 10 more minutes.
- While the cabbage and apples are cooking, melt butter in small saucepan and whisk in flour, forming a smooth paste. Stir in brown sugar, vinegar, salt, pepper and allspice and cook until slightly thickened.
- Pour sugar mixture over cabbage and toss to coat. Continue to cook over medium heat 10 minutes, uncovered. Remove and discard onion and bay leaf. Transfer cabbage and apples to serving dish. Serve warm.

Yield: 8 servings

Carrots with Horseradish

Liven up pork chops with zesty carrots

1½ **pounds baby carrots**
½ **cup mayonnaise**
1   **tablespoon prepared horseradish (or more to taste)**
½ **small onion, finely chopped**
½ **teaspoon salt**
½ **teaspoon white pepper**
1   **tablespoon butter, melted**
¼ **cup plain dry bread crumbs**

- Cook carrots in boiling water 10 minutes or until barely tender. Drain and place in greased 1-quart casserole.
- Preheat oven to 350°F.
- Combine mayonnaise, horseradish, onion, salt and pepper and spread evenly on top of carrots.
- Stir bread crumbs into melted butter until just moistened. Sprinkle on top of mayonnaise mixture and bake for 30 minutes.

Yield: 6 servings

Julienne of Carrots and Zucchini

Crisp-tender vegetables with a hint of herbs

4   **carrots, washed and peeled**
4   **medium zucchini, washed**
3   **tablespoons butter**
1   **tablespoon fresh basil leaves**
1   **tablespoon fresh rosemary**
    salt and pepper to taste
1   **lemon**

- Cut carrots and zucchini into ¼-inch thin strips, about 2 inches in length.
- In large, no stick frying pan, melt butter until slightly bubbling. Add carrots first and sauté 5 minutes or until crisp-tender. Sprinkle carrots with basil, rosemary, salt and pepper. Add zucchini, stirring to coat all vegetables with spices, and cook about 2 minutes more, but do not allow zucchini to get mushy.
- Remove carrots and zucchini from pan and transfer to serving dish. Squeeze lemon so that juice is sprinkled over vegetables. Serve immediately.

Yield: 4 servings

Dijon Butter

½ **cup butter softened**
2 **teaspoons Dijon mustard**
2 **teaspoons fresh lemon juice**
2 **teaspoons chopped fresh parsley**
¼ **teaspoon salt**
⅛ **teaspoon pepper**
- **Combine all ingredients in food processor. Process until fluffy. Chill. Serve on zucchini, broccoli or asparagus.**

Red Onion Butter

- 1 **stick plus 2 tablespoons butter**
- 1 **medium red onion, finely diced**
- 2 **tablespoons dry red wine**
- ¼ **teaspoon salt**

- **Sauté onion in 2 tablespoons butter until soft. Add red wine and cook until liquid evaporates. Allow to cool completely.**
- **Combine with remaining butter and salt in food processor. Process until fluffy. Chill. Serve with fresh corn or asparagus.**

You may substitute good quality frozen corn for 'fresh here, taking extra precaution not to over-cook.

Chile Corn Casserole

Corn gets spicy in a Mexican-inspired casserole.

4	**cups fresh white corn kernels, such as Silver Queen**
1	**cup grated sharp cheddar cheese**
1	**(8-ounce) package cream cheese**
1	**(7-ounce) can diced green chiles**
2	**teaspoons chili powder**
2	**teaspoons ground cumin**
½	**cup herb-seasoned stuffing mix**

- Preheat oven to 350°F.
- Mix corn, cheeses, chiles and spices until well combined.
- Place corn mixture into a greased 1½-quart baking dish. Sprinkle with stuffing mix.
- Bake for 30 minutes or until firmly set.

Yield: 6 servings

Summer Corn Pudding

A favorite of children for generations, sweet corn in a creamy but firm pudding

7	**ears fresh corn, any variety**
1	**egg, separated**
2	**tablespoons sugar**
2	**tablespoons butter, softened**
1	**teaspoon salt**
¼	**cup milk**
1	**teaspoon vanilla extract**

- Preheat oven to 350°F.
- Cut corn from cob about ⅔ down the kernel to measure a total of 3 cups.
- Combine corn, egg yolk, sugar, salt, butter, milk and vanilla, stirring until well combined and butter is smooth and even throughout.
- In a small bowl, beat egg white until stiff but not dry. Fold egg white into corn mixture.
- Spoon mixture into a lightly greased 8-inch square baking pan. Bake 35 to 40 minutes or until set. Allow to sit and firm up at least 5 minutes before serving.

Yield: 4 servings

Fresh Corn Fritters

Summer wouldn't be the same without corn-filled fritters sizzling on the stove.

6	ears fresh corn, any variety
3	eggs, separated, reserving yolks and whites
¼	cup all-purpose flour
½	teaspoon baking powder
¾	teaspoon salt
¼	teaspoon pepper

- Cut corn off cob, about ⅔ the depth of the kernel and scrape off cob into a medium sized mixing bowl.
- Separate eggs and set aside whites. Beat yolks and add to corn, stirring to mix well. Sift flour, baking powder, salt and pepper into corn mixture and mix together well.
- Beat egg whites until stiff peaks form. Fold egg whites gently into corn mixture.
- Drop corn mixture by spoonfuls onto hot greased griddle. Fry each fritter until brown, turn and brown other side. Place fritters on plate in warm oven until all are done and ready to serve.

Yield: 8 servings

Roasted Rosemary Potatoes

Substitute other herbs to create roasted thyme or tarragon potatoes if you prefer.

3	pounds small red potatoes
3	tablespoons olive oil
1	teaspoon paprika, divided
1	teaspoon black pepper, divided
1½	teaspoons fresh rosemary, divided
½	teaspoon salt
½	cup butter

- Wash potatoes well and cut into quarters, leaving skins on. (Cut smaller depending upon the size of potatoes you are able to find.)
- Mix one half of the paprika, pepper, rosemary and all of the salt into the olive oil. Toss potatoes in this mixture in large mixing bowl until potatoes are coated with the seasoning mixture.
- Preheat oven to 400°F.
- In large cast iron skillet, melt butter over medium heat. Add potatoes and stir continuously over medium heat until lightly browned. Add remaining herbs and spices and stir to coat evenly.
- Roast potatoes at 400°F for 35 to 40 minutes, stirring every 10 minutes for even browning. Serve hot.

Yield: 8 servings

Locally grown corn is available from June into September, however it is most plentiful in July and August. White corn produces smaller, sweeter kernels while yellow kernels are more flavor-packed. Once the ears are picked, corn's sugar begins its inevitable conversion to starch, diminishing its natural sweetness. It is best to buy corn as soon as possible once picked and also to cook or freeze within one day.

Grow your own rosemary for this and other dishes. The gray-green, needlelike leaves are fragrant and the pale blue flowers add a spot of color to your landscape during the winter. Rosemary thrives in full sun and slightly moist soil. It can be set outdoors 2 to 4 weeks before the last spring frost. Mist the foliage on hot summer days and enjoy cooking with this herb year-round.

Grilled Peppers Stuffed with Eggplant

Three varieties of peppers make a colorful presentation.

1	**medium eggplant**
	salt to taste
¼	**cup olive oil**
1	**cup plain bread crumbs**
3	**cloves garlic, minced to a paste with a pinch of salt**
½	**cup grated Parmesan cheese**
¼	**cup pine nuts**
¼	**cup chopped fresh Italian parsley**
1	**tablespoon chopped fresh oregano**
1	**tablespoon chopped fresh basil**
1	**egg, beaten**
2	**yellow bell peppers**
2	**red bell peppers**
2	**green bell peppers**

- Slice the eggplant into ¼-inch thick slices. Salt lightly and set aside on paper towels to drain for 30 minutes. Rinse, pat dry and chop coarsely.
- In a large skillet, heat oil and sauté eggplant over high heat until browned and tender, about 5 minutes.
- Chop the cooked eggplant again and mix with bread crumbs, garlic, Parmesan cheese, pine nuts, parsley and herbs. Add the beaten egg and mix well.
- Cut off the tops of the peppers, reserving tops, and remove the ribs and seeds from both the tops and the insides of peppers.
- Stuff the eggplant mixture loosely into the peppers. Secure the tops to the peppers with toothpicks.
- Cook the peppers on a covered grill over medium heat for 1 hour, turning occasionally to char peppers on all sides. Serve warm.

Yield: 6 servings

Stuffed Eggplant

An interesting variation of the previous recipe when the weather won't permit grilling.

2	medium eggplants
2	tablespoons extra virgin olive oil
1	clove garlic, pressed
	salt and pepper to taste.
	Filling (recipe follows)

- Preheat oven to 375°F.
- Cut the eggplant in half lengthwise with stems on. Scoop out the center, leaving a shell about ¼-inch thick. Reserve enough eggplant meat to equal 1 cup diced.
- Combine oil and garlic and brush the insides of the eggplant shells. Sprinkle inside of shells with salt and pepper to taste.
- Bake shells cut side down on a baking sheet until eggplant is tender, about 15 minutes.

Filling

2	tablespoons extra virgin olive oil, divided
1	cup finely chopped onion
	salt and pepper to taste
1	cup diced eggplant from shells
4	cloves garlic, pressed and divided
4	cups sliced fresh mushrooms
¼	cup dry white wine
2	sun-dried tomatoes packed in oil, drained and diced
2	tablespoons pine nuts, toasted and coarsely chopped
⅓	cup freshly grated Parmesan cheese, divided
2	tablespoons chopped fresh parsley, divided

- Preheat oven to 375°F.
- Heat 1 tablespoon olive oil in a large skillet. Add onion and a few pinches of salt and pepper. Sauté over medium heat until onions are tender, about 5 minutes.
- Add eggplant and half the garlic and continue to sauté until eggplant is tender, about 5 more minutes. Transfer eggplant-onion mixture to a bowl.
- In the same skillet, sauté mushrooms over high heat in remaining tablespoon of olive oil, adding a few pinches of salt and pepper. When the mushrooms are golden, add remaining garlic and cook 1 to 2 minutes more.
- Add wine to deglaze the skillet. Simmer mushrooms in wine 1 to 2 minutes, until pan is nearly dry.
- Chop the mushrooms coarsely and toss with the eggplant-onion mixture. Mix in sun-dried tomatoes and pine nuts, ½ cup Parmesan cheese and 1 tablespoon parsley.
- Spoon filling into eggplant shells. Place stuffed shells into a lightly greased baking dish.
- Bake, covered, 25 minutes.
- Sprinkle with remaining Parmesan cheese and bake 5 more minutes, uncovered.
- Sprinkle with remaining parsley just before serving.

Yield: 4 servings

Smooth-skinned and deep purple, eggplant is a fruit rather than a vegetable. It should be purchased firm and free of blemishes and stored unwrapped in the refrigerator. Eggplant is very perishable, so prepare it soon after purchase.

Paprika lends color to this updated comfort food. Add or substitute fresh parsley for additional appeal.

Creamy Scalloped Potatoes

Just right for Sunday dinner

1	large clove garlic, minced
1	shallot, chopped
$\frac{1}{2}$	teaspoon dried crushed red pepper
3	tablespoons butter, melted
$1\frac{1}{4}$	cups milk
$1\frac{1}{2}$	cups whipping cream
$\frac{1}{2}$	teaspoon salt
$\frac{1}{4}$	teaspoon freshly ground pepper
$2\frac{1}{2}$	pounds small red potatoes, unpeeled and cut into $\frac{1}{8}$-inch slices
1	cup shredded Gruyère cheese
$\frac{1}{4}$	cup freshly grated Parmesan cheese
$\frac{1}{2}$	teaspoon paprika

- Preheat oven to 350°F.
- In a large Dutch oven, sauté garlic, shallot and red pepper in melted butter about 2 minutes. Add milk, cream, salt and pepper, stirring well.
- Add potatoes to milk mixture, stirring to coat potatoes well, and bring to a boil over medium heat. Stir occasionally to prevent scorching.
- Once the mixture begins to boil, spoon into a lightly greased 12x8x2-inch baking dish. Sprinkle with cheeses and paprika.
- Bake for 45 minutes or until bubbly and golden brown. Allow to sit 15 minutes before serving.

Yield: 8 servings

Roasted Roquefort Potatoes

Spruced up potatoes for your steak crowd

1	tablespoon olive oil
1	pound small red potatoes
$\frac{1}{2}$	teaspoon salt
$\frac{1}{2}$	teaspoon freshly ground pepper
$\frac{2}{3}$	cup crumbled Roquefort cheese

Pick up potatoes at the Cary Downtown Farmers Market, one block north of Chatham Street, between Harrison and Academy, in the municipal lot at the depot. All produce sold by growers. Open Tuesday, 3-6 p.m.; Saturday, 8 a.m.-12:30 p.m. 367-1383.

- Preheat oven to 450°F.
- Wash potatoes thoroughly and halve, leaving skins on.
- Brush olive oil onto a nonstick baking sheet. Arrange the potatoes, cut side up, on the baking sheet. Sprinkle with salt and pepper and turn over so that cut side is down.
- Roast potatoes for 20 minutes or until browned on the bottom. Turn potatoes over, sprinkle with cheese and bake about 3 minutes until the cheese starts to melt off the potatoes. Serve immediately.

Yield: 4 servings

Oriental Spinach

A quick, healthy accompaniment to an Asian-inspired meal

1½ tablespoons olive oil
1   tablespoon butter
2   cloves garlic, pressed
1   teaspoon peeled, grated ginger root
1   pound fresh spinach leaves
1½ tablespoons soy sauce
1½ tablespoons dry sherry
1   teaspoon sugar

- Heat olive oil and butter over medium heat. Cook garlic and ginger in oil for about 30 seconds, then add spinach, stirring quickly until spinach is coated and begins to wilt, about 2 minutes.
- Sprinkle spinach with soy sauce, sherry and sugar. Continue to cook, stirring constantly, about 3 more minutes. Serve immediately.

Yield: 4 servings

Fines Herbes Butter

½ cup butter, softened
1   tablespoon chopped
    fresh parsley
1   tablespoon chopped
    fresh chives
1   teaspoon chopped fresh
    tarragon
1   teaspoon chopped fresh
    chervil
    pepper to taste

- **Combine ingredients in food processor. Process until fluffy. Chill. Serve on any green vegetable or on French bread.**

Spinach-Mushroom Bake

Layers of cheese, mushrooms and spinach melt together in a mouth-watering casserole.

2   tablespoons butter
1   pound mushrooms, sliced
2   (10-ounce) packages frozen chopped spinach
    dash of salt
½ small onion, chopped
1   cup grated sharp cheddar cheese, divided

- Preheat oven to 350°F.
- Sauté mushrooms in butter over medium heat 5 to 7 minutes or until tender. Remove from heat and set aside.
- Cook spinach according to package directions. Drain well and spoon into greased 1-quart casserole dish. Sprinkle with salt, onion and one half of cheese.
- Remove mushrooms from sauté pan with slotted spoon and place on top of spinach, cheese and onions. Top with remaining cheese and bake for 30 minutes.

Yield: 6 servings

Serve an all-kebab meal on one of those days too glorious to waste a moment indoors. Grill skewered meats and other vegetables with Striped Potato Kebabs and finish with brown sugar pineapple kebabs for dessert.

Tiger-Stripe Potato Kebabs

Your tummy will growl for this skewered side dish.

1	**pound small white potatoes**
1½	**pounds small sweet potatoes**
½	**cup water**
½	**cup olive oil**
2	**tablespoons chopped fresh parsley**
1	**tablespoon chopped fresh tarragon or 1 teaspoon dried tarragon**
¼	**teaspoon cayenne pepper**
¼	**teaspoon freshly ground black pepper**
½	**teaspoon salt**

- Peel potatoes and cut into 2-inch chunks
- Place potatoes and water in a 2-quart casserole. Cover and microwave on high 15 minutes, stirring once halfway through. Drain potatoes and place in large mixing bowl.
- In a small bowl, whisk together oil, parsley, tarragon, cayenne and black pepper and salt. Pour one half of oil mixture over potatoes and toss to coat, reserving remaining oil mixture.
- Thread potatoes onto metal grilling skewers, alternating white and sweet potato chunks. Arrange skewers on a prepared, oiled grill rack over medium coals or medium heat on a gas grill. Grill potato kebobs, brushing with the remaining oil mixture and turning frequently until a nice brown crust forms.

Yield: 6 servings

Nutted Mushroom Rice

When the temperature rises, serve this rice chilled.

4	**tablespoons butter or margarine**
5	**green onions, chopped**
1	**cup uncooked rice**
2¼	**cups (20 ounces) chicken stock**
½	**teaspoon salt**
⅔	**cup walnuts or pecans, toasted and finely chopped**
⅔	**cup finely chopped mushrooms**

For a quick accompaniment, cut a tomato into quarters, leaving intact at the bottom. Do not cut all the way through. Sprinkle with salt, pepper and Italian seasonings. Top with shredded parmesan or mozzarella cheese and broil for about 5 minutes, until cheese bubbles.

- Preheat oven to 350°F.
- Melt butter in casserole dish in oven. Add rice and onions and brown in oven.
- Add chicken stock and salt, cover and cook until rice is tender and stock is absorbed, about 30 minutes.
- Stir in nuts and mushrooms and cook 2 to 3 minutes longer.

Yield: 8 servings

Tomato-Basil Tart

½ (15-ounce) package refrigerated pie crusts
2 cups shredded mozzarella cheese
4 tablespoons fresh basil, divided
3 large ripe tomatoes, peeled and sliced
1 tablespoon olive oil
¼ teaspoon salt
¼ teaspoon pepper

- Preheat oven to 400°F.
- Place crust in a 10-inch pie pan and trim excess pastry around edges. Prick bottom and sides with a fork.
- Bake crust for 5 minutes.
- Sprinkle cheese evenly in baked crust. Top with three tablespoons basil
- Arrange tomato slices on top and brush with olive oil. Sprinkle with salt and pepper.
- Bake for 35 minutes.
- Top with remaining tablespoon fresh basil and let stand for 5 minutes before serving.

Yield: 8 servings

When it comes to gardening, tomatoes can be one of the most satisfying things to grow. Best of all, they can be grown anywhere that sun is plentiful. Patio varieties thrive in pots on apartment balconies and large vines grow skyward on stakes in large garden plots. With their use in sauces, sandwiches, salads and soups; eaten plain or with basil and mozzarella and a drizzle of balsamic vinegar, they are also one of the most satisfying things to eat.

Herbed Couscous and Vegetables

1 cup sliced fresh mushrooms
1 tablespoon butter
1 cup water
1 tablespoon snipped fresh parsley
½ teaspoon dried basil, crushed
¼ teaspoon salt
⅛ teaspoon dried oregano, crushed
   dash of pepper
⅔ cup couscous
1 medium tomato, peeled, seeded and chopped

- In a medium saucepan cook mushrooms in hot butter until tender.
- Stir in water, parsley, basil, salt, oregano and dash pepper.
- Bring to a boil. Remove from heat.
- Stir in couscous. Cover and let stand 5 minutes.
- Stir in tomato and serve immediately.

Yield: 4 servings

Basil Butter

½ cup butter, softened

½ cup chopped fresh basil
leaves

2 tablespoons chopped
fresh parsley

1 tablespoon fresh lemon
juice

¼ cup grated Parmesan
cheese

• Combine ingredients in
food processor. Process
until fluffy. Chill. Serve
with baked tomatoes or
green beans.

Baked Tomatoes with Broccoli and Cheese

Tomato shells encase a broccoli-cheese filling.

6 medium tomatoes
  salt and pepper to taste
½ pound fresh broccoli florets
1 cup grated Swiss cheese
1 cup plain dry bread crumbs
½ cup mayonnaise
1 tablespoon prepared horseradish
2 tablespoons minced onion
2 tablespoons freshly grated Parmesan cheese

• Cut approximately one-fourth off the top of each tomato and scoop pulp and
  seeds from the shell. Wash each tomato thoroughly. Sprinkle inside of shells with
  salt and pepper and invert each shell on a paper towel to drain while preparing
  the filling.
• Preheat oven to 350°F.
• Blanch broccoli florets in boiling water until just tender. Drain broccoli and chop
  coarsely.
• Combine chopped broccoli, cheese, bread crumbs, mayonnaise, horseradish and
  onion, stirring until ingredients are mixed thoroughly.
• Stuff tomato shells with broccoli-cheese mixture. Place in 9x13x2-inch baking
  dish; sprinkle tops with Parmesan cheese and bake for 30 minutes.

Yield: 6 servings

Roasted Rainbow Vegetables

Taste and color always marry well.

1	small eggplant
3	zucchini squash
2	Vidalia onions
1	yellow bell pepper
1	green bell pepper
1	red bell pepper
	salt and pepper to taste
5	tablespoons olive oil
1	tablespoon thyme
1	tablespoon rosemary
2	cloves garlic, crushed

- Preheat oven to 400°F.
- Wash eggplant and squash and cut into ½-inch thick slices, halving each slice if necessary. Slice onions into ½-inch thick rings. Wash and seed peppers and cut into ¼-inch strips. Place all in a large roasting pan and sprinkle with salt and pepper.
- In a small bowl, combine olive oil, thyme, rosemary and garlic, whisking to mix. Pour over vegetables and toss to coat.
- Roast for 20 to 30 minutes or until vegetables start to curl at edges.

Yield: 6 servings

> Find the freshest vegetables at the Fuquay-Varina Farmers Market, Main Street at Cooley Street. All produce sold by growers. Open Wednesday, 3 p.m.-6 p.m.; Saturday 8:30 a.m.-1 p.m. 387-1383.

Spicy Asian Noodles

Oriental pasta side becomes an entrée by tossing in a pound of cooked, peeled shrimp.

¼	teaspoon dark sesame oil
1	teaspoon hot chili oil
1	tablespoon very finely chopped fresh ginger
4	tablespoons soy sauce
½	teaspoon minced garlic
	salt and pepper to taste
12	ounces angel hair pasta, cooked al dente
	chopped green onions to garnish
	sesame seeds to garnish

- Whisk together sesame oil, chili oil, ginger, soy sauce, garlic, salt and pepper. Toss with pasta.
- Sprinkle with green onions and toasted sesame seeds on top of each serving.

Yield: 4 to 5 servings

Risotto with Grilled Vegetables

A light but substantial risotto

1	medium yellow onion
1	medium zucchini
1	red bell pepper
1	yellow bell pepper
3	tablespoons olive oil, divided
1	tablespoon butter
1	cup Arborio rice
3	cups chicken broth, divided
½	cup dry sherry
	pepper to taste
¼	cup pine nuts
½	cup freshly grated Parmesan cheese
2	tablespoons fresh chopped parsley

- Cut onion into ½-inch thick slices without separating rings. Insert wooden picks through slices to prevent rings from separating during grilling. Slice zucchini in half lengthwise. Seed peppers and half lengthwise.
- Brush vegetables lightly with 1 to 2 tablespoons of the olive oil and place on grill rack over medium coals or medium heat on a gas grill. Cover and cook until crisp-tender, about 5 minutes for zucchini and 20 minutes for peppers and onion. Cut grilled vegetables into bite-sized chunks and set aside.
- In 2½-quart saucepan, melt butter and 1 tablespoon olive oil. Add rice and cook over medium heat, stirring constantly, about 4 minutes until grains appear clear. Add ¼ cup of the chicken broth and all the sherry and continue cooking 5 more minutes, stirring constantly, until liquid is almost completely absorbed. Continue adding broth in ¾ cup amounts until grains are tender and mixture is creamy. Stir frequently to avoid sticking and to achieve creamy consistency.
- Stir in pine nuts and grilled vegetables and season with pepper. Do not allow dish to cook any longer, just heat vegetables through by stirring into rice. Before serving, sprinkle entire dish or individual servings with freshly grated Parmesan cheese and chopped parsley.

Yield: 6 servings

Patchwork Quilt Rice

Provides a colorful display next to roasted chicken or turkey

3	tablespoons butter
1	cup sliced celery
¾	cup coarsely chopped carrots
1	cup coarsely chopped onions
¾	cup coarsely chopped green onions
1	cup chopped unpeeled tart red apples
1	cup sliced mushrooms
1	(6¼-ounce) package long-grained and wild rice mix
1	(10½-ounce) can condensed chicken broth
¼	cup toasted slivered almonds

- In a large skillet, melt butter. Add celery, onions, carrots, and green onions. Sauté over medium heat until tender, about 8 to 12 minutes. Add apples and mushrooms and sauté 2 to 3 minutes longer. Add rice from mix and toss to combine. Stir in seasonings from rice mix.
- In glass measuring cup, combine broth with enough water to make 2 cups. Stir into rice mixture.
- Bring to a boil, cover, and simmer until broth is absorbed.
- Add almonds and toss to combine. Serve immediately.

Yield: 6 servings

Linguine with Fresh Tomatoes and Brie

Rich summertime pasta that easily stands as a main course

4	large tomatoes cut into ½-inch cubes
1	pound Brie cheese, rind removed, torn into bite-sized pieces
1	cup chopped fresh basil
3	cloves garlic, minced
1	cup olive oil
2	teaspoons salt
½	teaspoon pepper
1½	pounds fresh linguine

- Mix all ingredients except the linguine in a bowl and set aside at room temperature for 2 hours.
- Cook linguine al dente and toss with tomato mixture.
- Serve immediately.

Yield: 4 to 6 servings

Wine Recommendations: Dolcetto or Côtes du Rhone

Noted poet and author Maya Angelou, although originally from Arkansas, has called North Carolina home. When asked by *Bon Appétit* magazine about memorable foods from her childhood, she said, "We had rice at every meal. I thought everybody in the world ate rice all the time. If I have rice, onions, tomatoes, garlic and olive oil, I know I can make a wonderful dish."

Cooking Pasta al dente

Undercooked pasta is raw and chewy, overcooked pasta is mushy. To achieve perfectly cooked al dente pasta, lift a piece from the boiling water near the end of the cooking time. Bite into it, looking for tender-ness with a touch of resistance. If the pasta is done, remove from heat and drain immediately. Otherwise, test every 30 to 60 seconds until it is done.

Spaghetti Vinaigrette

Dress your spaghetti in more than marinara.

1   cup olive oil
1   cup red wine vinegar
1   tablespoon minced garlic
1½ teaspoons salt
    freshly ground pepper
1   (16-ounce) package spaghetti
12 fresh plum tomatoes, diced
1½ cups diced red onions
1   large or 2 small bunches arugula
    whole green onions to garnish

- For dressing, combine oil, vinegar, garlic, salt and pepper and set aside. This can be prepared ahead.
- Cook spaghetti in a large pot of rapidly boiling water, until tender but firm to the bite. Drain and transfer to a large bowl.
- Mix in half the dressing. Blend in vegetables and arugula, adding enough dressing to coat all ingredients lightly.
- Garnish with green onions.

Yield: 6 servings

Peppery Pasta with Feta Cheese

Simple yet bold

2   tablespoons olive oil
1   large red bell pepper, diced
1   large green bell pepper, diced
6   large cloves garlic, chopped
1   cup thinly sliced, stemmed, drained pepperoncini, about 1 (16-ounce) jar
½   cup chopped fresh basil or 2 tablespoons dried
1   (28-ounce) can Italian plum tomatoes with juices
1   pound bow-tie pasta, freshly cooked
8   ounces Feta cheese, coarsely crumbled

- Heat oil in a heavy pan over medium high heat.
- Add both bell peppers and garlic. Sauté until peppers begin to soften, about 4 minutes.
- Mix in pepperoncini, basil, and tomatoes. Simmer 15 minutes.
- Pour sauce over pasta and toss with Feta cheese.

Yield: 6 servings

Wine Recommendations: Rosé de Provence, a Macon or Pinot Grigio

Penne with Tomatoes, Olives and Two Cheeses

6   tablespoons olive oil
1½ cups chopped onion
1   teaspoon minced garlic
3   (28-ounce) cans plum tomatoes
2   teaspoons fresh basil
1½ teaspoons crushed red pepper flakes
2   cups low salt chicken broth
1   pound penne
⅓   cup kalamata olives
2½ cups grated Havarti cheese
½   cup freshly grated Parmesan cheese

- Heat 3 tablespoons oil in a heavy pan. Add onions and garlic and sauté 5 minutes.
- Add tomatoes, basil, red pepper flakes and bring to a boil.
- Reduce heat to medium and simmer until mixture thickens and is red, about 1 hour 10 minutes. (This can be prepared 2 days ahead and rewarmed before continuing.)
- Preheat oven to 375°F.
- Cook pasta, drain and return to pot. Toss with remaining 3 tablespoons olive oil.
- Pour sauce over pasta and toss. Mix in Havarti cheese.
- Put into a 13x9-inch glass casserole dish. Sprinkle with olives and Parmesan cheese.
- Bake 30 minutes.
- Sprinkle with basil.

Yield: 6 servings

Wine Recommendations: Chianti, Côtes du Rhone or California Rhone blend

When simplicity must prevail, a marinara fills the bill. This one takes 20 minutes, prepares ahead and freezes well.

4 large tomatoes, blanched, peeled and chopped
2 cloves garlic, chopped
10-15 fresh basil leaves
2 tablespoons olive oil
1 tablespoon Italian bread crumbs
  Parmesan cheese, grated

- Heat olive oil in heavy large skillet on medium high heat; add basil and garlic. Sauté until basil turns dark green.
- Remove from heat. Add chopped tomatoes, return to medium low heat, cover and cook until preferred tenderness. Add bread crumbs to thicken and serve warm. Top with grated Parmesan.

Pesto sauce is reason enough to grow a basil garden. It is quick and makes a good sandwich spread or pasta sauce. Since it freezes well, it also makes a thoughtful gift.

2 cups fresh basil leaves, washed in warm water and patted dry

2 garlic cloves

¼ cup pine nuts

¼ cup grated Parmesan cheese

½ cup olive oil
salt and freshly ground pepper to taste

- Place all ingredients but oil in food processor. Pulse until ingredients are finely minced, scraping down sides of bowl. Slowly add oil through feed tube and process until mixture becomes thick and smooth.
- To freeze, place in container with just enough oil to cover. Keeps 6 months.
- To serve with pasta, reserve up to ½ cup pasta cooking water to mix with pesto before tossing with pasta.

Pasta Cannonino

Freshly grated Parmesan cheese adds the finish to an elegant vegetarian dish.

1 (6-ounce) jar marinated artichoke hearts, cut up, marinade reserved

2 cloves garlic, minced

1 small onion, chopped

1 (15-ounce) can Great Northern white beans

1 (7-ounce) jar roasted red peppers in water, chopped and undrained

2 teaspoons Italian seasoning or 1 teaspoon basil and 1 teaspoon oregano
salt and pepper to taste

¾ pound freshly cooked bowtie or twist pasta
freshly grated Parmesan cheese
chopped parsley to garnish.

- Pour the marinade from the artichokes into a large non-stick skillet over medium heat.
- Sauté onion and garlic until translucent.
- Add beans, pepper with juices and seasonings.
- Cook until hot, about 15 minutes.
- Add salt and pepper to taste.
- Serve sauce over pasta with grated Parmesan cheese, garnished with parsley.

Variation: Add cut-up chicken breast. Sauté with onions and garlic.

Yield: 4 to 6 servings

Wine Recommendations: Pinot Grigio or California Sauvignon Blanc

Pasta Primavera

The name means springtime, and the taste is true to season.

1   (12-ounce) package linguine
2   cups broccoli cut into 1-inch pieces
2   tablespoons olive oil
1   (12-ounce) package mushrooms, each cut in half
1   small onion, minced
1   small carrot cut into matchstick-thin strips
1   small red pepper cut into ¼-inch thick strips
12 ounces heavy cream or half-and-half
2   teaspoons chicken flavored instant bouillon
1¼ teaspoons cornstarch
½   teaspoon salt
1   medium-sized tomato, seeded and diced
2   tablespoons grated Parmesan cheese
3   tablespoons chopped parsley

- In a large pot, prepare linguine per package directions. Drain and return to pasta pot.
- Put broccoli pieces and 1 inch water in a 2-quart saucepan. Bring to a boil. Reduce heat to low. Cover and simmer 2 to 3 minutes, stirring occasionally, until broccoli is crisp-tender. Drain.
- While broccoli is cooking, put oil in a 12-inch skillet. On high heat, cook mushrooms, onions and carrots, stirring frequently, until vegetables are golden and crisp-tender.
- Add red pepper strips and cook, stirring, until tender.
- In a 2-cup measuring cup, with a fork, mix cream or half-and-half, chicken bouillon, cornstarch and salt.
- Stir cream mixture into vegetables.
- Over high heat, bring to a boil.
- Add diced tomato, Parmesan cheese, parsley, broccoli and pasta, tossing to coat well. Heat through.

Yield: 6 servings

The Rose Garden adjacent to the Raleigh Little Theatre is a busy place in spring when it becomes a popular backdrop for weddings. In fact, Raleigh's green spaces have thrived ever since 1792 when William Christmas laid out the city's original gridwork plan to include four park squares that border the capitol building.

Side Dishes and Pasta

Linda Turner

The Dining Room
oil on canvas, 1996

From the private collection of M. Eleanor Fisher, Raleigh, NC.

Desserts

Pumpkin Pecan Cake

A moist and spicy alternative to carrot cake.

2	cups all-purpose flour
2	teaspoons baking powder
2	teaspoons baking soda
1	teaspoon salt
2	teaspoons ground cinnamon
2	cups pumpkin
2	cups sugar
1	cup vegetable oil
4	eggs, at room temperature
½	cup coconut
½	cup chopped pecans
	Cream Cheese Frosting (recipe follows)

- Preheat oven to 350°F.
- Sift together flour, baking powder, baking soda, salt and cinnamon. Set aside.
- With mixer at medium speed, combine pumpkin, sugar and oil. Add eggs, one at a time, beating well after each addition. Add flour mixture and blend well. Fold in coconut and pecans.
- Spoon batter into 3 greased and floured 8-inch round cake pans.
- Bake in center of oven for 30 minutes or until wooden pick inserted in center of cake comes out clean.
- Cool in pan for 10 minutes. Remove to wire rack and cool completely.

Cream Cheese Frosting

½	cup butter, softened
1	(8-ounce) package cream cheese, softened
3½	cups (about 16 ounces) powdered sugar
2	teaspoons vanilla extract
½	cup coarsely chopped pecans
30	pecan halves

- Cream butter and cream cheese. Slowly add powdered sugar, blending well. Stir in vanilla.
- Spread approximately 1 cup frosting between each layer. Spread remaining frosting on top and sides of cake.
- Lightly pat chopped pecans on sides of cake. Arrange pecan halves in a circle on top of cake.

Yield: 16 servings

With little effort, you can make cakes look bakery beautiful.

- **Combing the Frosting:** Smoothly cover the cake with frosting. Use a frosting comb from a kitchen goods store or a regular wide toothed comb (purchased exclusively for cake decorating) to create straight or curvy lines on the sides, then the top of the cake.

- **Decorating with Nuts:** Pecans are a good choice for decorating because of their uniform shape. Using a sharp knife, cut them into thin, vertical slices to lay in borders around the top or sides of a frosted cake. Coarsely chop nuts and press them into the icing on the sides of the cake for an encrusted look. Place whole pecans in patterns on top of the cake for an eye-appealing and tasty presentation.

Despite its extravagant appearance, this chocolate torte is not complex. It can be prepared ahead of time in four easy steps. Bake the cake and keep it in the freezer until the day it will be served. Prepare the cocoa frosting and hot fudge filling early in the day that the torte will be served. As a final step, assemble the torte and serve it on a plate garnished with fresh raspberries.

Triple Threat Chocolate Raspberry Torte

A party dessert featuring four chocolate layers with alternating hot fudge and raspberry filling, topped with a fluffy cocoa frosting.

½   **cup sour cream, at room temperature**
½   **cup vegetable oil**
1   **cup hot strong-brewed coffee**
1½ **cups all-purpose flour**
¾   **teaspoon baking soda**
½   **teaspoon salt**
2   **cups sugar**
2   **eggs, at room temperature, slightly beaten**
4   **ounces unsweetened chocolate, melted**
    Hot Fudge Filling (recipe follows)
    Chocolate Frosting (recipe follows)
    Raspberry Filling (recipe follows)

- Preheat oven to 350°F.
- In a small bowl, whisk together sour cream, oil and coffee. Set aside.
- Sift together flour, baking soda, salt and sugar. Add coffee mixture. Mix for 30 seconds with mixer at low speed. Add eggs, one at a time, mixing 15 seconds at medium speed after each addition. Add melted chocolate and mix 10 seconds or until batter is uniform in color.
- Spoon batter into 2 greased and floured 8-inch round cake pans.
- Bake in center of oven for 30 to 35 minutes or until wooden pick inserted in center of cake comes out clean.
- Cool completely in pan for 10 minutes. Remove to wire rack and cool completely.

Hot Fudge Filling

2   **ounces unsweetened chocolate**
2   **tablespoons unsalted butter**
⅓   **cup sugar**
6   **tablespoons hot water**
½   **teaspoon vanilla extract**

- Combine chocolate, butter, sugar and water in top of double boiler. Stirring occasionally, cook uncovered for 30 minutes or until chocolate is melted, sugar is dissolved and mixture is smooth.
- Pour into a small bowl. Stir in vanilla. Refrigerate for 2 hours or until mixture is thick and of spreading consistency.

(continued on next page)

Triple Threat Chocolate Raspberry Torte *continued*

Chocolate Frosting

1½ **cups heavy cream**
½ **cup sugar**
½ **cup cocoa**

* Whisk together cream, sugar, and cocoa. Chill for 1 hour.

Raspberry Filling

1 **cup seedless raspberry preserves**

* Split cake layers in half. Place one layer on cake platter. Spread with half of Hot Fudge Filling. Place another layer on top. Spread with raspberry preserves. Place another layer on top. Spread with remaining Hot Fudge Filling. Top with last layer.
* Whip Chocolate Frosting until stiff. Spread on top and sides of torte.
* Chill before serving.

Yield: 16 servings

Divine Coconut Cake

This make-ahead cake is worth the wait.

1 **box butter cake mix**
1¾ **cups sugar**
2 **cups sour cream**
4 **cups (about 1 medium) grated fresh coconut or 2 (6-ounce) packages frozen coconut, thawed**
1 **(9-ounce) package whipped topping, prepared according to package directions**

* Preheat oven to 350°F.
* Prepare cake mix according to package directions.
* Spoon batter into 2 greased and floured 8-inch round cake pans.
* Bake in center of oven for 30 to 35 minutes or until wooden pick inserted in center of cake comes out clean.
* Cool in pan for 10 minutes. Remove to wire rack and cool completely.
* Split cake layers in half. Combine sugar, sour cream and coconut. Reserve 1 cup sour cream mixture for frosting. Spread remainder of sour cream mixture between layers, split side up.
* Combine reserved sour cream mixture with whipped topping. Blend until smooth. Spread on top and sides of cake.
* Seal cake in an airtight container and refrigerate for 3 days prior to serving.

Yield: 16 servings

Grate fresh coconut the day before using. To open the coconut, pierce the "eyes" in the stalk end with an ice pick or metal skewer. Drain the liquid. Tap all around the girth with a hammer, tapping and turning until the coconut splits in half. Pry the flesh from the shell with a small, sharp knife. Use a vegetable peeler to peel away the dark outer skin. Finally, grate the coconut using a mandoline or the grating attachment of your food processor.

Family reunions offer the perfect opportunity to showcase a classic family recipe like Red Velvet Cake. Typically potluck collections of single dishes from family members, reunions are a good time to explore and record a family's cooking heritage:

- Hand-printed recipe cards placed next to each dish invite everyone to try the recipe at home.

- Interviews with older family members can yield clues to the family's ethnic heritage and customs.

- Some dishes are standards at wedding and baby showers, leading to stories of far-reaching branches of the family tree.

- Comparisons of today's grocery stores to yesterday's farmers' markets uncover interesting details about the day-to-day life of past generations.

Red Velvet Cake

1	tablespoon cocoa
1 to 2	ounces red food coloring, divided
2½	cups cake flour
1	teaspoon salt
1½	cups shortening
1½	cups sugar
2	eggs, at room temperature
1	cup buttermilk, at room temperature
1	teaspoon vinegar
1	teaspoon vanilla extract
1	teaspoon baking soda
	Frosting (recipe follows)

- Preheat oven to 350°F.
- Make a paste with cocoa and 1 ounce red food coloring. Set aside.
- Sift together flour and salt. Set aside.
- Cream shortening, sugar and eggs. Add cocoa mixture and mix well. Add flour mixture alternately with buttermilk. Stir in vinegar. Add vanilla and baking soda and mix well. Blend in enough additional food coloring to achieve a deep red color.
- Spoon batter into 2 greased and floured 8-inch round cake pans.
- Bake in center of oven for 30 minutes or until wooden pick inserted in center of cake comes out clean.
- Cool in pan for 10 minutes. Remove to wire rack and cool completely.
- Split cake layers in half.

Frosting

1	cup milk
3	tablespoons all-purpose flour
1	cup butter, softened
1	cup sugar
1	tablespoon vanilla extract

- In a small saucepan, combine milk and flour and cook until thick.
- Remove from heat and cool completely.
- Cream butter and sugar. Mix in vanilla. Add milk mixture gradually, beating constantly.
- Spread frosting between layers and on top of cake. Leave sides of cake unfrosted.

Yield: 16 servings

Tar Heel Cupcakes

Two layers of ingredients create a cupcake that is both eye-catching and delicious.

2   (3-ounce) packages cream cheese, softened
1⅓ cups plus 2 tablespoons sugar, divided
1   egg
1   cup (about 6 ounces) semisweet chocolate chips
½   cup chopped almonds
1½ cups all-purpose flour
1   teaspoon baking soda
½   teaspoon salt
¼   cup cocoa
1   cup water
⅓   cup vegetable oil
1   tablespoon vinegar
1   teaspoon vanilla extract

- Preheat oven to 350°F.
- Combine cream cheese, ⅓ cup sugar and egg. Mix well. Stir in chocolate chips. Set aside.
- Combine almonds and 2 tablespoons sugar. Set aside.
- Sift together flour, baking soda, salt, 1 cup sugar and cocoa. Add water, oil, vinegar and vanilla. Beat for 2 minutes with mixer at medium speed.
- Fill paper-lined muffin cups ½ full with batter. Top each cupcake with 1 tablespoon cream cheese mixture. Sprinkle almond-sugar mixture evenly over cream cheese mixture.
- Bake in center of oven for 30 minutes or until cream cheese mixture is light golden brown.
- Cool in pan for 15 minutes. Remove to wire rack and cool completely.

Yield: 18 cupcakes

There are no fewer than four versions of how North Carolina became known as the Tar Heel State, all relating to tar and its by-products produced in massive amounts from the teeming pine forests covering the state.

Legend has it that in 1781 British troops, led by Cornwallis, were en route to the Battle of Yorktown when they became mired down in tar poured by North Carolinians into the Tar River to prevent its capture.

The remaining stories date to the Civil War and attribute Robert E. Lee, Stonewall Jackson and Jefferson Davis as having coined the phrase. Tar was often stuck to the feet of anyone who worked or walked on North Carolina soil. As he praised the heroics of soldiers from the state, Lee stated in a speech, "God bless the Tar Heel boys."

Jackson, noting the tenacity of the North Carolina troops, said it was as if tar were stuck to their heels, keeping them rooted stubbornly in place during battle.

It is said of Davis that he offered to buy all the tar produced in North Carolina for use in Virginia, where he observed how North Carolina troops stuck to their posts during difficult battles.

Today citizens of the Old North State wear the name with pride, most prominently in Chapel Hill.

"My husband comes from German-Swiss stock, and his food motto is, 'If it has cinnamon in it, I'll eat it!' This is his absolute favorite dessert, a creation of his mom's, with a few minor modifications from me. It looks lovely on the plate, tastes great and smells even better. We like it with fall food, such as ham, bratwurst and dark bread."

Gran's Gingerbread with Streusel Topping

A spicy gingerbread with a decidedly made-from-scratch taste.

2	cups all-purpose flour
1	teaspoon baking soda
½	teaspoon salt
1	teaspoon ground cinnamon
1	teaspoon ground cloves
1	teaspoon ground ginger
1	teaspoon ground nutmeg
½	cup shortening, melted
½	cup sugar
½	cup molasses
1	cup hot water
	Streusel Topping (recipe follows)
	Whipped Cream (recipe follows)

- Preheat oven to 350°F.
- Sift together flour, baking soda, salt, cinnamon, cloves, ginger and nutmeg. Set aside.
- Combine melted shortening, sugar and molasses. Add flour mixture alternately with hot water. Mix well after each addition.
- Spoon batter into a greased and floured 6x10-inch baking pan.

Streusel Topping

½	cup all-purpose flour
1	cup brown sugar
½	teaspoon ground cinnamon
½	teaspoon ground nutmeg
6	tablespoons butter, softened
½	cup chopped nuts

- Combine flour, brown sugar, cinnamon and nutmeg. Cut in butter until mixture resembles coarse crumbs. Stir in nuts. Sprinkle evenly over gingerbread batter.
- Bake in center of oven for 40 to 45 minutes or until wooden pick inserted in center of cake comes out clean. Do not overcook.
- Cool completely.

(continued on next page)

(Gran's Gingerbread *continued*)

Whipped Cream

1   **cup heavy cream**
    dash of vanilla extract
1   **tablespoon powdered sugar**
    dash of ground nutmeg for garnish

- Just before serving, beat cream until soft peaks form. Blend in vanilla and powdered sugar. Beat until stiff peaks form.
- Cut gingerbread into squares. Place onto individual dessert plates and top with whipped cream and a dash of nutmeg.

Yield: 12 servings

Classic Southern Pound Cake

A staple at church and family events, pound cake takes its name from the tradition of tossing in a pound of everything, from butter to flour, to make the perfect cake.

3   **cups all-purpose flour**
3/4 **teaspoon baking powder**
1/4 **teaspoon salt**
1   **cup butter, softened**
1/2 **cup shortening**
3   **cups sugar**
6   **eggs, at room temperature**
1   **cup evaporated milk**
1   **teaspoon lemon extract**
1   **teaspoon vanilla extract**

- Preheat oven to 325°F.
- Sift together flour, baking powder and salt. Set aside.
- Cream butter, shortening and sugar. Beat until light and fluffy. Add eggs, one at a time, beating well after each addition. Add flour mixture alternately with evaporated milk. Mix well after each addition. Stir in lemon extract and vanilla.
- Spoon batter into a greased and floured tube pan.
- Bake in center of oven for 1 hour and 20 minutes or until wooden pick inserted in center of cake comes out clean.
- Cool in pan for 15 minutes. Remove to wire rack and cool completely.

Note: Wrap cake in aluminum foil to hold in moisture.

Yield: 16 servings

Enhance the appeal of a simple pound cake with a colorful fruit sauce, a lemon or berry curd, hot fudge or fresh fruit and whipped cream.

Peach-Blueberry Sauce

- **Combine 1/2 cup sliced peaches, 1/2 cup blueberries, 3/4 cup sugar, 1/8 teaspoon ground nutmeg and 1/3 cup water in a medium saucepan.**
- **Bring to a boil, reduce heat and simmer 10 minutes.**
- **Stir in additional 1/2 cup sliced peaches and 1/2 cup blueberries.**
- **Serve warm.**

**Grand Marnier Sauce adds
dazzle to a serving of
vanilla ice cream or lemon
sorbet, strawberry
shortcake, sliced fresh fruit
or a Belgian waffle with
whipped cream.**

Currant Pound Cake
with Grand Marnier Sauce

A traditional Southern favorite gets an update featuring the flavors of orange and currants.

3   cups all-purpose flour
½   teaspoon baking powder
½   teaspoon salt
1½ cups butter, softened
2¾ cups sugar
1½ teaspoons orange extract
1   teaspoon vanilla extract
6   eggs, at room temperature
1   cup sour cream, at room temperature
1   cup currants
     Grand Marnier Sauce (recipe follows)

- Preheat oven to 325°F.
- Sift together flour, baking powder and salt. Set aside.
- Beat butter and sugar until light and fluffy. Mix in orange extract and vanilla. Add eggs, one at a time, beating well after each addition. Add flour mixture alternately with sour cream. Mix well after each addition. Fold in currants.
- Spoon batter into a greased and floured bundt pan.
- Bake in center of oven for 1 hour and 20 minutes or until wooden pick inserted in center of cake comes out clean.
- Cool in pan for 15 minutes. Remove to wire rack and cool completely.

Grand Marnier Sauce

¼ cup sugar
1   tablespoon cornstarch
¾ cup orange juice
2   tablespoons Grand Marnier

- Just before serving, combine sugar and cornstarch in a small saucepan. Stir in orange juice. Stirring constantly, cook over medium heat until mixture boils and thickens. Stir in Grand Marnier. Drizzle over pound cake.

Yield: 16 servings

Raspberry Trifle with Custard Sauce

A light and delightful offering to serve after a special meal.

1   **(6-ounce) pound cake**
4   **tablespoons raspberry jam**
½   **cup sliced almonds, divided**
½   **cup sherry**
2   **tablespoons brandy**
3   **cups milk, divided**
2   **tablespoons cornstarch**
2   **tablespoons sugar**
3   **egg yolks, slightly beaten**
1   **teaspoon vanilla extract**
1   **cup heavy cream**
1   **tablespoon powdered sugar**
2   **cups raspberries, divided**

- Cut pound cake into 1-inch thick slices. Spread raspberry jam on one side of each slice. Place 2 to 3 slices, jam side up, in the bottom of an 8-inch glass serving bowl that is at least 3 inches deep. Cut remaining slices into 1-inch cubes and scatter over cake slices. Sprinkle with ¼ cup almonds. Pour in sherry and brandy and let steep at room temperature for at least 20 minutes.
- In a heavy saucepan, combine ½ cup milk and cornstarch. Whisk until cornstarch is dissolved. Add remaining 2½ cups milk and sugar. Stirring constantly, cook over medium heat until custard thickens and comes to a boil.
- Stir ¼ cup sauce mixture into egg yolks, then whisk egg mixture into remaining sauce. Stirring constantly, bring to a boil and cook for 1 minute.
- Remove from heat and stir in vanilla. Set aside.
- Beat cream until soft peaks form. Blend in powdered sugar. Beat until stiff peaks form. Set aside.
- Set aside 10 of the best raspberries. Scatter the rest over cake. Spread custard across top. Gently smooth half of whipped cream over custard. Using a pastry bag with a large rose tip, pipe remaining whipped cream decoratively around edge. Garnish with reserved raspberries and remaining ¼ cup almonds.

Yield: 10 servings

Spirited Blueberry Sauce

¼ cup sugar
¼ cup Grand Marnier
¼ cup water
2 pints blueberries

• Mix together sugar, Grand Marnier and water. Add blueberries. Let sit for 30 minutes.

Spiced Whipped Cream

1 cup heavy cream
½ teaspoon vanilla extract
2 tablespoons powdered sugar
¼ teaspoon ground cinnamon

• Beat cream until soft peaks form. Blend in vanilla, powdered sugar and cinnamon. Beat with chilled beaters until stiff peaks form.

Shortcake with Spirited Blueberry Sauce

This airy confection with a no-cook sauce refreshes quickly during blueberry season.

2 cups all-purpose flour
2¼ teaspoons baking powder
½ teaspoon salt
½ cup sugar
½ cup shortening
2 eggs
6 tablespoons milk
2 tablespoons butter, melted
  Spirited Blueberry Sauce
  Spiced Whipped Cream

• Sift together flour, baking powder, salt and sugar. Blend in shortening. Add eggs and milk. Mix until smooth. Dough will be very soft and sticky. Let dough sit at room temperature for 30 minutes.
• Preheat oven to 375°F.
• Turn dough out onto a well-floured surface. Pat dough to ½-inch thickness. Cut dough with a floured biscuit cutter.
• Place on an ungreased baking sheet.
• Bake for 14 to 16 minutes or until golden brown.
• Brush shortcakes with melted butter.
• Cool completely.
• Slice shortcakes and place on individual dessert plates. Top with Spirited Blueberry Sauce and Spiced Whipped Cream.

Yield: 12 servings

Bread Pudding with Fruit and Warm Whiskey Sauce

This bread pudding is luscious and sinful.

4   **cups milk**
10   **cups cubed bread**
1½   **cups sugar**
5   **eggs**
2   **tablespoons vanilla extract**
1   **cup blueberries or chopped peaches**
     Whiskey Sauce (recipe follows)

- Preheat oven to 325°F.
- In a large bowl, pour milk over bread cubes. Soak for 30 minutes.
- In a separate bowl, combine sugar, eggs and vanilla. Mix well. Stir egg mixture into bread mixture. Fold in fruit.
- Pour pudding mixture into a well-greased 13x9-inch baking pan.
- Cover with foil and bake for one hour and thirty minutes.
- Cool completely.

Whiskey Sauce

1   **cup butter, melted**
2   **cups powdered sugar**
2   **eggs**
⅓   **cup whiskey**

- Combine butter and powdered sugar. Whisk in eggs. Stir in whiskey. Serve warm over pudding.

Yield: 10 servings

A dazzling dessert be-
comes more so when
featured on its own table.
Highlight special desserts
in a separate room
complete with center-
piece, candles and warm
pots of coffee or tea. The
room should offer com-
fortable chairs, soft jazz
playing in the background
and dimmed lighting. A
fire in the fireplace is an
added enticement.

411 West Blueberry Chambord Cheesecake

This spectacular dessert is served at 411 West in Chapel Hill. Its sister restaurant, 518 West, is one of the first restaurants to revitalize South Glenwood Avenue in Raleigh.

1	egg
4	tablespoons milk
2½	cups all-purpose flour
½	teaspoon baking powder
¼	teaspoon salt
½	cup sugar
½	cup plus 2 tablespoons butter, softened
	Filling (recipe follows)
	Blueberry Sauce (recipe follows)

- Beat together egg and milk. Set aside.
- Sift together flour, baking powder, salt, and sugar. Cut in butter until mixture resembles coarse crumbs. Gently toss egg mixture into flour mixture until almost all dry ingredients are dampened.
- Form dough into a ball. Gently knead dough until smooth, no more than 1 minute, being careful not to overwork dough.
- Flatten dough into a 1½-inch thick disc. Wrap in wax paper and refrigerate for 1 hour.

Filling

32	ounces ricotta cheese
⅓	cup all-purpose flour
	pinch of salt
¾	cup sugar
¼	teaspoon ground cinnamon
	zest of 2 lemons
7	eggs, divided
2	tablespoons Sambuca
2	teaspoons vanilla extract
1	tablespoon water

- Preheat oven to 325°F.
- Purée ricotta in food processor or blender for 10 minutes or until very smooth.
- Transfer to a large bowl. Add flour, salt, sugar, cinnamon and lemon zest, gently mixing well after each addition. Add 6 eggs, one at a time, beating well after each addition. Gently mix in Sambuca and vanilla. Set aside.
- Turn dough out onto a lightly floured surface. Cut off ⅓ of chilled dough and set aside. Working quickly, roll remainder of dough into a ⅛-inch thick circle.
- Fold carefully into quarters and place with point in center into a 9-inch spring-form pan. Unfold and trim off excess pastry.

(continued on next page)

411 West Blueberry Chambord Cheesecake *continued*

- Pour filling into crust.
- Roll smaller portion of dough into a slightly thinner than ⅛-inch thick 11-inch circle. Cut into eight ¾-inch strips.
- Combine 1 egg with water and brush on top of strips. Gently place four strips 1 inch apart over filling. Adhere each strip firmly to crust with egg wash. Place remaining four strips 1-inch apart crosswise over first four, adhering to crust in same manner. Brush edges of crust with egg wash.
- Bake for 1 hour and 15 minutes or until cheesecake has puffed slightly, is browned on top and no longer jiggles in center.
- Cool completely. Remove sides of pan prior to serving.

Blueberry Sauce

½	**cup sugar plus sugar to taste, divided**
1	**tablespoon cornstarch**
	pinch of salt
1½	**cups cold water**
1	**tablespoon freshly squeezed lemon juice**
½	**teaspoon ground cinnamon**
	zest of 1 orange
1	**pint blueberries, divided**
2	**tablespoons Chambord**

- In a small saucepan, whisk together ½ cup sugar, cornstarch and salt until well combined. Whisk in water and lemon juice. Whisking constantly, bring to a boil over medium-high heat. Reduce heat to medium and simmer, whisking constantly, until slightly thickened. Add cinnamon, orange zest and half of blueberries. Whisking occasionally, simmer until blueberries are thoroughly cooked and have started to fall apart.
- Remove sauce from heat and purée in food processor or blender. Immediately add remaining blueberries while sauce is still hot.
- Taste sauce and add additional sugar if necessary.
- Cool completely and add Chambord.
- Serve over sliced cheesecake.

Yield: 12 servings

Top a plain cheesecake with colorful fresh fruit garnish.

- Begin with thinly sliced limes, lemons or oranges. Using a sharp knife, cut small V-shaped notches into the rind to form a cart-wheel. Or, make a twist by cutting into the center of a slice and twisting the ends in opposite directions.
- Slice a fresh strawberry several times vertically without cutting through the leafy top. Spread open the slices to create a fan.

As children canvas the neighborhood in search of Halloween candy, gather the adults for Orange Crème Brûlée and espresso at your house. Garnish plates with a sprinkling of candy corn and decorate the serving table with a glowing jack-o-lantern surrounded by fall leaves. After such a light dessert, your guests will still have room to sample candy from the children's trick-or-treat adventures.

Key Lime Cheesecake

Key lime juice adds a unique flavor to this delicately textured cheesecake.

32	graham cracker squares, finely chopped
½	cup butter, melted
2	(8-ounce) packages cream cheese, softened
1¼	cups sugar
¼	teaspoon salt
3	eggs, beaten
½	cup key lime juice
2	teaspoons vanilla extract
3	cups sour cream
2-4	drops green food coloring (optional)

- Preheat oven to 350°F.
- Combine graham cracker crumbs and melted butter. Firmly press mixture onto bottom and 1 inch up sides of a 10-inch springform pan.
- Beat together cream cheese, sugar, salt, eggs, lime juice and vanilla until smooth. Blend in sour cream. Add food coloring and mix well.
- Spoon filling over crust.
- Bake for 60 to 70 minutes or until edges are set. Center of cheesecake will be soft.
- Cool completely. Remove sides of pan prior to serving.

Yield: 16 servings

Orange Crème Brûlée

An elegant dessert with a hint of orange and a delightful consistency.

½	cup freshly squeezed orange juice, strained
2	cups heavy cream
½	cup sugar
6	large egg yolks, beaten
2	tablespoons Grand Marnier
2	teaspoons grated orange peel
1	teaspoon vanilla extract
2	tablespoons brown sugar

- Preheat oven to 350°F.
- In a heavy saucepan, boil orange juice for 5 minutes. Remove from heat.
- In a heavy saucepan, combine cream and sugar. Stirring constantly, cook over medium heat until sugar dissolves. Gradually whisk cream mixture into egg yolks. Add Grand Marnier and orange juice. Mix in orange peel and vanilla.

(continued on next page)

Orange Crème Brûlée *continued*

- Pour into 6 ungreased ¾-cup ramekins. Set ramekins in a shallow baking pan. Place in oven and add enough hot water to pan to reach halfway up sides of ramekins.
- Bake for 55 minutes or until custards are set in center.
- Remove ramekins from pan and cool completely.
- Cover custards loosely with plastic wrap and chill overnight.
- Set broiler rack so that custards will be 2 to 3 inches from heat and preheat broiler.
- Place ramekins on baking sheet. Sprinkle 1 teaspoon brown sugar over each custard.
- Broil for 2 minutes or until sugar is melted and caramelized. Rotate baking sheet for even broiling and watch closely to avoid burning.
- Chill for 20 minutes.

Yield: 6 servings

Coffee Crème Brûlée

Coffee liqueur adds a kick to creamy crème brûlée.

1   **egg**
6   **egg yolks**
²/₃   **cup sugar**
1¾ **cups heavy cream**
1¾ **cups milk**
2   **tablespoons Kahlúa**
1½ **tablespoons instant espresso powder**
¼   **cup brown sugar**

- Preheat oven to 325°F.
- Whisk together egg, egg yolks and sugar. Set aside.
- In a heavy saucepan, combine cream and milk. Stirring constantly, cook over medium-high heat until mixture just comes to a boil. Add Kahlúa and espresso powder. Stir until espresso powder dissolves. In a stream, add milk mixture to egg mixture. Whisk and skim off any froth.
- Pour into 8 ungreased ½-cup ramekins. Set ramekins in a shallow baking pan. Place in oven and add enough hot water to pan to reach halfway up sides of ramekins.
- Bake for 45 to 60 minutes or until custards are just set but still tremble slightly.
- Remove ramekins from pan and cool completely.
- Cover custards loosely with plastic wrap and chill for at least 4 hours.
- Set broiler rack so that custards will be 2 to 3 inches from heat and preheat broiler.
- Place ramekins on baking sheet. Sift brown sugar evenly over custards.
- Broil for 2 minutes or until sugar is melted and caramelized. Rotate baking sheet for even broiling and watch closely to avoid burning.
- Chill for 20 minutes.

Yield: 8 servings

Crème du Chocolate

The decadent chocolate taste belies this dessert's simplicity.

2   **eggs**
1   **tablespoon sugar**
    pinch of salt
1   **tablespoon brandy or liqueur**
1   **cup (about 6 ounces) semisweet chocolate bits, melted**
1   **cup hot milk**
    whipped cream

- In blender, combine eggs, sugar, salt, brandy or liqueur, chocolate bits and milk. Blend thoroughly.
- Pour into 4 individual dessert cups.
- Chill thoroughly.
- Top with whipped cream prior to serving.

Yield: 4 servings

Strawberry Soufflé

An airy dessert full of fresh strawberry flavor.

10 **eggs, separated**
2   **cups plus 2 tablespoons sugar, divided**
1   **quart strawberries, puréed**
¼ **teaspoon salt**
2   **(¼-ounce) envelopes unflavored gelatin**
½ **cup rum**
3   **cups heavy cream, divided**
    crystallized violets

- Beat egg yolks until light and fluffy. Gradually add 1 cup sugar. Beat until mixture forms a ribbon. Add strawberry purée and salt. Blend thoroughly.
- Transfer strawberry mixture to a heavy saucepan. Stirring constantly, cook over low heat until mixture thickens enough to coat the back of a spoon.
- Remove from heat and cool.
- In a small saucepan, sprinkle gelatin over rum. Set aside until solidified.
- Beat egg whites until foamy. Slowly add 1 cup sugar. Beat until mixture looks like marshmallow creme. Set aside.
- Beat 2 cups cream until soft peaks form. Set aside.
- Dissolve the gelatin mixture over very low heat. Stir into strawberry mixture. Fold in egg whites, then whipped cream.
- Fold a sheet of wax paper (long enough to fit around a 2-quart soufflé mold) in half lengthwise. Wrap it around the soufflé mold and fasten securely with a rubber band. Brush mold and collar with vegetable oil.
- Pour strawberry mixture into prepared soufflé mold. Refrigerate for at least 3 hours.

Yield: 10 servings

Strawberry Soufflé shows off beautifully with some added garnish. Prior to serving, remove collar from soufflé mold. Beat 1 cup cream until soft peaks form. Blend in 2 tablespoons sugar. Beat until stiff peaks form. Using a pastry bag with a star tip, pipe whipped cream into rosettes or stars on top of soufflé. Decorate with crystallized violets. Place the soufflé dish on a glass platter laden with pink rose blossoms.

Fearrington House Warm Chocolate Soufflés

Invite your guests to enjoy a taste from one of our area's premiere restaurants.

2 **tablespoons unsalted butter**
2 **tablespoons all-purpose flour**
1 **cup warm milk**
6 **tablespoons sugar**
   pinch of salt
2 **teaspoons vanilla extract**
8 **ounces unsweetened chocolate, melted and cooled slightly**
12 **egg whites**
½ **teaspoon cream of tartar**
   powdered sugar
   Chocolate Soufflé Sauce (recipe follows)
   whipped cream

- Preheat oven to 400°F.
- In a heavy saucepan, melt butter. Add flour. Stirring constantly, cook over medium heat for 2 to 3 minutes. Whisking rapidly, add milk all at once. Stir in sugar, salt and vanilla. Blend in melted chocolate.
- Beat egg whites until foamy. Add cream of tartar. Beat until stiff. Gently fold into chocolate mixture.
- Fill 8 greased 1-cup ramekins ⅔ full. Bake for 8 to 10 minutes.
- Dust tops of soufflés with powdered sugar.
- Serve immediately with Chocolate Soufflé Sauce and whipped cream.

Chocolate Soufflé Sauce

4 **ounces unsweetened chocolate, chopped**
1 **cup sugar**
⅛ **teaspoon salt**
¾ **cup heavy cream**
¼ **cup half-and-half**
1 **teaspoon vanilla extract**

- In a heavy saucepan, melt chocolate over low heat.
- Remove from heat and add sugar and salt. Set aside.
- Heat cream and half-and-half until just under a boil. Slowly whisk cream mixture into chocolate mixture. Stirring constantly, cook over low heat until completely smooth.
- Remove from heat and add vanilla.
- Cool to room temperature.
- Reheat in a double boiler.

Note: If necessary, adjust consistency with additional cream.

Yield: 8 servings

Second Empire Fresh Fruit Tart

The ornate Dodd-Hinsdale House in downtown Raleigh is home to the fine cuisine of the Second Empire Restaurant.

1¼ **cups all-purpose flour**
2   **tablespoons sugar**
    pinch of salt
½ **cup butter, cut into ½-inch cubes**
1   **egg yolk, slightly beaten**
    Pastry Cream (recipe follows)
    Fruit Topping (recipe follows)

- Sift together flour, sugar and salt. Cut in butter until mixture resembles coarse crumbs. Add egg yolk and mix gently until dough just holds together. If mixture is too dry, add a few drops of cold water or cream.
- Turn dough out onto a lightly floured surface. Gently knead dough a few times.
- Flatten dough into a disc. Wrap in wax paper and refrigerate for 30 minutes.
- Turn dough out onto a lightly floured surface. Roll dough into a 10-inch circle.
- Fold dough carefully into quarters. Gently lift and fit into a 9-inch tart pan with removable bottom. Prick bottom of tart shell with a fork.
- Freeze for 1 hour.
- Preheat oven to 375°F.
- Spray inside of foil square with nonstick cooking spray. Fit foil square snugly against tart shell.
- Bake for 12 to 15 minutes. Remove foil and bake for a few more minutes until pastry is lightly browned.
- Place on wire rack to cool completely.

Pastry Cream

2   **eggs**
½ **cup sugar**
7   **tablespoons all-purpose flour**
2   **cups whole milk**
1   **teaspoon vanilla extract**
1   **tablespoon butter, melted**

- Combine eggs, sugar and flour. Beat with mixer until thick and lemon-colored. Set aside.
- In a heavy, non-reactive saucepan, heat milk to boiling. Slowly whisk milk into egg mixture. Return to saucepan. Stirring constantly, cook over low heat until thick. Do not boil.
- Pour pastry cream into a clean bowl. Add vanilla. Coat surface with butter to prevent skin from forming. Cover with plastic wrap and chill.

(continued on next page)

Second Empire Fresh Fruit Tart *continued*

Fruit Topping

½	**cup apricot jam**
2 to 3	**tablespoons water**
1	**cup raspberries**
2	**bananas, peeled and sliced**
2	**kiwi fruit, peeled and sliced**
1	**pint strawberries, stemmed**
2	**oranges, peeled and sectioned**

- In a small saucepan, melt jam with water. Strain if lumpy. Lightly brush half of jam inside tart shell.
- Spoon pastry cream into tart shell.
- Decoratively arrange fruit in concentric circles on top of pastry cream, starting with raspberries and ending with oranges.
- Brush fruit lightly with remaining jam.
- Remove tart pan prior to serving.

Note: Seasonal fruits may be substituted for any of the above. For contrast, alternate colors of fruit.

Yield: 8 servings

Strawberry Crowned Chocolate Tart

The pecan crust is a surprising extra in this quickly assembled tart.

2	**cups pecans, toasted**
6	**tablespoons brown sugar**
¼	**teaspoon ground cinnamon**
¼	**cup unsalted butter, melted**
¾	**cup heavy cream**
6	**ounces semisweet chocolate, chopped**
2	**(16-ounce) packages strawberries, stemmed**
1	**(18-ounce) jar seedless raspberry jam**

- Preheat oven to 350°F.
- In a food processor fitted with steel blade, process pecans, brown sugar and cinnamon until finely chopped. Add butter and process until moist clumps form.
- Firmly press mixture onto bottom and up sides of a 9-inch tart pan.
- Bake for 30 minutes or until golden and firm to the touch.
- Place on wire rack to cool completely.
- Melt cream and chocolate in microwave. Stir until smooth.
- Pour chocolate mixture into cooled crust. Chill for 1 hour.
- Arrange strawberries, points up, on top of tart.
- Warm jam in microwave. Brush generously over strawberries.
- Spoon remaining jam over tart prior to serving.

Yield: 8 servings

Toast pecans in a conventional or microwave oven. Heat a conventional oven to 350°. Spread the pecans in a single layer on a baking sheet. Bake for 5 to 10 minutes or until light golden brown, stirring once.

For a microwave, spread pecans in a microwave-safe pan and heat on high for 4 to 8 minutes until lightly browned, stirring frequently.

Prepared in advance, chocolate garnishes add a quick, tasteful touch to individual desserts.
Chocolate Curls: Let a bar of milk chocolate come to room temperature. Carefully draw a vegetable peeler across the chocolate at an angle.
Chocolate Leaves: Use non-toxic leaves such as mint, ivy or strawberry. Brush melted chocolate on the underside of washed and dried leaves using a small paint brush. Wipe off any excess chocolate from the top of the leaf and place the leaf, chocolate side up, on a baking sheet covered with waxed paper. Chill or freeze until hardened. Peel the leaf away from the chocolate before serving.
Chocolate-Dipped Fruit or Nuts: Use confectioners' coating or melted milk chocolate for dipping. Wash and dry fresh strawberries, grapes or orange slices. Dried apricots work equally well, as do whole almonds and walnuts. Dip one half of the piece of fruit or nut into the melted chocolate and allow the excess to drip off. Place on waxed paper to dry.

Chocolate Seduction

Dress up this simple dessert to delight your favorite chocolate fan.

2   deep dish pie crusts
8   ounces unsweetened chocolate
2   cups butter
5   cups sugar
1   cup heavy cream
8   eggs, beaten
2   egg yolks, beaten
1   tablespoon vanilla extract
    whipped cream

- Preheat oven to 425°F.
- Prick pie crusts with a fork and bake for 5 minutes.
- Reduce heat to 350°F.
- In a large, heavy saucepan, melt chocolate and butter over low heat, stirring frequently. Add sugar and cream. Stir until sugar dissolves.
- Remove from heat. Gradually add eggs and egg yolks, stirring until mixture is smooth and thick. Blend in vanilla.
- Pour chocolate mixture into pie crusts.
- Bake for 25 to 30 minutes or until completely set.
- Top with whipped cream prior to serving.

Variation: To make tarts rather than pies, spoon chocolate mixture into 225 thumb size miniature tart shells and bake for 20 minutes or until almost set.

Yield: 16 servings

Coconut Chess Pie

A treasured southern tradition

1	pie crust
1½	cups sugar
1	tablespoon all-purpose flour
1	tablespoon cornmeal
½	teaspoon salt
5	eggs, lightly beaten
3	tablespoons butter, melted
3	tablespoons half-and-half
1	teaspoon vanilla extract
1	(4-ounce) can coconut

- Preheat oven to 425°F.
- Prick pie crust with a fork and bake for 5 minutes.
- Reduce heat to 375°F.
- Sift together sugar, flour, cornmeal and salt. Mix in eggs. Add butter, half-and-half and vanilla. Fold in coconut.
- Pour coconut mixture into pie crust.
- Bake for 30 minutes. Reduce heat to 300°F and bake for 30 additional minutes.

Yield: 8 servings

Use a food processor for homemade pie crust taste without the hassle. In a food processor fitted with steel blade, process 1 cup all-purpose flour and ¼ teaspoon salt, pulsing 4 times to combine. Add ⅓ cup shortening and pulse 5 or 6 times until the mixture resembles coarse crumbs. With food processor running, slowly add 2 to 4 tablespoons of ice water. Process just until dough begins to form a ball. Wrap dough in waxed paper and refrigerate for one hour. Turn dough onto a lightly floured surface and flatten into a 6-inch circle. Roll dough into a ⅛-inch thick 11-inch circle. Place in a 9-inch pie plate and trim excess pastry. Fold edges under and flute.

Fresh Lemon Pie

Finish off springtime meals with a lemony pie.

2   pie crusts
4   eggs, separated
½   cup butter, softened
1½ cups sugar
½   cup water
⅓   cup freshly squeezed lemon juice
       zest of 1 lemon
2   teaspoons all-purpose flour
1   teaspoon cornstarch
       whipped cream

- Preheat oven to 425°F.
- Prick pie crusts with a fork and bake for 5 minutes.
- Beat egg whites until stiff but not dry. Set aside.
- Cream butter and sugar until fluffy. Add egg yolks and beat well. Add water, lemon juice, lemon zest, flour and cornstarch. Blend well. Fold in egg whites.
- Pour lemon mixture into pie crusts.
- Bake for 10 minutes. Reduce heat to 325°F and bake for 20 to 25 additional minutes or until a knife inserted halfway between edge and center comes out clean. Cover loosely with foil for the last 10 to 15 minutes if top is browning too quickly.
- Remove from oven and place on wire rack to cool completely.
- Top with whipped cream prior to serving.

Yield: 16 servings

Cranberry Pie

A rustic-looking pie highlighting tart cranberries.

2	pie crusts
2	cups cranberries
1	cup sugar, divided
1/2	cup brown sugar
1	cup coconut
1	cup chopped pecans
1	cup all-purpose flour
2	eggs, beaten
1/3	cup butter, melted, plus enough vegetable oil to make 3/4 cup
1	teaspoon vanilla extract

- Preheat oven to 425°F.
- Prick pie crusts with a fork and bake for 5 minutes.
- Reduce heat to 350°F.
- Combine cranberries, 1/2 cup sugar, brown sugar, coconut and pecans.
- Pour cranberry mixture into pie crusts.
- Mix together flour, 1/2 cup sugar, eggs, butter and oil, and vanilla. Spread gently over cranberry mixture.
- Bake for 35 to 40 minutes.

Yield: 16 servings

Create decorative pie crusts in a few easy steps.

- **Sunburst Edges:** Trim the dough even with the pan edge. Cut 1/2-inch slits around the dough edge at 1/2-inch intervals. Fold each piece in half diagonally to form a triangle.

- **Cut-Out Decorations:** Trim the dough even with the pan edge. Use a canapé cutter or small cookie cutter to cut shapes from excess dough. Brush the edge of the crust with egg white and press the cut shapes onto the edge of the crust. Vary the cutouts to fit the season, using stars for Fourth of July or small leaf shapes for autumn.

- **Decorative Scallop:** Trim the dough even with the pan edge. Form a stand up rim with the dough and pinch it into scallops with your thumb and forefinger. Dip a fork into flour and press the tines gently into the center of each scallop.

42nd Street Apple Pie with Rum Sauce

Patrons frequent the 42nd Street Oyster Bar in downtown Raleigh not only for the seafood, but to sample this scrumptious apple pie.

1   pie crust
1½ cups plus 1¼ teaspoons all-purpose flour, divided
1⅓ cups plus ½ cup brown sugar, divided
¾   cup plus 1 tablespoon butter, melted
2   pounds (about 6 medium) cooking apples, peeled and chopped
½   teaspoon ground cinnamon
¼   teaspoon ground nutmeg
¼   cup water
    Rum Sauce (recipe follows)

- Preheat oven to 425°F.
- Prick pie crust with a fork and bake for 5 minutes.
- Reduce heat to 300°F.
- Combine 1½ cups flour and 1⅓ cups brown sugar. Add melted butter and mix well. Set aside.
- In a very large saucepan, combine apples, ½ cup brown sugar, cinnamon, nutmeg and water. Bring to a boil, then simmer until liquid is almost a glaze.
- Remove from heat. Stir in 1¼ teaspoons flour and 1 cup brown sugar mixture.
- Pour apple mixture into pie crust. Top with remaining brown sugar mixture.
- Bake for 50 minutes. Raise heat to 350°F and bake for 15 additional minutes.

Rum Sauce

1½ cups plus 2 tablespoons butter
1¾ cups plus 2 tablespoons brown sugar
¼   cup honey
3   ounces dark rum

- In a large, heavy saucepan, combine butter and brown sugar. Stirring every 10 minutes, cook over low heat for 50 minutes.
- Whisk in honey and cook for 10 additional minutes or until honey is dissolved.
- Turn off heat and stir in rum. Mixture will bubble up when rum is added.
- Spoon over pie prior to serving.

Note: Do not refrigerate.

Yield: 8 servings

Seasonal Fruit Cobbler

Cobblers are easy, flexible and fast. Fresh fruit cobblers are best, but canned fruit will work in a pinch.

4   **cups fruit, sliced if necessary**
1½ **cups plus 2 tablespoons sugar, divided**
½   **cup butter, softened**
2   **eggs, slightly beaten**
     dash of vanilla extract
1   **box pie crust mix**
½   **teaspoon ground cinnamon**
½   **teaspoon ground nutmeg**

• Preheat oven to 350°F.
• Spread fruit in a greased 13x9-inch baking pan. Sprinkle with 2 tablespoons sugar.
• Cream butter and 1½ cups sugar. Add eggs, vanilla, pie crust mix, cinnamon and nutmeg. Blend until mixture looks like gooey cookie dough. Spread topping over fruit.
• Bake for 30 minutes or until topping is golden and bubbly.

Yield: 10 servings

Grandma's Blackberry Dumplings

Surprise your family with a berry season treat.

1   **quart blackberries**
1   **cup plus 1 tablespoon sugar, divided**
¾   **teaspoon salt, divided**
½   **teaspoon lemon extract**
1½ **cups all-purpose flour**
2   **teaspoons baking powder**
¼   **teaspoon ground nutmeg**
⅔   **cup milk**
     whipped cream

• Preheat oven to 400°F.
• Combine blackberries, 1 cup sugar, ¼ teaspoon salt and lemon extract in a large ovenproof Dutch oven. Bring to a boil, then reduce heat and simmer for 5 minutes.
• Combine flour, baking powder, ½ teaspoon salt, 1 tablespoon sugar and nutmeg. Stir in milk until just blended. Drop dough by tablespoonfuls onto hot blackberry mixture.
• Bake for 35 minutes or until golden.
• Top with whipped cream prior to serving.

Yield: 6 servings

"One year when I was a child I requested blackberry dumplings instead of birthday cake for my December birthday. Of course, blackberries weren't available in the middle of winter. My mother remembered to freeze extra berries during the summer to prepare my favorite dessert on my next birthday."

Apple Dumplings

A warm, apple-infused sauce adds to the appeal of crisp dumplings.

1½ cups all-purpose flour
½   teaspoon baking powder
½   teaspoon salt
½   cup shortening
¼   cup orange juice
6½ tablespoons sugar
1   teaspoon ground cinnamon
½   teaspoon ground nutmeg
6   tablespoons butter, softened
3   red cooking apples, peeled, reserving peelings, and chopped
    Sauce (recipe follows)

- Sift together flour, baking powder and salt. Cut in shortening until mixture resembles coarse crumbs. Gradually stir in orange juice until dough holds together.
- Form dough into a ball. Wrap in wax paper and refrigerate for 1 hour.
- Preheat oven to 375°F.
- Sift together sugar, cinnamon and nutmeg. Set aside.
- Turn dough out onto a lightly floured surface. Roll dough into a ⅛-inch thick 18x12-inch rectangle. Cut into six 6-inch squares. In the center of each square, spread 1 tablespoon butter. Place at least 2 tablespoons apples in the center of each square and sprinkle with 1/6 of sugar mixture. Gather corners of pastry and pinch together.
- Place in a greased 8-inch round cake pan with edges touching.
- Bake for 45 minutes or until golden brown.

Sauce

    reserved apple peelings
1½ cups water
¼   cup butter
1   tablespoon all-purpose flour
1   cup sugar
    juice of ½ lemon

- Boil reserved apple peelings in water until reduced to ¾ cup. Discard peelings and set liquid aside.
- Melt butter. Blend in flour. Gradually add peeling liquid. Stir in sugar and lemon juice. Stirring constantly, cook until thickened. Serve warm over dumplings.

Yield: 6 servings

Chocolate Cloaked Pears

Elegant pears are even more exquisite when served on a pool of crème anglaise.

5   cups water
1¼ cups sugar
2   (3-inch) cinnamon sticks
3   whole allspice berries
6   whole cloves
8   small ripe Bosc pears, peeled and rubbed with a lemon half
20 amaretti cookies, crumbled
2   tablespoons rum
8   ounces semisweet chocolate
2   tablespoons unsalted butter
1/6 cake of paraffin
     chocolate leaves, crystallized violets or fresh mint leaves
2   cups crème anglaise

- In a large pot, combine water with sugar, cinnamon, allspice and cloves. Stirring occasionally, cook over medium heat until sugar dissolves. Turn heat to low and simmer for 30 minutes.
- Core pears from the bottom, leaving stem end intact. Add pears to syrup and simmer for 20 minutes or until just tender. Cool in syrup for 24 hours.
- Remove pears from syrup and dry thoroughly with paper towels.
- Mash cookies and rum together with a fork, adding a small amount of water if necessary to make a firm mixture. Pack cookie mixture into pear cavities.
- In top of double boiler, melt chocolate, butter and paraffin over barely simmering water. Dip pears in chocolate, coating them evenly. If necessary, smooth chocolate with a spatula. Place upright on a wax paper lined baking sheet until set.
- Decorate with chocolate leaves, crystallized violets or fresh mint leaves. Serve on a pool of crème anglaise.

Note: Leftover syrup can be used to make spiced apples. Boil sliced apples in syrup for 5 minutes or until they reach desired tenderness.

Variation: Prepare syrup. Cool completely. Preheat oven to 350°F. Combine 2 cups syrup with the juice of half a lemon and 2 tablespoons Frangelico. Dip raw Bosc pears in syrup mixture and place on an ungreased baking sheet. Sprinkle each pear with ⅓ cup sugar. Bake for 1 hour and 30 minutes.

Yield: 8 servings

Crème Anglaise

- **Combine 2 cups milk, 3 tablespoons sugar and a 1-inch piece of vanilla bean, split and scraped, in a medium saucepan.**
- **Cook over low heat, stirring occasionally, until sugar is dissolved.**
- **Remove from heat.**
- **Slightly beat 4 egg yolks and whisk in a small amount of the hot milk.**
- **Add the eggs to the remaining hot milk mixture.**
- **Stir constantly over low heat for ten minutes or until the custard coats a wooden spoon.**
- **Strain the custard, then replace the vanilla bean and chill.**

Ginger is a plant grown for its gnarled root. The root's buff colored skin must be peeled away for the spicy flesh underneath. An everyday spoon makes the best tool for peeling ginger. Fresh, mature ginger is available in the produce section of most supermarkets and oriental markets. Young ginger, which needs no peeling, is more difficult to find.

Puff Pastry Domes with Caramelized Bananas and Ginger Ice Cream

Unusual flavors combine to impress your special guests.

6   tablespoons butter
6   small, ripe bananas, halved lengthwise then crosswise
6   tablespoons sugar
¼   cup chopped pecans, toasted
½   cup rum
     Puff Pastry (recipe follows)
     Ginger Ice Cream (recipe follows)

- Melt butter over medium heat. Add bananas and cook until coated with butter, about 30 seconds on each side. Stir in sugar and pecans. Remove from heat and add rum. Return to heat and sauté for 30 seconds until sauce coats bananas.
- On individual dessert plates, arrange 3 banana pieces in a fan design. Spoon sauce over bananas. Place a puff pastry on top of bananas and a scoop of Ginger Ice Cream to the side.

Puff Pastry

1½ pounds puff pastry
1   egg yolk
3   tablespoons heavy cream

- Preheat oven to 400°F.
- Turn dough out onto a lightly floured surface. Roll dough to ⅜-inch thickness. Cut dough into 2x4-inch rectangles. Place on greased baking sheet.
- Whisk together egg yolk and cream. Brush on pastries.
- Bake for 20 minutes or until pastries are puffed and golden.
- Remove to wire rack to cool completely.

Ginger Ice Cream

¼   cup Szechwan peppercorns
1¾ cups half-and-half, scalded
8   ounces fresh ginger, peeled and chopped
¾   cup sugar
¼   cup water
9   egg yolks, at room temperature
1   teaspoon vanilla extract
     pinch of salt
1   cup heavy cream

- Stirring occasionally, cook peppercorns in a small skillet for 4 minutes. Mix with scalded half-and-half. Cool completely.

(continued on next page)

Puff Pastry Domes *continued*

- In a heavy saucepan, cook ginger, sugar and water over low heat until sugar dissolves. Increase heat to a simmer and cook for 25 minutes or until ginger is tender.
- Combine egg yolks, vanilla, salt and peppercorn mixture. Whisk in ginger mixture.
- Return to saucepan. Stirring constantly, cook over medium low heat 10 minutes or until thickened.
- Remove from heat and whisk in cream.
- Strain custard. Cover and chill.
- Process in an ice cream freezer according to the manufacturer's directions.

Note: Szechwan peppercorns can be purchased at Asian markets.

Yield: 8 servings

Maple Mousse Ice Cream
You don't need an ice cream freezer to make this uniquely flavored ice cream.

3   **eggs, well beaten**
¾   **cup maple syrup**
2   **cups heavy cream, whipped**

- Combine eggs and maple syrup in the top of a double boiler. Stirring constantly, cook until thickened.
- Cool completely.
- Fold whipped cream into maple syrup mixture.
- Pour into a chilled freezer tray. Freeze until firm, stirring 2 to 3 times.

Yield: 8 servings

Maple Mousse Ice Cream is a mouth-watering base for a waffle sundae. Top a warm waffle with ice cream, fudge sauce, toasted nuts and whipped cream sprinkled with cinnamon. For children, spread a thick layer of ice cream between two cinnamon graham crackers and smooth the ice cream around the sides with a knife. Wrap the sandwich in plastic wrap and freeze until slightly firm.

For maximum volume when beating egg whites, bring them first to room temperature. Be sure the bowl and mixer are clean and dry. Even a small amount of grease or a speck of yolk will prevent the whites from whipping properly. Copper bowls work best. Begin beating slowly, gradually increasing speed as the whites begin to foam. Beat continuously until the egg whites hold the desired shape, either stiff or soft peaks.

Peppermint Ice Cream in Meringue Cups

Delicious during the holidays or on a hot summer day

4   egg whites
1⅓ cups sugar
½   teaspoon baking powder
1   teaspoon vanilla extract
    Peppermint Ice Cream (recipe follows)

- Preheat oven to 200°F.
- Beat egg whites until foamy. Slowly add sugar, baking powder and vanilla. Beat until stiff.
- Spoon meringue into 8 equal portions onto an ungreased, foil-lined baking sheet. Using the back of a spoon, shape meringues into 4-inch circles. Using the tip of a spoon, make a well in the middle of each meringue.
- Bake for 1 hour and 30 minutes.
- Turn off heat. Leave meringues in oven to cool overnight.

Peppermint Ice Cream

½   gallon vanilla ice cream, cut into small pieces
2   cups heavy cream
⅔   cup powdered sugar
½   teaspoon vanilla extract
½   cup finely crushed soft peppermint sticks
8   drops red food coloring

- Place ice cream in a chilled bowl. Let soften slightly in the refrigerator.
- Beat cream until soft peaks form. Blend in powdered sugar and vanilla. Beat until stiff peaks form.
- Quickly blend together softened ice cream, whipped cream mixture, peppermint sticks and food coloring.
- Pour into a chilled freezer tray and freeze until firm.
- Place meringue cups on individual dessert plates.
- Top with a scoop of Peppermint Ice Cream.

Variation: Top meringue cups with a scoop of vanilla ice cream and sugared berries.

Yield: 8 servings

Frozen Mocha Torte
with Amaretto Cinnamon Sauce

Layers of chocolate, coffee and cinnamon ice cream with a heavenly sauce

36	graham cracker squares
²/₃	cup slivered almonds
¹/₃	cup butter, cut into small pieces
1	quart chocolate ice cream, softened
1	quart coffee ice cream, softened
1	quart vanilla ice cream, softened
2¹/₂	teaspoons ground cinnamon
	Amaretto Cinnamon Sauce (recipe follows)

- Preheat oven to 375°F.
- In a food processor fitted with steel blade, process graham crackers and almonds until finely chopped. Add butter and process until blended.
- Firmly press mixture onto bottom and 1 inch up sides of a 10-inch springform pan.
- Bake for 10 minutes.
- Place on wire rack to cool completely.
- Beat chocolate ice cream with mixer at low speed. Spread onto bottom and 1 inch up sides of crust. Freeze until firm.
- Beat coffee ice cream at low speed. Spread over chocolate ice cream. Freeze until firm.
- Beat vanilla ice cream and cinnamon at low speed until blended. Spread over coffee ice cream. Freeze for 8 hours.

Amaretto Cinnamon Sauce

³/₄	cup honey
³/₄	cup Amaretto
¹/₄	teaspoon ground cinnamon
¹/₃	cup slivered almonds, toasted

- In a small saucepan, combine honey, Amaretto and cinnamon. Stirring occasionally, cook over medium heat. Cool to room temperature prior to serving.
- Cut torte into wedges. Place onto individual dessert plates. Sprinkle with toasted almonds and drizzle with Amaretto Cinnamon Sauce.

Yield: 12 servings

When a local supper club was featured in *Southern Living* magazine, the photo shoot turned into a memorable weekend. "The photographer came in October and shot our group here in Raleigh at our house. It was very chilly that day. We all had to wear summer clothes and pretend it was July. I was calling neighbors ahead of time, asking to borrow still-blooming plants for our yard. The food editor said the photographer would only stay an hour or two. We had such a great time, he stayed all day and the next. I even gave him tickets to the State Fair!"

Raleigh's blissfully long porch season allows us additional time to enjoy the outdoors, to escape the sun's direct heat and to casually entertain neighbors and friends who happen by. Providing a focal point for the invitation to come up and sit for a spell is important. A hand-cranked ice cream freezer gets everyone involved and lengthens the stay of drop-in guests. The promise of ice cream served fresh from the dipper keeps everyone's attention riveted.

Summer Fruit Ice Cream

Fresh strawberries, raspberries or peaches flavor homemade ice cream.

2   quarts milk, divided
4   eggs
2   cups sugar, divided
1   heaping tablespoon all-purpose flour
4   cups ripe fruit, chopped if necessary

- In a heavy saucepan, combine 1 quart milk, eggs, 1 cup sugar and flour. Stirring constantly, cook over medium heat for 5 minutes or until mixture comes to a boil. Remove from heat.
- Combine fruit with remaining 1 cup sugar. Fold into milk mixture. Add remaining 1 quart milk.
- Process in an ice cream freezer according to the manufacturer's directions.

Yield: 12 servings

Champagne Peach Sherbet

A celebration of fruit with the sparkle of champagne.

½   cup sugar
½   cup water
5   very ripe peaches, peeled, pitted and cut into 1-inch pieces
1   tablespoon freshly squeezed lemon juice
    well-chilled champagne, divided
1   egg white

- Combine sugar and water in a 2-cup glass measuring cup. Stirring once, cook on high in microwave for 1½ minutes or until sugar is dissolved.
- In a food processor fitted with steel blade, process peaches until smooth, stopping occasionally to scrape down sides of bowl. Add syrup and lemon juice and process for 5 seconds. Cover and refrigerate until well chilled.
- Stir 1 cup champagne into peach mixture.
- Process in an ice cream freezer according to the manufacturer's directions. When slushy but not quite frozen, mix in egg white and finish freezing.
- Just before serving, scoop sherbet into champagne glasses. Pour champagne over sherbet and serve.

Yield: 5 servings

Matt's Watermelon Ice

Offer this simple fruity cooler as a treat to check the heat of the summer.

4	cups cubed watermelon, seeded
2	tablespoons lime juice
½	cup sugar

- In a food processor fitted with steel blade, process watermelon, lime juice and sugar until sugar dissolves and mixture is smooth.
- Process in an ice cream freezer according to the manufacturer's directions or freeze for 2 hours in chilled freezer trays, stirring occasionally.

Yield: 6 servings

Refreshing Berry Sorbet

Make more than one batch using different berries for a colorful, tasteful presentation.

3	cups blackberries, raspberries or strawberries
½	cup cold water
1	cup sugar
1	tablespoon lemon juice
1	tablespoon vodka or berry liqueur

- In a food processor fitted with steel blade, process berries and water until smooth, stopping occasionally to scrape down sides of bowl.
- Strain purée into a metal bowl set over a larger bowl filled with ice water. Add sugar, lemon juice and vodka or berry liqueur. Stir occasionally for several minutes until sugar has dissolved. To see if sugar has dissolved, rub finger along bottom of bowl.
- If necessary, cover and refrigerate until well chilled.
- Process in an ice cream freezer according to the manufacturer's directions.
- Cover and ripen in freezer for 1 to 2 hours.

Yield: 4 servings

Raleigh is home to the State Farmers Market, a multi-building complex carrying everything in season: field-fresh produce, homebaked goods, cut flowers, gardening supplies and herbs for planting. An outing to the market on a fine morning is a delight any time of year. In summer the individual stands are crowded with stacks of fruits and vegetables from nearby farms. In October the pumpkins, squash and hand-painted Halloween cutout decorations seem to go on forever. Around Christmas, the freshest fir trees from the North Carolina mountains fill the air with the scent of evergreens.

Sinful Caramel Squares

Rich, sweet squares layered with chocolate, caramel and pecans

1	**(14-ounce) package caramels**
⅔	**cup evaporated milk, divided**
1	**box German chocolate cake mix**
¾	**cup butter, melted**
1	**cup chopped pecans, divided**
2	**cups (about 12 ounces) semisweet chocolate chips**

- Preheat oven to 350°F.
- Melt caramels with ⅓ cup evaporated milk over low heat, stirring until smooth. Keep warm.
- Combine remaining ⅓ cup evaporated milk, cake mix and melted butter. Mix well.
- Press half of cake mixture into bottom of greased and floured 13x9-inch baking pan.
- Bake in center of oven for 6 minutes.
- Sprinkle ¾ cup pecans and chocolate chips over crust. Top with caramel mixture, spreading to edges of pan. Drop teaspoons of remaining cake mixture over top of caramel. Press gently to spread. Sprinkle with remaining ¼ cup pecans.
- Bake for 20 additional minutes.
- Cool completely. Cut into 2-inch squares.

Yield: 24 squares

Frosted Chocolate Kahlúa Bars

A combination of chocolate and coffee in a dense bar cookie

1¼ **cups all-purpose flour, divided**
¼   **cup sugar**
½   **cup butter, softened**
½   **teaspoon baking powder**
½   **cup cocoa**
1   **(14-ounce) can sweetened condensed milk**
1   **egg**
2   **tablespoons Kahlúa or 1 teaspoon instant coffee dissolved in 1 table-
      spoon hot water**
1   **teaspoon vanilla extract**
¾   **cup chopped nuts**
     Frosting (recipe follows)

- Preheat oven to 350°F.
- Sift together 1 cup flour and sugar. Cut in butter until mixture resembles coarse crumbs.
- Press flour mixture firmly into bottom of greased 13x9-inch baking pan.
- Bake in center of oven for 15 minutes.
- Combine remaining ¼ cup flour, baking powder, cocoa, sweetened condensed milk, egg, Kahlúa or dissolved coffee and vanilla. Mix well. Stir in nuts. Spread over crust.
- Bake for 20 additional minutes or until center is set.
- Cool completely.

Frosting

¾   **cup butter, softened**
2   **cups powdered sugar**
1   **tablespoon milk**
½   **teaspoon vanilla extract**
½   **(1.55-ounce) milk chocolate bar, grated**

- Cream butter with mixer at medium speed. Gradually add powdered sugar, beating until light and fluffy. Add milk and beat until spreading consistency. Stir in vanilla. Spread frosting on cooled brownies.
- Sprinkle with chocolate shavings.
- Cut into 2-inch squares.

Yield: 24 squares

At casual gatherings of
book clubs or garden
clubs, a simple spread of
freshly perked coffee, hot
tea and, of course,
something made of
chocolate, stands as the
perfect refreshment.
Add these special touches
to your coffee bar:

- Flavored creams to stir
  into coffee or tea
- Flavored sugars to
  sweeten everyone's
  drink (store a small
  container of sugar
  containing a whole
  vanilla bean in the
  pantry to have on hand)
- A basket of varied tea
  packets, including
  decaffeinated spice or
  herbal teas
- Your real china teacups
  or a generous ceramic
  mug for everyone
- Matching plates and
  napkins for stacks of
  sweets
- A centerpiece to fit your
  theme, such as a
  grouping of books or a
  pot of herbs.

Fudgy Mint Brownies

Basic brownies show off with a swirl of color and mint flavor.

1   (8-ounce) package cream cheese, softened
2¼ cups sugar, divided
5   eggs, divided
1   teaspoon mint extract
4   drops green food coloring
1   cup butter
4   ounces unsweetened chocolate, chopped
2   teaspoons vanilla extract
1   cup all-purpose flour
     Frosting (recipe follows)

- Preheat oven to 350°F.
- Beat cream cheese and ¼ cup sugar until smooth. Add 1 egg, mint extract and food coloring. Mix well. Set aside.
- Stirring frequently, melt butter and chocolate in a large, heavy saucepan over low heat.
- Remove from heat and cool slightly.
- Stir in 2 cups sugar and vanilla. Add 4 eggs, one at a time, beating well after each addition. Stir in flour. Mix well.
- Spread brownie mixture into a greased and floured 13x9-inch baking pan. Carefully spoon cream cheese mixture over brownie mixture and lightly swirl the two together.
- Bake in center of oven for 45 to 50 minutes or until set.
- Cool completely.

Frosting

¼   cup butter
¼   cup light corn syrup
¼   cup water
4   ounces unsweetened chocolate, chopped
2   teaspoons vanilla extract
2   cups powdered sugar

- In a heavy saucepan, bring butter, corn syrup and water to a rolling boil.
- Remove from heat. Add chocolate and stir until melted. Stir in vanilla and powdered sugar. Beat until smooth. Spread frosting on cooled brownies.
- Cut into 2-inch squares.

Yield: 24 brownies

Raleigh's Best Ever Cookies

Cookies so loaded with ingredients they need to be made monster size.

½ **cup butter, softened**
1 **cup sugar**
1 **cup plus 2 tablespoons brown sugar**
2 **teaspoons baking soda**
¼ **teaspoon salt**
3 **eggs**
¾ **teaspoon light corn syrup**
¼ **teaspoon vanilla extract**
2 **cups (about 18 ounces) crunchy peanut butter**
4½ **cups rolled oats**
1 **(10-ounce) bag candy coated milk chocolate pieces**
1 **cup (about 6 ounces) semisweet chocolate chips**

- Preheat oven to 350°F.
- Combine butter, sugar, brown sugar, baking soda, salt, eggs, corn syrup, vanilla and peanut butter. Mix well. Mix in oats. Stir in candy coated milk chocolate pieces and chocolate chips.
- Drop 2 inches apart by heaping tablespoonfuls onto a greased baking sheet.
- Bake in center of oven for 10 to 12 minutes.
- Transfer cookies to a wire rack to cool completely.

Yield: 48 cookies

Before storing cookies of any type, allow them to cool completely. Keep soft cookies moist and chewy by storing them in an airtight container. A small slice of apple or bread placed in the container will help keep them from drying out. Crisp cookies are best stored in a container with a loose fitting lid. Bar cookies keep well in their baking pan covered tightly with aluminum foil or plastic wrap.

Angel Kisses

An airy cookie with crunchy chocolate chips and pecans.

2 **egg whites**
⅔ **cup sugar**
   pinch of salt
1 **tablespoon vanilla extract**
1 **cup (about 6 ounces) semisweet chocolate chips**
½ **cup chopped pecans**

- Preheat oven to 350°F.
- Beat egg whites until foamy. Slowly add sugar, salt and vanilla. Beat until stiff. Gently fold in chocolate chips and pecans.
- Drop onto an ungreased foil-lined baking sheet.
- Place in oven. Turn off heat and leave overnight.

Note: Store in a metal tin to keep cookies from getting soggy.

Yield: 48 cookies

Meringue cookies bake up best on a non-humid day, not an easy proposition in the steamy Carolina summertime. To vary Angel Kisses for special occasions, substitute butterscotch chips or dried cherries for the chocolate chips. A few drops of food coloring mixed into the batter turns them pink for Valentine's Day or a rainbow of pastel colors for Easter.

Glazed Apple Cookies

Hearty cookies with a tipsy taste

2	cups all-purpose flour
½	teaspoon baking soda
½	teaspoon salt
¾	teaspoon ground cinnamon
½	cup butter, softened
1¼	cups brown sugar
1	egg
¼	cup buttermilk
1	cup (about 1 medium) chopped cooking apples
1	cup raisins
1	cup chopped walnuts
	Glaze (recipe follows)

- Preheat oven to 350°F.
- Sift together flour, baking soda, salt and cinnamon. Set aside.
- Cream butter. Gradually add brown sugar, beating well. Beat in egg. Add flour mixture alternately with buttermilk, beginning and ending with dry ingredients. Fold in apples, raisins and walnuts.
- Drop two inches apart by heaping tablespoonfuls onto a greased baking sheet.
- Bake in center of oven for 15 minutes or until golden brown.
- Transfer cookies to a wire rack placed over wax paper.

Glaze

1	cup powdered sugar
3	tablespoons apple juice or brandy

- Combine powdered sugar and apple juice or brandy. Spoon over hot cookies.

Yield: 30 cookies

Painted Sugar Cookies

A painted-on glaze makes these sugar cookies fun to make and eat. Great for children's parties!

3¾ cups all-purpose flour
1½ teaspoons baking powder
1   teaspoon salt
1   cup butter, softened
1½ cups sugar
2   teaspoons vanilla extract
2   eggs
       Glaze (recipe follows)

- Sift together flour, baking powder and salt. Set aside.
- Cream butter, sugar and vanilla until fluffy. Add eggs, one at a time. Slowly add flour mixture and blend well.
- Form dough into 2 balls. Wrap in wax paper and refrigerate for 1 hour.
- Preheat oven to 375°F.
- Turn dough out onto a lightly floured surface. Roll dough to ¼-inch thickness. Use cookie cutters to cut into desired shapes.
- Place 2 inches apart on an ungreased baking sheet.
- Bake in center of oven for 7 to 10 minutes.
- Cool on pan for 1 minute. Transfer cookies to a wire rack to cool completely.

Glaze

1½ cups powdered sugar
3   tablespoons light corn syrup
2   tablespoons milk
¼   teaspoon vanilla extract
       food coloring, as desired

- Combine powdered sugar, corn syrup, milk and vanilla. Divide and color as desired with food coloring.
- Place cookies on wax paper. Paint glaze onto cookies using a pastry brush for large areas and a small artist's brush for details.
- Allow glaze to dry before storing.

Yield: Varies depending on size of cookie cutters

Invite family members of all ages to gather around the table and decorate these sugar cookies once they are cool. For extra shine, paint the cookies with a layer of white glaze and allow them to dry before decorating with additional colors. Buy a new package of inexpensive paint brushes in any size to brush on the colorful glaze. Wide pastry brushes work best for covering the cookies with glaze and small watercolor brushes are easiest for kids to use for more detailed decoration. Provide individual containers of glaze in a variety of colors and other decorations, such as sprinkles or edible glitter, to spark everyone's imagination.

"I developed this cookie after a trip to Austria, where I scoured the bakeries of Linz for a slice of Linzertorte, a famous dessert featuring apricot jam. Alas, I was told that, 'no one in Linz eats Linzertorte.' I returned home enlightened but refusing to give up on the concept of combining chocolate and apricot. These lend an elegant touch to a tea tray or a Christmas party. If you prefer your chocolate with raspberry, simply switch to raspberry jam."

Chocolate Glazed Linzer Cookies

Enjoy these Austrian-inspired cookies with coffee or tea.

1   cup butter, softened
½   cup sugar
2   cups all-purpose flour
1   cup ground pecans
     Glaze (recipe follows)

- Cream butter and sugar until fluffy. Mix in flour and pecans.
- Form dough into 2 balls. Wrap in wax paper and refrigerate for 1 hour.
- Preheat oven to 350°F.
- Turn dough out onto a lightly floured surface. Roll dough to ¼-inch thickness. Cut with small round or oblong cookie cutter.
- Place 2 inches apart on an ungreased baking sheet.
- Bake in center of oven for 10 to 12 minutes or until set but not brown.
- Cool on pan for 1 minute. Transfer cookies to a wire rack to cool completely.

Glaze

1   cup (about 6 ounces) semisweet chocolate chips
1   tablespoon shortening
     apricot or seedless raspberry jam

- Melt chocolate chips and shortening in microwave. Stir until smooth.
- Stir jam to break up lumps. Spread on bottom side of cookie. Top with second cookie. Dip end in glaze, then place on wax paper until chocolate hardens.

Yield: Varies depending on size of cookie cutters

Marbled Chocolate Peanut Butter Bark

Easy enough for anyone to make

18 ounces white chocolate, divided
1½ cups crunchy peanut butter
8   ounces semisweet chocolate

- Melt 16 ounces white chocolate and peanut butter in microwave. Stir until smooth.
- Spread evenly into a well-greased jelly-roll pan.
- Melt semisweet chocolate in microwave. Stir until smooth. Drizzle stripes over peanut butter mixture. To marbleize, draw lines through peanut butter mixture perpendicular to stripes using a sharp knife.
- Melt remaining 2 ounces white chocolate in microwave. Stir until smooth. Drizzle stripes over peanut butter mixture. To marbleize, draw lines through peanut butter mixture perpendicular to stripes using a sharp knife.
- When candy is firm, turn it out onto a cutting board. Cut into diamonds with a knife or use canapé cutters to make heart, star or flower shapes.

Yield: 2½ pounds

Chocolate Peanut Clusters

Crunchy clusters featuring peanuts in a chocolate coating.

2	tablespoons peanut butter
1	cup (about 6 ounces) butterscotch chips
1	cup (about 6 ounces) semisweet chocolate chips
2	cups salted Spanish peanuts

- Melt peanut butter, butterscotch chips and chocolate chips in microwave. Stir until smooth. Stir in peanuts.
- Drop by rounded teaspoonfuls onto wax paper.

Yield: 48 clusters

Chocolate Hazelnut Truffles

The taste of hazelnuts makes these truffles irresistible.

1½	**pounds semisweet chocolate**
½	**cup heavy cream**
3	**tablespoons Frangelico**
½	**cup cocoa**
2	**teaspoons ground cinnamon**
40	**hazelnuts, shelled**

- Melt chocolate in microwave. Stir until smooth. Add cream and Frangelico. Stir until well blended.
- Cool to room temperature, then beat until fluffy.
- Chill for 1 hour or until firm but pliable.
- Sift together cocoa and cinnamon. Set aside.
- Shape chocolate mixture into ¾-inch balls around hazelnuts. Roll in cocoa-cinnamon mixture.
- Chill until firm.

Variation: Substitute 3 tablespoons Grand Marnier for Frangelico. Shape chocolate mixture into ¾-inch balls (no nuts). Roll in cocoa-cinnamon mixture.

Yield: 40 truffles

Tips for Melting Chocolate

- **Double Boiler: Place chocolate in a double boiler or a metal bowl placed over a simmering pot of water. Stir over medium heat until chocolate begins to melt. Remove from heat and continue stirring until smooth.**
- **Microwave Oven: Place chocolate in a micro-wave-safe bowl or measuring cup. Micro-wave on high power until soft enough to stir until smooth. Stir every minute during heating to avoid scorching.**

Although Raleigh is called "The City of Oaks," pecan trees are prominent in the yards and parks of the city. This rich, buttery nut has the highest fat content of any nut and is perfect for baking. Pecans start falling from the trees in late autumn. The outer husks peel away and the smooth, oblong nut inside is ready to be scooped off the ground just in time for holiday pie baking.

Old-Fashioned Caramels with Pecans

Mass-produced candy cannot compete with the buttery taste of homemade caramels.

2   cups brown sugar
    pinch of salt
1   cup light corn syrup
1   (14-ounce) can sweetened condensed milk
½   cup butter
1   teaspoon vanilla extract
2   cups chopped pecans

- Combine brown sugar, salt, corn syrup and sweetened condensed milk in a heavy saucepan. Stirring frequently, cook over low heat for 15 minutes. Add butter. Stirring constantly, cook for 15 additional minutes or until caramel mixture reaches the firm ball stage (approximately 244°F).
- Remove from heat and stir in vanilla and then pecans.
- Spread evenly into a well-greased 13x9-inch baking pan.
- Cool completely. Cut into 1-inch pieces and place in miniature muffin cups.

Yield: 120 caramels

Using a candy thermometer is the most accurate test for doneness when making candy. Make sure the bulb of the thermometer is completely submerged in the boiling mixture, but don't let it touch the pan bottom. The temperature rises quickly as the candy nears doneness, so watch the thermometer closely. Almond Crunch is done at the hard crack stage, between 300° and 310°. If a candy thermometer is not available, use a cold water test. Remove the pan of candy from the heat. Immediately drop a few drops of the candy syrup into a cup of very cold water. At the hard crack stage, the syrup will separate into brittle threads.

Almond Crunch

Almond Crunch disappears quickly and is perfect for gift giving.

1   cup butter
1⅓ cups sugar
1   tablespoon light corn syrup
3   tablespoons water
1¾ cups finely chopped almonds, toasted and divided
2   cups (about 12 ounces) semisweet chocolate chips, melted

- Melt butter in a large, heavy saucepan. Add sugar, corn syrup and water. Cook to hard crack stage (approximately 300°F), stirring frequently with a wooden spoon. Add 1 cup almonds.
- Spread evenly into a well-greased cookie sheet. Cool completely.
- Spread melted chocolate onto candy. Sprinkle with remaining ¾ cup almonds.
- When chocolate is firm, turn candy out onto wax paper and break into pieces.

Yield: 1½ pounds

Contributors

The Junior League of Raleigh, Inc. wishes to thank our Provisional, Active and Sustaining members, families and friends for submitting their treasured recipes, for diligently testing the many selections, and for steadfastly supporting the development of this cookbook. The Cookbook Development Committee received more than 1,600 recipes for consideration and many of these were double- or triple-tested for accuracy and clarity. We are truly grateful to all these individuals who contributed so generously to **You're Invited.**

Jackie R. Abbott
Marie Abee
Chris Allen
Charlene Askew
Amy Avram
Anna K. Baird
Beth Bartelt
Jane Jeter Black
Lee Black
Nancy Bolen
Rachel Bowen
Beth Bradley
Ginny Broughton
Perrin Burton
Joanne Butler
Parker Call
Hope Derby
  Carmichael
Sonya Carwile
Ann Cathcart
Allison Cayton
Lois Chamblee
Meredyth Champ
Rebecca Christian
Marion Johnson Church
Becky Clark
Pam Clark
Suzanne Coleman
Kim Connare
Gina Brooks Cornick

Henni Corbin
Catherine Cox
Fredrika Van Vleck Cox
Lisa Magnone Coyle
Valerie Cozart
Linda Gardner Crandall
Kim Nielsen Cummings
Rae Marie Czuhai
Nancy Henry Dameron
Pam Davis
Marion Deerhake
Carolyn Dickens
Gisela Donovan
Florence Bickel Doud
Edna Edwards Dougher
Lisa Duke
Lu Dumas
Irish Dunlap
Janis Dunn
E. Bryan Elks
Diane Ellison
Laura Ferguson
Linda Otten Fitch
Mary Lynn Fitzgerald
Penney Fox
Sarah Wesley Fox
Cynthia Franken
Catherine Garda
Marynell Gehrke
Charlotte Griffin

Marcia Griffin
Sally Grogan
Andrea Groon
Sandra A. Gulierrez
Sally Habermeyer
Libby Haggerty
Donna Halat
Sue Hane
Susan H. Harley
Denise Harper
Kelly Harris
Diane Hatcher
Jennie Hayman
Laurel Harvey
Donna Heffring
Mary M. Henning
Larry Young Hines
Allison Holmes
Sue Hood
Dena Aretakis Horn
Lynne Hornaday
Janis Houlihan
Martha Beach Howard
Kim Huff
Jane Hunt
Eleanor White Hunter
Beth Boney Jenkins
Mary Charles Jenkins
Karen Johnson
Cindy Jones

Bertina Jones
Mary June Jones
Claire Joyce
Chancy M. Kapp
Betty M. Kapp
Elaine Karchner
Jane Kidd
Helen Kirven
Maria Kling
Terry Flanagan Knott
Emily Knuckley
Sara Lawrence
Janice Layne
Martha Councill Leak
Liz Lee
Cathy Lepley
Cindy Lewis
Elizabeth Lewis
Mary Helen Wilson
  Long
Julie Lowe
Sheila Ryan Loyd
Greer Lysaght
Leslie Mahan
Mary Ann Maisto
Lucy Newton Maloney
Paige Marsh
Jean Maupin
Susan Mayes
Susan McAllister

Thanks

Alice McCall

Margaret Mundy McCoy

Cornelia McPherson

Peggy Schafer Meares

Martha Michaux

Mary H. Mitchiner

Susan M. Moore

Danita Morgan

Betsy Mosley

Kim Murray

Lindsay Newsome

Linda Nunnallee

Cindy Lanier Oates

Dolores O'Connor

Virginia Parker

Dida Parrott

Suzy Pearson

Elizabeth Davis Peeler

Holly Pegram

Carol Pennisi

Linda Piccola

Lynn Place

Sydnor Presnell

Courtney Procter

Mary Ruth Pupa

Suzy Purrington

Susan Dietz Ramquist

Melanie Rankin

Debbie Ray

Susan P. Remling

Violet Barwick Rhinehart

Margot Richter

Liz Riley

Lisa Robinson

Ann S. Robinson

Anne Rogers

Marsha Russo

Leslie Schappell

Edwina Shaw

Sue Shearin

Jennifer Slepin

Blair Wall Smallman

Kelly K. Smith

LeGrande Lister Smith

Rachel S. Smith

Anne Smithson

Margie Springer

Susan Stanhope

Miller Stanley

Judith Starritt

Becky Steadman

Mary Stevenson

Caroline Stirling

Toni Talton

Tammy E. Taylor

Kathy Teague

Jayne Teel

Geralin Thomas

Mary Duncan Thompson

Nicole Trail

Donna Tucker

Linda Donnell Turner

Erd Venable

Cornelia Vick

Ellen Vitek

Barbara Wagner

Janie Wagstaff

Emily Beahm Walser

Jayne Nelson Walton

Carol Ward

Kathy Warren

Betty Warren

Terri Weidle

Joanna Wells

Janet B. White

Beth Whittaker

Stacey Speight Wiley

Mary Clark King Williams

Barbara Williford

Cecelia Winslow

Karin Winslow

Kate Davenport Wisz

Melissa Wittmeier

Sherry Cameron Worth

Mary Brent Wright

Marlena Yates

Mary Youngblood

Alice Yow

Committee

Cookbook Development

Editor
Valerie Cozart

Assistant Editors
Martha Howard
Sara Lawrence
Martha Grattan

Computer Administrator
Donna Heffring

Graphics Design Chair
Marty Peterson

Testing Chair
Marie Abee

Recipe Chair
Ellen Vitek

Section Editors
Hope Carmichael
Geralin Thomas
Lynn Place
Maria Kling
Sara Lawrence
Miller Stanley
Suzy Pearson
Karin Winslow

Concentrated Testers
Beth Bradley
Karen Bornhofen
Lois Chamblee
Lori Church
Pam Clark
Elizabeth Dempster
Shelia Elliott
Laura Ferguson
Kim Hoft
Liz Lee
Cindy Lewis
Tracey Parker
Susan Ramquist
Cindy Smith

Co-Chair
Lucy Maloney
Cindy Oates

Public Relations Chair
Alice McCall

Marketing Chair
Marcie Gordon

Assistant Marketing
Diane Lawrence
Toni Talton

Administrator
Sara Barefoot

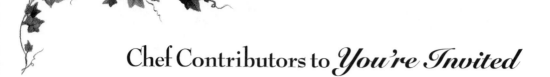

Chef Contributors to *You're Invited*

Bloomsbury Bistro, Five Points - Raleigh	(John Toler)
Fearrington House, Pittsboro	(Cory Mattson)
518 West Italian Cafe, Raleigh	(Nick Maglieri)
411 West, Chapel Hill	(Zenzi Gaddon)
42nd Street Oyster Bar, Raleigh	(Mark Edelbaum)
Lofton's, North Raleigh Hilton, Raleigh	(Bob Maciel)
Margaux's, Raleigh	(Richard Hege)
Portobello Restaurant, Raleigh	(Andrew Booger)
Second Empire, Raleigh	(Daniel Schurr, Shari Novak)
The Grill, Prestonwood Country Club, Cary	(Ed Kaminski)
The Rockford, Raleigh	(Jeff Stewart)
Tír na nÓg, Raleigh	(Dan Hurley, Randy Wilder)

Wine Consultants for *You're Invited*

Wine pairings throughout the cookbook are courtesy of the Carolina Wine Company, 6601 Hillsborough Street, Raleigh.

About the Junior League of Raleigh

The Junior League of Raleigh is a not-for-profit organization of more than 1500 women who share a commitment to volunteer service. The League is dedicated to promoting voluntarism, developing the potential of women, and improving our community through the effective action and leadership of trained League volunteers.

Since its establishment in 1930, the League has contributed more than $2 million to community projects and programs in such areas as education, children's services, health and the welfare of women. In addition, the League has contributed more than one million hours of volunteer service to the community through the action of its trained volunteers.

The League is proud of its support for community projects and programs in the following areas:

Children's Services: We believe that every child has the right to mature in an environment free from physical and emotional neglect and abuse. The Junior League established SAFE*child*, a not-for-profit agency committed to the elimination of child abuse and neglect. The League has continued to support SAFE*child* with volunteers and funding.

Education: We are committed to ensuring that all individuals have access to educational opportunities that will provide them with the skills necessary to be productive members of our society. We support programs designed to enhance educational opportunities and support legislative initiatives to achieve these goals.

Health Services: We believe that every individual should have access to quality health services in order to safeguard their physical and mental health. We support programs and services that enhance the complex health service needs of our citizens, regardless of age, sex, race, disability or economic status.

The purpose of the Junior League of Raleigh is exclusively educational and charitable. Funds raised through *You're Invited* will be used to support our volunteer efforts, community programs and projects.

About the Artists

Margaret Hill

Still Life With Peaches And Melon, oil on canvas, 1997.

A native of Albemarle, North Carolina, Raleigh-based artist Margaret Hill has studied painting with several locally and nationally renowned artists. She has shown her paintings in numerous art exhibitions throughout North Carolina and in New York City. Margaret has been a member of The Junior League of Raleigh for many years, serving on the board and as a docent at the North Carolina Museum of Art.

Marriott Little

You're Invited, pastel, 1998.

Megg's Cups, watercolor, 1994.

Marriott, an art history major from Duke University, has been a professional artist for many years, working in oils and pastels. She has won numerous awards in regional and national exhibitions. Her work has shown in many private and corporate collections both nationally and internationally. Marriott has served as a member of the Junior League of Raleigh for many years. In addition, she has been the president of the Artspace Artists Association, a past board member of the Raleigh Fine Arts Society, vice president of Wake Visual Arts Association, and vice president of the Watercolor Society of North Carolina.

Tracey Parker

Fleur-de-lis, oil on canvas, 1998.

Tracey is from Raleigh and has been painting for several years, preferring to work with oils. She has enjoyed studying under well-known local artists to develop her skills. Tracey is also a member of the Junior League of Raleigh, where she fulfilled one placement testing recipes for *You're Invited.*

Marinda Sapp

Summer Spread, oil on canvas, 1998.

Marinda is a native of the Raleigh-Durham area. Having painted since she was thirteen years old, Marinda went on to receive a Bachelor of Fine Arts in painting and art history from Virginia Commonwealth University.

Nora Shepard

Places I Have Been, oil on canvas, 1997.

Nora was born in Raleigh, grew up in Asheville, and returned to Raleigh several years ago. Nora, too, has studied painting from many well-known area artists. She is very involved in arts in the community and the Junior League of Raleigh. She rewrote the Art In Schools program for the Wake County Department of Public Instruction. She is also the founding president of Arts Together. In addition, Nora was the first president of the Docent Association for the North Carolina Museum of Art and also served in the education department at the museum for three years.

Linda Turner

Breakfast - Dappled Shade, oil on canvas, 1997.

Provence Luncheon, oil on canvas, 1998.

The Dining Room, oil on canvas, 1996.

Linda grew up in Oklahoma and went to college on a full art scholarship at the University of Oklahoma. Over the years Linda has exhibited her paintings in numerous local and regional art shows, as well as studied with many well-respected artists and art critics. A longtime member of the Junior League of Raleigh, Linda has served as a vice president and board member among her many other activities.

Index

Index

Index

Index

Index

Index

Index

Index

Index

Index

Index

Index

Index

Index

Index

Junior League of Raleigh, Inc.
4020 Barrett Drive, Suite 104
Raleigh, North Carolina 27609
(919) 785-0530 Cookbook fax
(919) 787-1103, pound (#) 120 Cookbook voice mail

Please send me _____ copies of **You're Invited**   @ $21.95 each_____

North Carolina residents add sales tax   @   1.32 each _____

Postage and handling   @   4.00 each _____

Name _____

Address_____

City _____ State _____ Zip_____

Daytime Phone_____

Make checks payable to the Junior League of Raleigh
Or include your credit card information as follows: (CIRCLE ONE)   VISA   MasterCard

Card number _____ Expiration Date _____

Signature of Authorization _____

- -

Junior League of Raleigh, Inc.
4020 Barrett Drive, Suite 104
Raleigh, North Carolina 27609
(919) 785-0530 Cookbook fax
(919) 787-1103, pound (#) 120 Cookbook voice mail

Please send me _____ copies of **You're Invited**   @ $21.95 each_____

North Carolina residents add sales tax   @   1.32 each _____

Postage and handling   @   4.00 each _____

Name _____

Address_____

City _____ State _____ Zip_____

Daytime Phone_____

Make checks payable to the Junior League of Raleigh
Or include your credit card information as follows: (CIRCLE ONE)   VISA   MasterCard

Card number _____ Expiration Date _____

Signature of Authorization _____